REVIEW COPY

CURATORS AND CULTURE

History of American Science and Technology Series

General Editor, LESTER D. STEPHENS

CURATORS AND CULTURE
The Museum Movement in America, 1740–1870

JOEL J. OROSZ

The University of Alabama Press
Tuscaloosa and London

Copyright © 1990 by
The University of Alabama Press
Tuscaloosa, Alabama 35487–0380
All rights reserved
Manufactured in the United States of America

∞

The paper on which this book is printed meets the minimum
requirements of American National Standard for Information
Science-Permanence of Paper for Printed Library Materials,
ANSI A39.48-1984.

Library of Congress Cataloging-in-Publication Data

Orosz, Joel J.
    Curators and culture : the museum movement in America. 1740–1870 /
Joel J. Orosz.
        p. cm.—(History of American science and technology series)
    Bibliography: p.
    Includes index.
    ISBN 0-8173-0475-4 (alk. paper)
    1. Museums—United States—History. 2. Museum curators—United
States—History. 3. United States—Popular culture--Museums—
History. I. Title. II. Series.
AM11.076   1990
069'.0973—dc20   89-33865
                                                                      CIP

British Library Cataloguing-in-Publication Data available

For my parents,
Joseph Orosz and Caroline Orosz,
my first and best teachers

Contents

Preface

This book will argue that a small, loosely connected group of men constituted an informal museum movement in America from about 1740 to 1870. As they formed their pioneer museums, these men were guided not so much by European examples, but rather by the imperatives of the American democratic culture, including the Enlightenment, the simultaneous decline of the respectability and rise of the middle classes, the Age of Egalitarianism, and the advent of professionalism in the sciences. Thus the pre-1870 American museum was neither the frivolous sideshow some critics have imagined, nor the enclave for elitists that others have charged. Instead, the proprietors displayed serious motives and egalitarian aspirations.

The conflicting demands for popular education on the one hand and professionalism on the other were a continuing source of tension in American museums after about 1835, but by 1870 the two claims had synthesized into a rough parity. This synthesis, the "American Compromise," has remained the basic model of museums in America down to the present. Thus, by 1870, the form of the modern American museum as an institution which simultaneously provides popular education and promotes scholarly research was completely developed.

This work is offered, of course, as a contribution to the history of American museums, but it is not intended to be limited to an audience of scholars. The author hopes that practicing museum professionals will read it in order to gain an insight as to why the institutions that they serve developed as they did.

Acknowledgments

In the course of nearly eight years' labor, I have accumulated a number of obligations. The greatest is to my coadviser, Dr. Patsy Gerstner, who first suggested this topic to me and who provided me with much of my thesis. Her deep and insightful knowledge of early museum history, and her unstinting labors in reading and rereading the manuscript have proved invaluable to me. Dr. David Van Tassel, my other coadviser, has given freely of his profound understanding of the development of American culture, and has kept a sharp eye on style. Thanks are due as well to Dr. Carl Ubbelohde, who translated the eternal mysteries of graduate school requirements. These three, and Drs. Darwin Stapleton and David Hammack, formed a superb committee. Dr. Kathleen D. McCarthy and Dr. Sally Gregory Kohlstedt read the entire manuscript and corrected many errors. The dean of museum historians in America, Dr. Edward P. Alexander, graciously offered many suggestions which materially improved certain chapters of this work. Dr. David Strauss reviewed the early chapters. To them belongs the credit for much that is right with this book; to me belongs the responsibility for all errors.

During the course of my research I extensively corresponded with and/or visited twenty-four manuscript repositories. In every case, I encountered courteous, helpful, and professional archivists and curators, only the most outstanding of whom can be mentioned here. Gordon Marshall of the Library Company of Philadelphia took extra time to share his knowledge of Philadelphia museum history, as did Peter Parker at the Historical Society of Pennsylvania. Carol Spawn, at the Academy of Natural Sciences, frequently went beyond the call of duty to assist me, as did Billie Broaddus of Cincinnati's History of Health Sciences Library and

Museum. Eugene Gaddis of the Wadsworth Atheneum was a source of both sound advice and pleasant company.

The highest praise, however, must be reserved for five truly remarkable people at the Smithsonian Institution. Nathan Reingold and Marc Rothenberg of the Joseph Henry Papers exerted themselves to accommodate my needs, and the incomparable staff of the Smithsonian Institution Archives—Harry Heiss, Libby Glenn, and Bill Deiss—made me feel more like visiting royalty than a visiting scholar. The Smithsonian is fortunate to have them all as staff members.

The Graduate Alumni Fund of Case Western Reserve University has been very generous in support of this work. Several of the research trips were made possible through its assistance. Jan Huddleston, manuscript editor for The University of Alabama Press, rooted out many errors and edited sensitively.

Special thanks go to my dear friends, Sarah Borgeson, Lisa Nagler, and Katherine Rorimer, who have added so much to this work. Elizabeth Upjohn and her late husband, Burton, provided crucial support on many occasions. The Kalamazoo law firm of Fox, Thompson, Morris, Stover, and O'Connor (now Early, Lennon, Fox, Thompson, Crocker, and Peters) was helpful in ways too numerous to enumerate, as were the management and staff of the W. K. Kellogg Foundation of Battle Creek, especially Sandra Brookmyer and Rosalie Gaudrault. Sandra in particular left a lasting imprint upon this book. My parents, Joseph and Caroline Orosz, were a constant source of encouragement. My wife, Florence, deserves tremendous credit for her support, both moral and financial, during the past half-decade. She also prepared the lion's share of the index.

Finally, I wish to thank the following repositories for sharing their superb knowledge resources, and for giving permission to publish excerpts of letters, diaries, and publications from their collections:

Library of the Academy of Natural Sciences of Philadelphia
American Philosophical Society
The Barra Foundation, Inc.

The Cincinnati Historical Society
The Connecticut Historical Society
Archives of the Gray Herbarium, Harvard University
The Historical Society of Pennsylvania
The Library Company of Philadelphia
Library of Congress
The Maryland Historical Society
The Metropolitan Museum of Art
The New-York Historical Society
The New York Public Library, Rare Books and Manuscripts
    Division, Astor, Lennox and Tilden Foundations
Smithsonian Institution Archives
Wadsworth Atheneum

CURATORS AND CULTURE

Prologue: Thesis, Definitions, and Structure

The thesis of this book is essentially a refutation of two points of view regarding the pre-1870 history of museums in America, which I shall call the professional criticism and the democratic criticism. These approaches are utterly contradictory, and just as completely unfounded, but they have until now completely shaped our view of the first century of museum history in America. Both criticisms will be considered in detail in the Epilogue, but it is necessary here to summarize them.

The professional criticism is the more venerable of the two, for Joseph Henry, the first secretary of the Smithsonian Institution, had sketched it out as early as the 1840s. It received a full statement in the first formal attempt at American museum history, "Museum-History and Museums of History," by George Brown Goode, the assistant secretary of the Smithsonian Institution in charge of the National Museum. Goode, an early museum professional, speaking to the third annual meeting of the American Historical Association, dismissed these early institutions, saying that they were "a chance assemblage of curiosities . . . rather [than] a series of objects selected with reference to their value to investigators, or their possibilities for public enlightenment."[1] The professional criticism, then, holds that pre-1870 American museums consisted of spectacular or bizarre objects with no scientific or educational value; in short, they were sideshows aimed at public gratification.

The democratic criticism takes an opposing view. Goode, whose thought on the subject of museum history was complex and wide ranging, was the first to take this position as well. John Cotton Dana, the director of the Newark Museum in the early part of the twentieth century, refined it, and Theodore L. Low perfected it. In 1942, while still a graduate student, Low was commissioned by the Committee on Education of the American Association of Museums to define the ideal educational mission of the museum in America, and to measure how well that ideal was being met in practice. Low produced *The Museum as a Social Instrument*, a blunt critique of contemporary museum practice. He sketched a grim picture of curators so obsessed with collecting that they shamelessly ignored their educational responsibilities. In the course of criticizing the museum world of 1942, Low made some unsupported assumptions regarding American museum history. Museum staffs had so closely imitated elitist European models, he asserted, "that museums soon became little more than isolated segments of European culture set in a hostile environment."[2] The democratic criticism, then, holds that the pre-1870 museums developed from an alien, antiegalitarian background antithetical to the egalitarian culture of America, that is to say, that museums are, and always have been, run by the elite for the elite.

These two contradictory criticisms have exerted a great influence over the small corpus of historiography of American museums, as is discussed in detail in the Epilogue. These views of the museum as sideshow and the museum as elitist enclave have filtered down to the general public, coloring the popular conception of the pre-1870 museums. The two views share a contempt for the first century of museum history in America, for they assert that the early institutions were backward and primitive. Both approaches also share a glaring methodological error: They are based on hearsay and assumption rather than fact. The authors who invented and perpetuated these criticisms scarcely consulted any secondary sources and certainly did not search for primary evidence. The originators made unproven sweeping assumptions and their successors repeated and elaborated upon them. Both criticisms, therefore, are essentially wrong.

This work aims to show that the museums founded in America from 1740 to 1870 were not predominantly sideshows or elitist enclaves, but rather were direct products of the American democratic culture and developed in synchronization with the evolution of the wider cultural climate. A study of a sample of these institutions will show that, while a small proportion of these museums did degenerate into sideshows or elitist enclaves, the great majority had serious and egalitarian aspirations. It will also show that the community of museum proprietors was so small and the interconnections among them so common, that it is useful to say that there was a loosely knit informal museum movement abroad in the land. There was, obviously, no formal museum movement before 1870; no professional organization was formed, no official journal was published, and no one person was recognized as the premier spokesman for museums. Yet there was a network of museum proprietors who communicated among themselves, who were simultaneously influenced by the same cultural factors, and who were doing the same things at the same time for the same reasons. Hence, it seems sensible to refer to the totality of their actions as a "movement," although with the caveat that it was never a movement in a rigid, institutionalized sense. Finally, the work will show that the evolution of American democratic culture caused museums to go through many stages, including one period when popular education was emphasized and another when professionalism was ascendant, and that by 1870 these two had been fused into a synthesis that determined the form of the modern American museum: an institution devoted simultaneously to discovering new truths and educating the public about them. In short, from 1740 to 1870 the American museum was born and grew to maturity, serving as a model for all that would follow.

Today, we understand a "museum" to be an institution that collects tangible objects, makes them available for scholarly research, and exhibits them to the general public as a means of popular education. The pre-1870 museum proprietors, however, understood the term to mean something different. To them, a museum was a cultural center, the purpose of which was the intellectual and moral improvement of the general public. Intellectual improvement was accomplished by the collection and exhibition of three-dimensional objects, by conducting experiments open to the public, and by sponsoring edifying lectures. Moral improvement was achieved by means of didactic recitals, moral messages inserted into labels, and by the inspiring nature of art and natural history itself. Most cabinets were privately owned, either by individuals or by corporations, and were expected to make a profit for their proprietors. Such institutions are naturally called proprietary museums. They were, however, distinctly understood to be public institutions in one crucial sense: they were beholden to the general public for their very survival.

The forerunner of the museum was the cabinet, which implies a collection of objects belonging to an individual or an organization, not open to the general public. A curio cabinet is a pejorative term that suggests a collection formed without system or order. Hence a cabinet, which resembles a museum in physical form, has an entirely distinct purpose, being private, not public.

Many of the early museum proprietors were self-consciously patriotic in the realms of art, science, and history. They understood and envied Europe's cultural primacy in these fields and sought to promote American achievements in them. This effort to cultivate American accomplishments in intellectual endeavors, to the exclusion of European influences, will be referred to as cultural nationalism.

The distinction between the amateur and the professional will be very important in this work. The amateur is defined as a person who did museum work as a hobby or as an adjunct to his actual career. He may have been proud of the work he did in museums, but he considered himself a member of another calling, not a curator. The professional, on the other hand, thought of himself as a curator, and pursued museum work as his livelihood. He imposed upon himself more rigorous standards of practice and behavior than the amateur, and often looked down upon the amateur's efforts as inferior to his own.

It will also be important to understand some terms relative to the structure of American society before 1870. In the colonial era and lasting into the first years of the young republic, American society was divided into two great classes, the "respectability" and the "lower orders." There were, of course, further divisions, from the merchant and planter aristocracies at the top of the social order to the slaves at the bottom, but the most important division separated the respectability from the lower orders. The distinction between the two main classes was based upon wealth, property, and standing; those who had one or more of these things were members of the respectability, and those who had none belonged to the lower orders. The country's social and political systems were administered on the basis of a "deferential-participant" model; that is, the lower orders deferred to their social betters, and the respectability were the participants in the power structure. In return for the deference accorded them by the lower orders, the respectability was expected to administer social and political systems in the best interests of their social inferiors.[3]

The years following 1800 witnessed the progressive decline of the deferential-participant system. A new group, the middle class, consisting, among other callings, of physicians, attorneys, prosperous farmers, and merchant proprietors, was rising from the lower orders. Although they did not have the social standing of the aristocracy, they had independent and self-reliant habits and the means to indulge them. The emergent middle class refused to defer to the higher levels of the respectability and asserted their right to any office in the land, including the presidency. By 1820, they had gained the upper hand against the respectability, and the next two decades would be remembered as the Age of Jackson, after their leader-hero. A better term would be the Age of Egalitarianism, for it was their belief that all native white men were born equal and should have an equal opportunity to earn a livelihood and hold public office. If their watchword was egalitarianism, their program stressed education for all, so that all could discharge their public and private duties.

The respectability could either accommodate itself to the new social order or withdraw from it. Those who chose the latter course became elitists. Elitists are those who reject the notion of the essential dignity and equality of all people. They make distinctions among people based upon criteria such as wealth, descent, or education, and vary their treatment of others accordingly. The term *elite*, however, is less pejorative, merely denoting a group that has more wealth or education, or a higher social standing, than the average person. It follows that one may be a member of an elite, but still reject elitism as an attitude. Many of the pre-1870 museum proprietors came from elite backgrounds, but were zealous in their egalitarian sentiments.

With these terms made explicit, it is now possible to consider the form of this work. The evolution of museums in America before 1870 can be divided into six periods, and this book will be divided thus to accommodate them. Periodization can be a dangerous technique, for it can reduce diversity to uniformity and lead to arbitrary distinctions made to fit preconceived "key dates." The historian is obliged to use this technique, however, when it provides the best model for explaining past events. In order to use it profitably, the historian must always remember that periodization is a helpful model, not a species of determinism. In each of these six periods, then, significant changes in the cultural climate of the United States caused changes in the development of American museums.

The first period is the longest, stretching from the 1740s, when the Library Company of Philadelphia commenced forming a cabinet of curiosities, to 1780. During this period, the idea of the European curio cabinet was transplanted to the new world in Philadelphia, Boston, and Charleston. These institutions represented a beginning, but only a tentative one, for their collections were randomly formed and not accessible to the public.

The second phase of pre-1870 museum history, which was more sophisticated and will be called the Moderate Enlightenment, lasted from 1780 to 1800.[4] Museum founders in this period tended to come from the respectable classes and were better educated and wealthier than the average American. They were greatly influenced by the optimistic ideas of the British Enlightenment and were especially taken with the idea that museums may be able to suppress vice by means of rational amusement and pleasurable instruction. They also believed that the museum, by impressing upon the visitor an appreciation of the order and beneficence of God's creation, became a secular house of worship that promoted reverence and piety. Such goals were benign and optimistic, and demanded free access for the public in order to be effective.

During the Didactic Enlightenment, which lasted from 1800 to 1820, the proprietors of the cabinets were from the same class, but their optimistic outlook had given way to pessimism. The excesses of the French Revolution had eroded their confidence in democracy, and the very social order that codified their supremacy had begun to crumble with the election of Jefferson in 1800. They now saw museums as the guardians of the social order and as a means of social control, to be used as a bulwark of the established classes by teaching "acceptable" behavior to the people. The members of the respectability were losing their grip as the deferential mode of society declined, and they tried to use their museums to cling to their position and power. This was the closest thing to an elitist phase of museum history. Yet even during this period, the museums, in order to fulfill the social agenda of their proprietors, had to be accessible to the public.

The rising middle classes could not be denied; by 1820, they had taken over most museums, thus launching the Age of Egalitarianism, which lasted until 1840. The new proprietors were in step with the reform impulse that was sweeping the nation, and they made museums into centers for self-culture, especially self-education. They considered it essential for every man to gain all possible knowledge in order to discharge the duties of citizenship and assure the health of the republic. The museum was thus an integral part of the educational system, which also included the public school, the lyceum, and the public library, the combination of which helped train the sovereign individual to take his rightful place in society. At the same time, the burst of cultural nationalism following the War of 1812 led Americans to reject European authority, and tended to make the museum more than ever a product of American culture.

While this emphasis on popular education would never be expunged from American museums, it was briefly eclipsed during the Age of Professionalism, from 1840 to 1850. Since the collections of most American museums were still top-heavy with natural history specimens, their curators were strongly influenced by events in the world of science. The rise of professional scientists, which had begun around 1820, took a sudden surge during this decade, and their disdain for amateurism resulted in a decline of museum efforts in popular education. The end of the Jacksonian era in 1840, the prolonged economic hardship following the panic of 1837, and the rise of scientific professional organizations also contributed to the decline in popular education, and its replacement by an emphasis on aiding the scholarly researcher.

The sixth and final period, which lasted from 1850 to 1870, witnessed a synthesis of the claims of popular education and scholarly research. This accommodation was so crucial that the period will be referred to as the age of the American Compromise. Several factors accounted for the relative decline of professionalism and the resurgence of popular education during this era. The scientists self-consciously reined in their drive for professionalization because they sensed that they were beginning to violate shared cultural values and were becoming perceived as dangerously elitist by the general public.[5] The free labor ideology, most powerful in the North, but influential all over the nation, emphasized popular education so that each man may have every advantage in his attempt to rise in life.[6] The nascent preservation movement and the fledgling world's fair movement also began to diffuse the museum idea and weaken the grip of the professionals. Finally, during the Civil War, museums became important as teachers of national loyalty and patriotism. Sanitary fairs advanced the museum idea and reinforced the concept of popular education. By 1870, scholarly research and popular education had become fully accepted as equal goals of the American museum. This achievement will be called the *American* Compromise, for it was in the United States that it was first realized. With this accomplishment, the form of the modern American museum was determined.

This book refutes Theodore Low's vision of the pre-1870

American museum as merely a third-rate imitation of European models. The evidence to be presented will demonstrate that American museums were founded, for the most part, by Americans, in response to American cultural needs, and developed according to the imperatives of the changing American culture. This is not to deny that American museum proprietors were influenced by developments in the European museum world; indeed, these inspirations are noted in the text whenever appropriate. It is to say, however, that the primary impetus for the development of American museums came from America. It should be noted that this work is not in any sense a comparative exercise; such would require a separate study.

It would have been ideal to have traced the cultural changes from the beginnings of the museum in the United States through the achievement of the American Compromise by examining every American museum. In point of fact, however, museums proliferated so rapidly after the Revolution that it would be simply impossible to analyze them all within the scope of a single book. It became necessary to select representatives from their number, examine them, and apply the results to the larger universe whence they were selected. This study focuses on eleven museums, namely the three Peale museums in Philadelphia, Baltimore, and New York; Du Simitière's museum and the Academy of Natural Sciences, both of Philadelphia; the New-York Historical Society, the American Museum, and the Elgin Botanical Garden, all in New York; the Wadsworth Atheneum in Hartford; the Western Museum of Cincinnati; and the National Museum of the Smithsonian Institution in Washington, D.C. In addition, the last chapter will briefly examine the effect of the American Compromise on the great metropolitan museums: the Boston Museum of the Fine Arts and New York's two great institutions, the American Museum of Natural History and the Metropolitan Museum of Art.

These institutions were chosen carefully on the basis of type, geographical location, and philosophy. As to the first of these criteria, the Wadsworth Atheneum was one of the first art museums in the nation, and the Academy of Natural Sciences, the

Smithsonian Institution, and the Elgin Botanical Garden special-ized in natural history. The others, although having general col-lections, had significant concentrations in different fields. The Peale museums were strong in both science and art. Du Simitière's and the New-York Historical Society were among the earliest historical museums in the nation, and both the Western and American museums held significant collections of natural history.

The geographical mix provided by these institutions is both balanced and diverse. They extend north and east to Hartford, west to Cincinnati, and south to Baltimore and Washington. They also span the era from 1783 to 1870, thus covering nearly all of the crucial first century of museum development in America.

Finally, they run the gamut of museum philosophy. On the one hand is the aloof elitist stance of the New-York Historical Society; on the other the wide-open popular orientation of the Western and American museums. All of the various shades of approaches between these two extremes are well represented by Du Simitière's, the three Peale museums, the Wadsworth Athe-neum, the Academy of Natural Sciences, the Elgin Garden, and the National Museum.

This microcosm of the American museum world to 1870 should present a reasonable facsimile of the whole, and it will be explored in relation to that larger picture. For although the spotlight will be on these eleven institutions, it is important to remember that they fit into a loosely connected, somewhat amor-phous, but nonetheless discernible matrix. Taken as a whole, they also mirror a century that witnessed the spectacular development of American museums from infancy to maturity. This record of achievement and eventful development has been forgotten during the intervening decades. The records have been accessible, for the most part, but have been ignored, and lost to our collective con-sciousness. They tell the story of a cultural adventure that had its first tentative beginnings before the nation itself was born. The cradle city was Philadelphia, for it was there that the Euro-pean curio cabinet was first transplanted onto American soil.

1

The Curio Cabinet Transplanted to the New World, 1740–1780

The American museum was not, as Theodore Low supposed, transferred fully developed from Europe. In point of fact, the European model first imitated by Americans was not the museum, but the cabinet. During the 1740s and for some years thereafter, there were no true museums in Europe for Americans to copy. There were the vast collections belonging to the monarchies of France, Britain, Spain, and Russia; there was the magnificent collection owned by the Catholic Church; there were universities with cabinets like Oxford's Ashmolean and even a few private collectors with vast aggregations, such as Sir Hans Sloane, but all were essentially cabinets, accessible only to a privileged few. Even the best of these contained an eclectic assortment of natural history specimens, items with historical associations, objets d'art, and things that could only be labeled "curiosities." In fact, the contents gave the generic name to these collections, for they were widely known as curio cabinets. This was the state of the European "museum" world in the 1740s.

Across the water, in the new land of America, the provincials were struggling to transplant European cultural institutions to a land they had occupied for scarcely more than a century. Churches and schools and even universities had been successfully begun. Libraries would be next, and with them would come the first cabinets. However, any provincial who attempted to bring European culture to America soon found himself confronting a dilemma neatly summed up by J. Hector St. John Crevecoeur: "What then is the American, this new man? He is either a European or the descendant of a European. . . . *He* is an American, who leaving behind him all his ancient prejudices and manners, receives new ones from the new mode of life he has embraced, the new government he obeys, and the new rank he holds."[1]

Crevecoeur's famous lines from *Letters from an American Farmer* concisely state the dilemma of the eighteenth-century American. On the one hand, he was proud of his European heritage and fancied himself a participant in the intellectual and scientific revolutions that comprised the Enlightenment—those vast social changes that seemed to be unlocking the very secrets of God's creation. He eagerly read the ideas of the philosophes and recreated the experiments of the scientists, attempting to expand on them whenever possible. He felt that he was a kindred spirit to the best minds of his age. On the other hand, he realized that his libraries lacked the books and his laboratories lacked the apparatus to participate on a par with Europe. Given these shortcomings he must always improvise, always adapt the activity to fit the situation. These were negative considerations, but there were positive ones to ponder: the American was proud of his (relatively) clean streets, the absence of paupers, the abundance of resources, and the blessings of freedom and opportunity in this new land. He could not help but believe that Europe was in many ways filthy, oppressed, and decadent, on a downhill path just as surely as America was in the ascendant. So the American saw Europe both as a superior and an inferior, as a mentor and a pupil. This was certainly ambivalent, but the ambivalence stemmed directly from the nature of European society, which encompassed both brilliance and squalor. In practical terms it meant that the American would always be willing to learn from Europe, but that he would never be a slavish imitator. While he recognized the value of European ideas, the American knew that he would have to alter them to fit the American environment, and in any case, he believed that not every European idea was good enough for America.

If one wishes to understand the history of museums in America, one must begin with the Enlightenment and America's reaction to it. The Enlightenment as a concept is not difficult to grasp. The scientific advances of the sixteenth and seventeenth centuries were the basis for an intellectual ferment equaling in many respects the height of the Renaissance. This movement had regional variations, but several elements were common to every nation it affected: a respect for the achievements of the classical past, a faith in progress up to and including the perfectability of man, an ardent humanitarianism, a strong belief in political and intellectual freedom, a faith in a cosmic system directed by the laws of nature formulated by nature's God, and, above all, a belief in the power of reason to both discover those laws and to induce conformity to them. Enlightened men made a fetish of reason, and they demanded proof to substantiate claims. This need for evidence gave the museum, for the first time, a strong raison d'être. Before the Enlightenment, cabinets had served as reliquaries, as storehouses, and as treasuries. With very few exceptions (such as Paolo Giovio's Museum Jovianum, begun about 1520, and Rogier de Gaiginere's natural history museum of the early eighteenth century), they had had little, if any, intellectual justification for their existence.[2] Now they had become indispensable for the preservation of the artifacts of history, the taxonomy of the natural world, the apparatus of science, and the legacy of great art from the past.

The philosophes wished to make the sovereign collections of England, France, Spain, and the Papacy—amassed to satisfy the vanity of the mighty—serve instead the needs of the scholar. In his article "Louvre" for his *Encyclopedie*, Denis Diderot advocated transforming the Louvre into a museum, library, and home for various scholarly societies. It was to be an instrument of the educated, not an instrument for education. Not even the philosophes could conceive of a museum for the masses. When the Enlightenment ideas in general and the museum idea in particular arrived in America, they underwent a metamorphosis to fit the American environment. This was inevitable, for unlike Europe, the American environment did not offer much of a heritage. In the 1720s, Americans could look back on only slightly more than a century of history. The surroundings conveyed no artistic reminders of a glorious classical past to be admired, as in Europe, nor was there an oppressive and entrenched oligarchy, inherited from earlier times, against which to raise the banner of reform. And Americans, aside from the reprehensible institution of slavery, had few examples of barbarism to oppose. If, however, they were relatively unburdened by history and inhumanity, they evinced an even stronger commitment than did Europeans to the ideas of political and intellectual freedom, a more ardent belief in the perfectability of man, and a deeper faith in the efficacy of reason to order society. These facts, especially the lack of constraints from the past, made Americans more pragmatic and more open to experimentation than Europeans. The Enlightenment in America would be more optimistic and more fluid than its counterpart across the water.[3]

The museum idea, too, was modified to suit the American environment. The lack of a long history and a great artistic tradition immediately limited the idea's scope. In Europe the collections of the monarchs and the prelates, centuries in the making, could be readily transformed into museums; in this new land, collections must first be formed. Europe had patrons with surplus capital to create collections for reasons of acquisitiveness, aesthetics, or use; America, which desperately needed capital for development, would welcome museums if and only if they were formed for some practical, useful purpose. In a country with an abundance of undescribed species of flora and fauna, it was inevitable that taxonomy should become one purpose of the early cabinets. Another would be experimentation in the sciences, since the pioneer collections were natural depositories for scientific apparatus. These first efforts at museum-making, then, were essentially attempts to set up centers to satisfy the demand for scientific knowledge in an enlightened age. These were the impulses that lay behind the first serious attempts to form museums in America.

Beginnings until the Revolution

The history of the museum in America is a uniquely American story.[4]

Although the germ of the museum idea came from Europe, its development did become a truly American story. Far from its native shores, the European curio cabinet blossomed into something more open and more useful than it had been in its initial manifestation. In short, it grew to fit the needs of the American cultural climate. Its story begins far earlier than most suppose, well before the Revolution transformed the British provinces into a new nation.

Most histories of American museums begin with the Charleston Museum, founded in 1773 as a child of that city's Library Society. Indeed, this seems the natural place to begin, for this was the first American cabinet to call itself a museum. However, Charleston was hardly the earliest attempt at museum-making in the American provinces; in fact, it was only an old idea called by a new name. The earliest prototypes of that idea were collections of curiosities which were from time to time shown in some colonial cities in the early years of the eighteenth century. But it was not until well into the eighteenth century that provincial cities could support a serious attempt to form a cabinet.

It is only fitting that America's paragon of the enlightened man should have played a major role in the founding of its earliest cabinet. Benjamin Franklin inadvertently provided the impetus in 1727, when he founded the renowned "Junto." This group consisted of the young printer and a small group of like-minded friends, who met for discussions aimed at mutual intellectual improvement. In 1730, acting on Franklin's suggestion, they pooled their books in order to form a common library. Although everyone agreed that it was a useful experiment, the attempt collapsed within a year. This failure taught Franklin that a library needed a more substantial base in order to succeed, so he sought support from the wider community. On July 1, 1731, he and fifty other subscribers drew up the Instrument of Association of an institution they named The Library Company of Philadelphia. Each pledged to contribute forty shillings initially, and bound himself to contribute additional annual sums. Thus was founded the "mother of all the N. American Subscription Libraries," as its father aptly called it.[5] The subscribers laid a firm foundation indeed, for this venerable institution recently celebrated its "quarter-millennium" anniversary.

By degrees the Library Company began to form a cabinet. The precise date of the arrival of the first object is a mystery, but members seemed to have commenced depositing curiosities rather early. By the late 1740s they began to regard this miscellaneous collection as a cabinet, and commenced the first efforts to arrange it. The value of the collection sharply escalated after Captain Charles Swaine tried and failed to find the Northwest Passage during voyages in his schooner *Argo* in 1752 and 1753. He returned with "a fine collection of Eskimo garments and artifacts, which, when presented to the Library . . . became one of the most popular exhibits in its growing collection."[6] Actually this statement is slightly misleading, because the artifacts were accessible to members only, exhibited to widen the scope of their knowledge, not to enlighten the populace. The members became so zealous in this pursuit that they soon began to barter shares in the company for curiosities. Some may have thought that preserved animals, fossils, and coins were "strange things with which to burden a library." Not so the directors of the Library Company; "indeed they asserted [them] to be directly in support of their objective, which was 'the Improvement of Knowledge.'"[7]

The Library Company never was a museum, with exhibits open for public viewing; it was a private organization with a collection. As time wore on that collection became more valuable, especially in the available materials of coins, medals, and fossils. But the members did not make it accessible, so it remained a private cabinet, without power to reach the broad public.

The Library Company was soon joined by other cabinets, both in Philadelphia and elsewhere. The Pennsylvania Hospital in Philadelphia established a teaching cabinet in 1757 when it acquired a skeleton. Five years later the great Quaker physician of London,

James Fothergill, donated to the collection anatomical specimens, casts, and drawings valued at £350. These and subsequent acquisitions were placed in a separate room and opened to the public, but only under rather restrictive conditions. Visitors were admitted only if they paid the equivalent of a Spanish silver dollar, which was a prohibitive price for the time. Professors offered lectures to the public for a somewhat smaller fee; the first series of lectures, given by the renowned Philadelphia physician, Dr. William Shippen, Jr., in 1763, was very well attended, due partially to the reasonable cost. Although public interest was strong, the trustees made no effort to lower the price of admission to the collection itself. Such inaction could be justified—the collection was meant for training physicians, not enlightening the public—but the continued high prices effectively kept the people out and prevented the collection from becoming a museum in a wider sense.[8]

A similar situation prevailed to the north at Harvard College. The roots of this pioneer cabinet can be traced to a gift of a telescope by Governor John Winthrop in 1672. A few other donations came sporadically until, in 1727, an Englishman named Thomas Hollis endowed a chair in mathematics and natural philosophy, and included with the endowment five chests filled with a varied assortment of "philosophical apparatus." The Hollis Professor was to use these for class demonstrations. This gift stimulated others, and the college even began to purchase equipment to fill gaps. The presence in the Hollis Chair, starting in 1739, of John Winthrop IV was undoubtedly a great inducement to expand the collection. Winthrop was acknowledged as a scientist of great achievements; Europeans considered him second only to Franklin among American scientists.

Winthrop's stature became crucial to the college after the disastrous night of January 24, 1764, when Harvard Hall burned to the ground, taking with it virtually the entire philosophical cabinet. The General Court, the administration, and the graduates rallied around the school, and rebuilding began at once. Winthrop personally oversaw the reconstruction of the cabinet, which was placed in the Philosophy School (later Philosophy Chamber) of the new Harvard Hall. Interestingly, one of the rooms in the hall was named the "Musaeum," but this was meant in the older sense of the word, as a room for study.

The new cabinet began to attract more than philosophical apparatus; soon stray minerals and natural history specimens were being deposited. It was not, however, until the years between 1793 and 1800 that the cabinet really began to grow. In 1793 John Coakley Lettsome, an English physician, donated a valuable mineral collection, which was followed in 1795 by a large bequest of minerals made as a gesture of Franco-American solidarity by the Committee of Public Safety of the French Republic, and in 1796 by a substantial collection of marble specimens from James Bowdoin. Dr. Benjamin Waterhouse of the Harvard faculty was designated keeper of the mineral cabinet, and he arranged the minerals in an "elegant mahogany Cabinet" in the Philosophy Chamber for "the inspection of the curious." But the "curious" at Harvard, as at the Pennsylvania Hospital, were only those who were members of the corporation, not the general public. Harvard did not yet have a collection for everyone.[9]

Back in Philadelphia, still another institution of note began to accumulate a cabinet, and again Benjamin Franklin was a founding father. In 1743 Franklin established the American Philosophical Society in the hope that it would become the Royal Society of the New World. Instead it expired of acute apathy within three years; in fact, the heedlessness was so pronounced that no one knows exactly when it died. The fallen torch was raised in 1750 by the Young Junto, a secret club modeled on Franklin's celebrated group of the same name. It had a promising launching, but by 1762, it too was defunct. The Young Junto was revived in 1766, gradually opened its membership, and later that year rechristened itself the American Society for Promoting and Propagating Usefull Knowledge, held in Philadelphia. By 1767 they had adopted as their goal the application of science to economic improvement, and began to attract a somewhat wider membership.

The American Society soon found it had a competitor. Dr. Thomas Bond, a member of Franklin's original American Philosophical Society, founded another organization by the same name at the end of 1767. Bond had many motivations, but perhaps the strongest was his feeling that the American Society was far too exclusive in its membership practices. He saw to it that the new APS had a very broad-based policy; this in turn forced the American Society to further liberalize its own standards. The older group broached an offer to merge the two societies, but was rebuffed by the APS. The two then engaged in a struggle for new members that proved invigorating to both. By the end of 1768, however, sensible men in both camps realized that Philadelphia could not support two scientific societies. The American Society repeated its offer, and after extensive negotiations, the APS accepted it. The two societies pooled their resources, consolidating everything except their already none too short titles: the institution was henceforth to be known as the American Philosophical Society Held at Philadelphia for Promoting Usefull Knowledge.

Despite the ungainly name, the two societies melded together quite nicely. The infant organization already had a tiny cabinet at the time of the merger. On March 13, 1768, Lewis Nicola, a sometime British army officer and now a Philadelphia educator, gave the American Society, of which he was a member, a collection of fishes and other natural curiosities. The Philosophical Society does not appear to have added any artifacts to the union, but the newly minted APS soon became rather active in the collecting game. The new bylaws called for the creation of three curators whose sole responsibility it was to look after the artifacts, an indication of the importance the society placed on arranging and exhibiting its collection. Gifts began to come in from all over the provinces of North America: Massachusetts, Maryland, even Pensacola, Florida, were represented in the *Proceedings*. The collection was heavily weighted toward natural history; the halls soon became crowded with sharks, lizards, birds, and quadrupeds of every description. By 1770, with the addition of the splendid collection of natural history objects formed by Philadelphian William Johnson, the society's collection rivaled that of the Library Company.

The Revolution interrupted the society's meetings for seven

years. In 1785, the APS missed a chance to buy a significant part of Pierre Eugène Du Simitière's valuable collection, but did manage, in 1789, to move into spacious new quarters. In 1794 they secured the services of Charles Willson Peale as curator. The energetic Mr. Peale presided over the rapid expansion of the collection. The APS never solicited donations, nor, it appears, did they frequently refuse them. Growing, as Whitfield Bell put it, "without plan or even clear purpose," the cabinet became ever more various and harder to classify. Moreover, it, like every other cabinet, was open to members only; only those who had the right credentials could see it.[10]

Philadelphia, by the early 1770s, had become a hotbed of interesting cabinets. The Library Company, the Pennsylvania Hospital, and the APS all had collections that were rapidly expanding. An "ill-arranged but interesting assortment of Indian relics"[11] resided at the Society of Fort St. David about this time. Philadelphia's most interesting attraction, however, was to be found at Vidal's Alley off Second Street. This was the home of the extremely colorful Dr. Abraham Chovet (1704–1790). Chovet was born in England, where he learned surgery and medicine. Traveling first to France, he began in 1732 to experiment with wax as a means of making anatomical models. Sometime around 1740, Chovet left for the West Indies, and lived in Antigua and Jamaica.

Finally, sometime before 1774, he settled in Philadelphia. By the end of that year he had established himself as a physician with a growing practice and as the proprietor of a cabinet notable for its quality.

The doctor inspired strong opinions by virtue of his singular personality. Peter S. Du Ponceau, the noted lawyer, linguist, and doyen of Philadelphia cultural life, warmly described him as "witty and good-natured," altogether "humane and benevolent," and, above all, possessing an "excellent heart." Even Du Ponceau, however, had to admit that Chovet was "severe on vulgar people" and had "a constant habit of swearing. With almost every word he would rap a big oath."[12] Chovet's biting tongue and peculiar habits put off many people; the visiting Marquis De Chastellux would declare, more charitably, but still pointedly, "He was to me a greater curiosity than his anatomical models."[13]

All agreed, however, that Chovet's anatomical manikins were of high quality. The manikins provided Chovet with a method of teaching anatomy without having to snatch bodies or offend religious opinion regarding the dissection of cadavers. In Philadelphia, he extended the idea to include popular exhibition, netting profit for Chovet and enlightenment for the populace. Just when he opened his collection to the public is not known, but on October 14, 1774, John Adams, in Philadelphia to attend the Continental Congress, visited and afterwards wrote glowingly in his diary: "Went in the morning to see Dr. Chevott and his skelletons and wax work—most admirable, exquisite, Representations of the whole Animal Æconomy. Four complete Skeletons. . . . Two compleat bodies and Wax. . . . This exhibition is much more exquisite than that of Dr. Shippen, at the Hospital. . . . These wax works are all of the doctor's own hands."[14]

Time did not temper Adam's enthusiasm. In a letter to his wife Abigail, dated May 10, 1777, he favorably compared Chovet's establishment to a rival wax works, saying it was "much more pleasing to me."[15]

Adams, although an acute observer, may have been blinded by nationalistic sentiments during these inflammatory years. But foreign observers, lacking such prejudices, agreed with his conclusions. The critical Chastellux, during his visit on December 5, 1781, judged that Chovet's wax models were "superior to those of the institute at Bologna," and was moved to exclaim that Chovet had carried "this art to the highest degree of perfection."[16]

Baron Von Closen, visiting nearly a year later, was thoroughly impressed by two life-size models of a man and a pregnant woman, opened so that the viscera were visible, with the organs made detachable. He commented, "The faces and other parts are imitated so naturally, the location of the nerves, the loins, and muscles is so well marked, that it is impossible to see them without a certain shock."[17] There can be little doubt that Chovet's collection combined a first-rate teaching tool and a popular attraction and that it was the first American cabinet to gain the respect of visiting Europeans: no small achievement for a provincial institution.

This collection took its life from its creator, and Chovet was unstable. Chastellux had noted of the doctor during his visit, "He is a real eccentric: his chief characteristic is contrary-mindedness."[18] This contumacy was exacerbated by age; long before his death Chovet sank into a pitiful state of offensive garrulousness. After his passing, the Pennsylvania Hospital purchased his collection and in turn presented it to the University of Pennsylvania in 1824, where it was completely destroyed by fire in 1888. Although no tangible record of his work remains, Chovet did manage to prove that respectable cabinets could be established in the New World.

It is perhaps significant that none of these pioneer collectors ever formally called their aggregations a "museum." The term had been in use in its modern sense as early as 1520, and there had been plenty of precedents, among them, of course, the British Museum, dating from 1753. But all of the early American institutions stuck to "cabinet" or "philosophical chamber." Perhaps it was a tacit admission that they did not yet deserve the honor of the appellation.

All this changed in 1773 with the advent of the Charleston Museum. Charleston was *the* cultural center of the colonial South. No ban was placed upon the theater (as there was, for instance, in Boston) and English and American dramatics flourished. Beginning in 1737 the St. Cecilia Society provided excellent concerts, and a varied social menu of lectures, horse races, and elegant balls was to be had. And in 1748 a library was founded there. The leader in this effort was Peter Timothy, son of the Library Company of Philadelphia's first librarian. Within two years the society had 160 members and a small endowment. After gaining a charter in 1755, the society grew rapidly, and by the outbreak of the Revolution, the library's endowment had swollen to £18,000.[19]

As the endowment grew, so too did the scope of the institution. The gentlemen of Charleston, imbued with the Enlightenment urge to pursue knowledge in its totality, naturally sought to widen their field of activities. Alexander Garden, who arrived in Charleston in 1752, was to play an important, if accidental role in this development. A Scottish physician with a strong ambition to be a first-rate botanist, Garden earned the respect of European naturalists by dint of his hard work. In 1772 Garden "wrote to some young men of the province who were attending universities in Great Britain to visit the British Museum. . . . These young men returned with determination to establish the . . . first [museum] in America at Charles Town."[20] On January 12, 1773, the Library Society, at the suggestion of its president, Dr. William Bull, appointed a committee with the ambitious mission of collecting materials in order to promote a "full and accurate natural history of South Carolina, and to support a faculty of professors in order to carry out the charge."[21] The first goal fell by the wayside, but four curators were named, including such leaders of South Carolina's social and political life as Thomas Heyward, Jr., and Charles Coatsworth Pinckney. The four took out a newspaper advertisement appealing for public support, and the donations began to trickle in, the first recorded acquisition being "a drawing of the head of a bird."[22] Soon a bewildering variety of objects were being donated, including "an Indian hatchet, a Hawaiian woven helmet, [and] a Cassava basket from Surinam.[23]

The unifying theme of the institution was scientific. The library and museum purchased a Rittenhouse orrery, a Manigault telescope, "a Camera obscura, a hydrostatic balance and a pair of elegant globes."[24] The founding of the museum was truly "an attempt to establish a center for the study of science,"[25] and the effort was well launched by the time of the Revolution. But the destruction wreaked during the struggle laid a heavy hand on Charleston, and fire, the greatest nemesis of museums in their first century of existence, wiped out nearly all of the museum's collections in 1778. The museum was slow to recover from this blow. As recent authors have stated, the Revolution had "directed intellectual energy towards politics and away from science and literature," and it took some time to reverse this trend.[26] Nothing of substance could be achieved until there was a building, and it was not until 1792 that the third floor of the courthouse was reserved for the struggling institution. Even then the effects of the devastation lingered on, for the collection grew only slowly during the following quarter-century, mainly because of the museum's isolation. It was the only museum south of Philadelphia (with the exception of ephemeral efforts in such cities as Washington, D.C., and Richmond), and it resided in a town that boasted no scientific societies, no medical schools, and only a feeble college. The museum enjoyed a rebirth of sorts in 1815, when the Charleston Library Society donated it to the new Literary and Philosophical Society. The society's energetic president, Stephen Elliot, saw to it that the museum had (for a time) a paid curator, and an ever-increasing collection. The collection was housed in a structure on Chalmers Street and styled the Museum of South Carolina. Elliott, however, failed in an attempt to raise funds for a new building, and in 1828, the society moved the collection to the Medical College, although they retained full ownership. Elliot's death in 1830 proved a blow to the society and the museum, and by the 1840s, the museum was in a state of dormancy.[27]

The museum did not regain its old dynamism until the great scientist and museum director Louis Agassiz, during visits to Charleston in 1847 and 1850, recognized its potential, and convinced the trustees of the College of Charleston to absorb it. After 73 years of relative inactivity, America's oldest museum began once more to take its place at the forefront of the museum movement.

In a real sense, however, the catastrophic fire of 1778 was a beneficial influence on the American museum movement as a whole. In its early years, the Charleston Museum was the child of the Charleston aristocracy, really more a cabinet than a museum. While this select group was neither so elitist nor so exclusive as European aristocracies, it was nonetheless a closed corporation with many antiegalitarian views. As Carl Bridenbaugh noted, "Unlike the Library Company of Philadelphia . . . the trustees made no gesture toward including the lower orders in their undertaking."[28] This is not to say that there was rampant leveling occurring in Philadelphia; however, artisans and other persons among the lower orders in society could belong to the Library Company. That was almost unheard of in the Charleston Library Society. The Charleston Museum established, and for a brief time fostered, an elitist model for American museums. The flames that gutted this model also assured that the American museum would be a more open place than its European counterpart.

The legacy of the Revolution was a new nation gripped by a new nationalism, both political and cultural. The Reverend Jedidiah Morse spoke for his countrymen when he cried, "We are independent of Great Britain and are no longer to look up to her for a description of our own country."[29] That feeling had tremendous consequences for the pioneer cabinets.

The pride and the dignity of a free nation demanded that it gain cultural, as well as political, independence from the mother country. As a consequence, the old "cabinet of curiosity," the European model of a museum—a cabinet for the edification of the few—must be replaced by a distinctly American style, one open to all and useful to all.

The old cabinets did not disappear overnight, of course—indeed, some still survive today—but their ascendancy was clearly doomed. At the Library Company, the Philosophical Society, Harvard, the Pennsylvania Hospital, and Charleston, the cabinets were, by the end of eighteenth century, more or less appendages, and of the five, only Charleston survives today as a lineal descendant of the original institution.

It is important, however, to remember the contributions these institutions made to American museum history. First, they broke the barren ground, planted the seeds of an idea, and nurtured them into a frail germination. Second, by linking their infant establishments to important cultural resources like hospitals, colleges, and libraries, they assured that museums would be viewed as vital institutions in American life. Finally, they began forming collections and inculcated in the American public of the eighteenth century an appreciation for the curious and the historical. They prepared the postrevolutionary era for museums, and, beginning in 1783, museums began to rise with a vengeance.

2

The Moderate Enlightenment, 1780–1800: The Museum for the Respectability

It was the Enlightenment, and America's reaction to it, that completed the transformation of cabinets into museums. As previously noted, during the years 1780 to 1800, the old exclusive "for members only" cabinet began to fade away, to be replaced by the more democratic and open museum. It is important to remember, however, that the exclusivity did not fall away overnight. The owners of these pioneer museums were themselves members of the respectability. Necessity drove them to open their museums to the public, but once they had taken this step, the proprietors came to realize that their museums could be socially useful. The "lower orders"—hired hands, menial laborers, merchant sailors, and the like—sought entertainment and needed education. The museum could be used to give both. At first, of course, these efforts were somewhat tentative. The museum's audience was wider than the cabinet's, but it was still not as broad as it would be later.

The key to understanding the transformation from cabinet to museum is the Enlightenment in America. Like museums, the Enlightenment changed in America to fit the American culture. America had no classical past, no royalty or nobility, no strong established church; in short, there was little against which to rebel. The Enlightenment in America was less contentious than in Europe, although it was not static. Henry May, in his important work *The Enlightenment in America,* divided the Enlightenment into four phases, the Moderate, Skeptical, Revolutionary, and Didactic. He held that the Moderate Enlightenment, mainly a British invention, was dominant in England from the time of Newton and Locke to about 1750, and in America to about 1800. The Skeptical and Revolutionary Enlightenments, both centered in France, had little effect on America. The Didactic Enlightenment, originating in Scotland, took the United States by storm in the first quarter of the nineteenth century.[1] It was the Moderate and the Didactic enlightenments that strongly affected American museums.

The Moderate Enlightenment, like any complicated social phenomenon, sprang from a number of causes. Its founding fathers were Newton and Locke. Newton had bequeathed to the world an understanding of a cosmic system governed by explicable and regular laws and a "faith in Reason as competent to penetrate the meaning of those laws and to induce conformity to them."[2] Locke added to it a belief in the freedom of the human mind, and an ardent humanitarianism. As the Enlightenment developed, other concepts were added: the doctrine of progress, a faith in the perfectability of man, and the desire for balance, order, and moderation in all things. Certain philosophes came truly to believe that if the laws governing the universe could be discovered, and if people could be persuaded to conform to them, the result would be universal happiness and the perfection of mankind.

The Moderate Enlightenment emigrated from Britain to America in the 1750s, just as it was waning in the mother country, and deeply affected the first generation of museum proprietors. There is no mystery why this should be so. According to Henry May, "As in England, the ideas of the Moderate Enlightenment— the formulae of balance, order, and rationality—were especially attractive to the urban, the successful, the striving, the up-to-date."[3] Urban, striving and up-to-date—these are qualities that described the pioneer curators, Pierre Eugène Du Simitière, Charles Willson Peale, and Gardiner Baker. Donald Meyer, in his study, *The Democratic Enlightenment,* confirmed May's insight, saying, "To be sure, the Enlightenment was an elitist (though not an aristocratic movement)—theoretically welcoming all free and inquiring minds, but, in fact, limited to those with talent and the opportunity to participate in the intellectual life."[4] The pioneer curators were all members of the respectability, and had both the talent and the opportunity to participate in the intellectual life of their communities by building a museum.

They were thus members of a privileged class, but they were not content to merely enjoy life without contributing to their society. J. R. Pole neatly summed up the feelings of the respectability in the 1770s: "Privilege certainly existed in America and so did distinctions of class and fortune. But privilege was not a principle; even the privileged tended to see themselves as earning their social keep."[5]

Imbued by this sense of obligation to society, and fired by the Moderate Enlightenment beliefs in reason, humanitarianism, order, balance, and progress, the pioneer proprietors invited to their museums all who could afford the price of admission, and they set these prices low, so that most could buy a ticket. Du Simitière, Peale, and Baker all expected to make a living from their institutions, so there was an admission charge; but the fee had to be kept reasonable, so as to attract a clientele. Nor would they offer mere mindless entertainment. Again and again in their writings, these men reiterated three goals of their museums: rational amusement, pleasurable instruction, and the promotion of piety. Each goal deserves to be examined in turn.

Any man, even an enlightened one, needed amusements and diversions. Too often, however, these diversions were tainted with vice, as in drunkenness and gambling. The museum provided an alternative to sinful pastimes, for it offered entertainment that was innocent and, above all, rational. The early proprietors, then, saw their museums as potent weapons in the war on vice.

Americans had translated earlier the Moderate Enlightenment imperative to search for the natural laws of the universe into the practical goal of education. The pioneer museum proprietors seized upon this idea as worthwhile. They were careful to distinguish, however, between the unpleasant rote memorization that passed for learning in most schools, and their brand of education, which they preferred to call "pleasurable instruction." They felt that the visitor to the museum could not help but learn from the objects displayed, for all men had an innate desire to learn, and the artifacts imparted knowledge in an enjoyable fashion. This too could provide an alternative to unsavory amusements.

The museums also became, in the eyes of their proprietors, secular temples. The evidence of the creator's beneficent plan was on view there; the visitor could begin his consideration with the humblest of animals, continue up the ladder to the sublime creation of man, and from there make a leap to contemplate God Himself. The general formula for this experience was to "look through nature, up to nature's God." To the enlightened man, museums provided the physical proof of the wisdom and order of God's creation. Taken together, these three concepts promoted the Moderate Enlightenment goals of moderation, balance, rationality, progress, and faith in the perfectability of man. They also combined in the museum the functions of a theater, a school, and a church.

It was with these high aspirations that the proprietors began their museums. They looked to European models and found few to imitate, for most were elitist cabinets, or so expensive of entry that they were virtually closed off, even from the respectability. Moreover, they ran museums at a time "when the new nation was struggling toward a national identity, a sense of moral particularity."[6] The victorious conclusion of the Revolution, the ratification of the Constitution, and the jingoistic calls for war with France all occurred between 1780 and 1800, and all promoted cultural nationalism. These new museums would thus develop along American lines, and self-consciously join in the attempt to define a new American culture.

This transition from the cabinet for the classes to the museum for the masses was a slow, evolutionary process, one that was not so much carefully planned as it was improvised. The cradle city was once again Philadelphia, and the unlikely midwife to the birth was not an American cultural nationalist, but a Swiss émigré who was anything but a democrat: Pierre Eugène Du Simitière.

The Transition from Cabinet to Museum: The Experience of Pierre Eugène Du Simitière

There is a gentleman here of French Extraction whose name is Dusimitière, a painter by Profession. . . . This Mr. Dusimitière is a very curious Man. He has begun a Collection of Materials for an History of this Revolution.[7]

John Adams, who wrote these words to his wife Abigail in 1776, was in error regarding the ancestry of Pierre Eugène Du Simitière, who was of Swiss rather than French extraction, but certainly correct about Du Simitière's professions. Indeed, Pierre Eugène Du Simitière is remembered today as an artist and a historian, but rarely given the credit he deserves as a pioneer of American museums. There are several reasons for this failure of our collective memory. Du Simitière's museum proprietorship was short, lasting barely two years, and his premature death, in 1784 at the age of forty-seven, brought a sudden end to his efforts. The considerable achievements of Charles Willson Peale, who like Du Simitière lived in Philadelphia, eclipsed memories of the Swiss. By 1980, Du Simitière's reputation had sunk so low that Peale's biographer, the late Charles Coleman Sellers, sneered that Du Simitière's American Museum was "a magpie's nest of historical and scientific rarities."[8] Such a glib dismissal, however, does not square with the facts. For instance, many worldly European travelers who were critical of most things American had praise for Du Simitière and his museum. Nor does such a harsh assessment recognize that Du Simitière was the first in America to transform a private cabinet into a public museum, and the first to mention the possibility of establishing an American national museum. Most importantly, he pioneered the formation of a museum that simultaneously catered to "middling" and elite audiences, a duality then unknown in Europe, which would become a distinguishing trait in American museums. It is important to remember that these innovations were inspired by an attempt to make a living as a museum proprietor, rather than by an idealism on Du Simitière's part, but they are no less important for that.

Very little is known about Du Simitière's early life, save that he was born in Geneva, of French Protestant parents, on September 18, 1737. He grew to manhood in Geneva, and by the time he turned twenty he had decided to produce a guide to the natural history of the entire Caribbean, illustrated by his own drawings. From 1757 to 1774 he embarked on an odyssey in pursuit of his dream, visiting every major island in the Caribbean, and the principal cities in the North American provinces, supporting himself by his painting. He began to collect natural history specimens immediately and soon started gathering historical and anthropological artifacts as well. As his collection expanded, so did the scope of his project, so that he contemplated a civil and natural history of the Caribbean and North American provinces. During this time, he was collecting purely to document his historical project, which he hoped to publish when he returned to Switzerland.

Du Simitière, however, would never go home again. Instead, he settled in Philadelphia in 1774, where he had lived briefly on three earlier occasions. There he seems to have realized the enormity of his undertaking and decided to condense his plans; he would now limit his natural and civil history to the American provinces. His winnowing notwithstanding, the project remained daunting and he was no doubt alert for a patron to back his plans.

The budding historian returned to the most culturally mature city in the American provinces. "The Paris of the new world" was *the* center of American science. Here lived Benjamin Franklin, who had "tamed the lightning"; David Rittenhouse, one of the world's foremost astronomers; and Benjamin Rush, the preeminent physician in the provinces. All three, and many others besides, gathered at the meetings of the American Philosophical Society. The cabinet of the APS had by now grown to a respectable size, as had that of the Library Company, which also offered its stockholders borrowing privileges from a collection of books already numbering in the thousands. The Pennsylvania Hospital still allowed a visit to its cabinet for a dollar, and Dr. Chovet was undoubtedly the best show in town.

Du Simitière settled comfortably into the intellectual life of Philadelphia. He belonged to the APS and thus had access to Philadelphia's cultural elite. He continued his search for a patron to publish his history project, and in the meantime, continued to augment his collection. He corresponded extensively with those who might be helpful, such as the commander of a western fort, whom he wrote asking for "Things in Use among the Indians . . . Subjects of Natural History . . . all the different kinds of . . . Shells found in the alleghenny . . . [and] any Samples of minerals . . . found in your district."[9] A fair proportion of the historian's correspondents sent donations, and his rooms soon were literally overflowing with artifacts of science, history, natural history, and art. It was fortunate that he received gifts, for his income from painting was never really sufficient to cover his expenses. Du Simitière was constantly in financial trouble.

The outbreak of the Revolution in 1775 complicated Du Simitière's life immensely. It exacerbated his financial problems and placed him in the middle between hostile parties. His response to the crisis of these years illuminates his character as nothing else could. Idealism, nationalism, patriotism—all of these sentiments were unknown to Du Simitière. The American Enlightenment was at its zenith, but one searches his writings in vain for any sentiments extolling moderation, balance, or order. He was a Swiss national, but his surviving manuscripts show no evidence of any affinity for Switzerland. He did make numerous references to his love for the American people, but these always occurred in the writings promoting either his history project or his museum. The Swiss's biographer, Paul Sifton, noted that Du Simitière used his detachment to advantage: "It is evident that Du Simitière enjoyed the ability to be both a 'European in America' and a 'Naturalized American'; that either one pose or the other would assist him in a given situation."[10]

Sifton was absolutely correct in identifying Du Simitière as a consummate pragmatist. The Swiss was put to the test when he was drafted to serve in the Pennsylvania militia in 1777, as the British closed in on Philadelphia. Du Simitière, who had not the money to hire a substitute, appealed his conscription to Thomas Wharton, president of the Executive Council of the commonwealth of Pennsylvania: "Your memorialist . . . begs leave upon this occasion to present to the Honourable Council that he is a foreigner and native of the Republic of Geneva. . . . in all countries strangers travelling in them are exempted from such regulations as are calculated solely for the particular inhabitants thereof."[11]

Du Simitière, who had lived in America for nearly thirteen of the preceding fourteen years, was standing on dubious ground when he claimed to be a foreigner. Moreover, he omitted that on May 20, 1769, he had become a naturalized citizen of the province of New York. Du Simitière, innocent of ideology, devoid of nationalism, and ever watchful for the main chance, saw no percentage in serving the country he professed to love, so he shamelessly lied to avoid it.

Du Simitière continued to be a citizen of the world during the British occupation of Philadelphia from September 1777 to May 1778. He entertained British officers and patriot leaders with complete impartiality, and managed to retain friends in both camps. After the British withdrawal, far from apologizing for his collaboration with the enemy, Du Simitière, on July 22, 1779, wrote a memorial to the president of the Continental Congress asking support for his proposed civil and natural history of America. Interestingly, his request was entitled "Memorial of Pierre Eugène Du Simitière, Native of the Republic of Geneva and Citizen of the United States of America."[12] Now that it suited his purposes, he once again claimed American citizenship. Congress denied his request. Du Simitière then turned to the Pennsylvania legislature, which awarded him a grant of £200, but by the time it was finally approved in 1781, the Pennsylvania money had stopped circulating and was therefore literally worthless.

The would-be historian accepted these rebuffs unhappily but pragmatically. He needed to increase his income; if his historical project would not serve, perhaps his artifacts would. In truth, his collection had been evolving into a museum for some time.

The first recorded patron came to his door in 1775. The Continental Congress was meeting in Philadelphia, and one of its members, Richard Smith, took advantage of a day of adjournment to visit the learned Swiss. Smith's diary reads simply, "Thursday 28 Septr. No Congress. . . . I amused myself all the morning in M. Du Simitière's museum."[13] Smith erred, for at this point Du Simitière had a collection, or at most a private cabinet, not a museum open to the public. Smith's brief account, however, reveals one useful fact: Du Simitière must have already assembled a substantial cabinet if he could amuse a visitor for an entire morning.

Over the next six years, Du Simitière's collection gradually evolved into a quasi-public institution. His notebooks reveal he frequently lent books and other articles from his collection to his fellow townspeople and he occasionally experienced difficulty in retrieving them. Unlike other cabinets, which were expensive of entry, a tour of Du Simitière's cabinet was free to any person of the respectable classes. The volume of visitors must have suggested the monetary expedience of opening a museum.

Certainly more requests were coming in from people anxious to see the virtuoso's collection. On August 20, 1780, Du Simitière, in replying to a correspondent, wrote, "I shall be very happy to see you at my house, and to entertain you with my collection, which has increased considerably, and which is in much better order than when you saw it before."[14] Later that year, the German soldier Baron Ludwig Von Closen, in the midst of a trip to Philadelphia, paid Du Simitière a visit. Von Closen apparently meant to list in his journal the curiosities he had observed, but failed to do so. What he did note, however, is interesting: "After seeing all these fine things, I could not help telling him of my amazement at finding, in the very middle of them, a poor pair of little strong-boots, at which we laughed a great deal. He assured us that for some years they had attracted the attention of many gentlemen, who took them for *Charles XII's* shoes because of his jest that he had obtained them from *Sweden*!!! His sport has certainly been spoiled since the arrival of the French army on the Continent."[15]

Von Closen went on to label Du Simitière "a likable charlatan"[16] but that assessment seems too harsh. Von Closen himself spoke of the many "fine things" exhibited by his host, and implied that Du Simitière's arrangement was good, for otherwise it would not have shocked him to find the boots as a part of it. This approbation is significant, for the baron was used to seeing fine things. As for Du Simitière's "jest," it was just that, a jest. The Swiss seems to have enjoyed occasionally poking fun at the pretensions of the rather gullible Americans who surrounded him.

Another distinguished foreign visitor, the Marquis Du Chastellux, arrived about three months after Von Closen took his leave. Chastellux later wrote of the cabinet that it "was rather small and rather paltry [but] very renowned in America because it had no rival there; it was formed by a painter from Geneva called 'Cimitière,' whose cemeterial name is better suited to a doctor than to a painter."[17] The marquis was undoubtedly measuring the developing institution by the standard of the great galleries of the Continent, and it cannot be surprising that it should suffer in the comparison. Chastellux noted, however, that Du Simitière's collection had already achieved some fame in the young nation, a remarkable achievement for a cabinet not yet open to the public. The perceptive Chastellux added of the proprietor, "He is still a bachelor and still a foreigner, a very uncommon thing in America, where the titles of husband and of citizen are generally acquired without delay."[18] Once more, Du Simitière had decided he was not an American citizen, evidence again of his peculiarly detached nature, a man without strong convictions living in an age full of enthusiasms. This aloofness, however, does not mean that he did not understand the prevailing cultural currents, for though he never legally became a United States citizen, he understood what Americans wanted.

By the end of 1781, with his historical scheme hopelessly moribund and his bills mounting, Du Simitière began to consider seriously opening his collection to the public. Du Simitière seems to have been motivated initially only by financial need.

He fixed the date of opening in a letter to a foreign correspondent: "You will probably have seen in our newspapers of last April and May that I have been induced to open my collection of [sic] the public."[19] This initial opening in April of 1782 was announced by small notices in the newspapers. Thus quietly, for the first time in American history, a private cabinet had been transformed into a public museum. That which was formerly open only to friends and acquaintances of Du Simitière was now open to anyone who could manage the relatively affordable entrance fee of fifty cents. The Swiss would take care to keep his museum a respectable place, for he never offered spectacular entertainments. On the other hand, he also needed to attract the "middling" orders to remain solvent, hence his advertisements in the popular press. This was the first experiment in the tenuous balance between the elite and the popular that would become the hallmark of the American museum.

Unfortunately, Du Simitière's opening was too quiet, and he failed to get many visitors. The aspiring museum proprietor took quick action. On June 1, 1782, he purchased newspaper advertisements and distributed broadsides, both boldly entitled "American Museum." He explained: "The subscriber, having been induced from several motives to open his Collection for the inspection of Gentlemen and Ladies . . . who are desirous to see the curiosities it contains, thinks it incumbent upon him to subjoin for their information a short enumeration of the subjects of which it is composed."[20]

Du Simitière classified his collection according to the standard divisions of the eighteenth century, "Natural" and "Artificial" curiosities. Under the Natural heading, he listed marine productions, land productions, petrifications, and botany; under the Artificial, antiquities, weapons, ornamental dresses of both the American Indians and the natives of the East and West Indies, artifacts from certain African tribes, and a "Collection of curious paintings in Oil, Crayons, Water-Colours."[21] Certainly there was much to attract visitors in this wide-ranging aggregation, particularly when "a number of miscellaneous Curiosities of various kinds" were included in the bargain.[22]

Du Simitière proceeded to list his policies. He planned to be open four days per week: Tuesday, and Thursday through Saturday. He would sell tickets, at fifty cents each, every forenoon

American Museum.

THE Subscriber having been induced from several motives, to open his Collection for the inspection of the Gentlemen and Ladies, Strangers in this City, and their Friends, who are desirous to see the Curiosities it contains, thinks it incumbent upon him, to subjoin for their information, a short enumeration of the subjects of which it is composed, collected from most parts of America, the West-Indies, Africa, the East-Indies, and Europe.

NATURAL CURIOSITIES.

MARINE PRODUCTIONS. A very large and complete Collection of the most rare and beautiful Shells, Sea-eggs, Corals, Sea-plants, Fishes, Tortoises, Crabs, Sea-stars, and other curious animal productions of the sea.

LAND PRODUCTIONS. Rare Birds, and parts of Birds and Nests; a variety of Snakes, Lizzards, Bats, Insects, and Worms, the most of them from different parts of the West-Indies.

FOSSILS. Ores of various metals, Platina, and other mineral substances, Agates, Moccos, Jaspers, Cornelian, Onyx, Chrysolites, Crystals, Sparrs, Quartzes, Asbestas, and other curious and rare-figured, pellucid and diversely coloured Pebbles.

PETRIFICATIONS, of various kinds of wood, Plants, Fruits, Reptiles, Insects, Bones, Teeth, and of those subjects that once belonged to the sea; such as Shells, Sea-eggs, Sea-worms, Shark's Teeth, Corals, and Madrepores: As also curious concretions of petrified waters, and stony incrustations over several kinds of bodies, natural and artificial.

Likewise, Fossil substances produced by the eruptions of Volcanos.

BOTANY. A very considerable Collection of the most curious Plants of the West-Indies, together with the several productions of those Plants; such as their Wood, Bark, Fruits, Pods, Kernels, and Seeds, all in the highest preservation.

ARTIFICIAL CURIOSITIES.

Antiquities of the Indians of the West-Indies, and of the North American Indians.

Ornamental Dresses of the modern Indians of North and South-America, with their Weapons and Utensils.

Curious ancient European and East-Indian Weapons; also a valuable curiosity from the Island of Otaheite.

Various Weapons, Musical Instruments and Utensils of the Negroes, from the coast of Guinea, and the West-Indies.

A Collection of curious Paintings in Oil, Crayons, Water-colours, Miniature, Enamel, China, with specimens of the ancient and modern transparent painting on glass, and a curious deception of perspective.

Besides a number of miscellaneous Curiosities of various kinds.

The days of admittance are Tuesday, Thursday, Friday and Saturday, and the hours for each company at Eleven and Twelve o'clock in the forenoon, and at Three, Four and Five o'clock in the afternoon, allowing an hour for each company; which to avoid inconveniency to themselves, he hopes will not exceed six, or at most eight in one sett. By sending for tickets a day or two before, the day and hour that suit the company will be particularly mentioned.

He takes this public opportunity to return his grateful thanks to all those persons who for several years past have from various parts of this Continent contributed to increase his Collection, and hopes he will continue to be favoured with such articles as may fall in their possession, more particularly as he intends his Cabinet to be hereafter the foundation of the first American Museum.

TICKETS to be had in the forenoon of every day, Sundays excepted, at his house in Arch-street, above Fourth-street, at HALF A DOLLAR each.

P. E. DU SIMITIERE.

Philadelphia, June 1, 1782.

PRINTED BY JOHN DUNLAP.

Broadside announcing the opening of Pierre Eugène Du Simitière's American Museum, June 1, 1782 (Courtesy of The Library Company of Philadelphia)

Monday through Saturday. The purchasers would then arrange with the proprietor to return later. He would keep strict control over his patrons, decreeing, "The hours for each company [will be] at Eleven and Twelve o'clock in the forenoon and at Three, Four and Five o'clock in the afternoon, allowing an hour for each company; which to avoid inconveniency to themselves, he hopes will not exceed six, or at the most eight in one sett [*sic*]."[23]

In restricting visitors to tours of short duration, Du Simitière was following the lead of the British Museum, which, although it was much larger, herded visitors through its galleries in about the same amount of time. Unfortunately the self-imposed maximum of eight persons per tour would limit him to a gross income of eighty dollars per week, hardly adequate for the support of a growing collection.

This calculation seems to have escaped Du Simitière, for he concluded the broadside with an optimistic, almost visionary wish: "He intends his Cabinet to be hereafter the foundation of the first American Museum."[24] Here is the first articulation of a dream that would echo for more than seventy years to come: a national museum for the United States. It is doubtful if Du Simitière was motivated by idealism in making this declaration. Once again, the canny virtuoso made an appeal to the patriotism and cultural nationalism of the era, by both calling his new establishment the "American Museum" and by hinting that he would some day make it a national institution. The cultural nationalism of the 1780s was a potent force. Scholars have long noted that after the Revolution there was an enormous demand for American artists, scientists, and authors to divorce their work from that of their counterparts in Europe in order to build—self-consciously—a distinctively *American* culture.[25] In naming his museum, then, Du Simitière was climbing on the cultural bandwagon.

The newly opened museum was destined to have a brief life of less than two and one-half years. This short existence left almost no trace behind it; there are no records of attendance or special events, and only sketchy accession records. Thus many crucial questions about the quality of Du Simitière's museum can be answered only tentatively, if at all. Only the accounts of a handful of visitors remain to document this pioneering effort at museum-making.

Baron Von Closen had spoken of the many "fine things"[26] he saw in the virtuoso's collection, and even the critical Marquis Du Chastellux admitted, "[I] satisfied my eyes,"[27] at Du Simitiere's cabinet. They were not the only ones to appreciate his efforts. A German physician named Johann David Schoepf praised the Swiss's museum: "Mr. du Simitière of Geneva, a painter, is almost the only man in Philadelphia who manifests a taste for natural history. Also he possesses the only Collection, a small one, of natural curiosities—and a not inconsiderable number of well-executed drawings of American birds, plants and insects."[28]

Schoepf's approbation is significant, for he had received extensive training in natural history and would have been offended by a poorly arranged cabinet full of trivial curiosities. The verdict of the visitors seems clear: Du Simitière's collection was small, but of reasonably high quality, and tolerably well arranged. If his museum was worthy of a generally favorable assessment from well-traveled Europeans, it almost certainly pleased less-traveled Philadelphians and American tourists.

Unfortunately, there were neither enough people in Philadelphia, nor enough tourists visiting it, to constitute an ample clientele for Du Simitière. He wrote several times of having received "a number of visitors" after opening his museum, but this early success did not last. By September of 1782, he was lamenting his ticket sales: "[T]his has confirmed my expectations very well for some time, but it is not continuing. I find it exceedingly difficult to keep together what I have been collecting for a great number of years & I find hardly any prospect of enjoying the fruits of my toils and labours."[29]

The despair so evident in this passage was premature, for business began to pick up shortly thereafter. Then in March 1783 disaster struck; an illness required the amputation of a joint from a finger on his left hand. This operation left him in terrible pain and unable to work for some weeks thereafter. The loss of income was a terrible blow, and was exacerbated by a move to more commodious (and expensive) quarters at Arch above Fourth Street in May. By the time Schoepf arrived in Philadelphia in late July 1783, the situation was becoming serious. Schoepf declared, "It is to be regretted that his activities, and his enthusiasm for collecting, should be embarrassed by domestic circumstances, and that he should fail of positive encouragement from the American public."[30] Despite the fact that by August 8, 1783, there were sufficient patrons to keep Du Simitière home "every forenoon" to attend them, his museum income was not enough to cover his bills.[31]

Du Simitière never really fully recovered from the operation, which severely hampered his artistic ability and thus cut further into his already depleted income. At the end of 1783 his writing abruptly ceased, as his health began to fail him. By December of 1783 he had taken on drawing pupils, among them Thomas Jefferson's daughter Martha, in a desperate attempt to make ends meet. A letter Jefferson wrote Martha reveals just how impecunious Du Simitière had become by February of 1784. "With respect to the paiment [sic] of the guinea," wrote Jefferson, "I would wish him to receive it, because if there is to be a doubt between him and me, of which of us acts rightly, I would chuse [sic] to remove it clearly off my own shoulders."[32] Du Simitière's grasping for money was understandable, for he was penniless. The obvious answer was to sell his collection, but he could not bring himself to do it. He died on October 10 or 22, 1784, at the age of forty-seven. After a careful study of the few scraps of remaining evidence, Paul Sifton theorized that the cause of death was starvation.

The American Museum died along with its proprietor. Some members of the Pennsylvania legislature wished the commonwealth to purchase the collection intact for the University of Pennsylvania, but their efforts failed. Two administrators, including the bookseller Ebenezer Hazard, were named to take charge of the estate. Although Hazard later claimed that he took the post "with a view to prevent his museum from being scattered,"[33] he and his partner worked with dispatch to do just the opposite. On March 19, 1785, the contents of the American Museum were sold at public auction in Philadelphia, comprising thirty-six large lots. Among them were eighteen lots of books, nine of drawings and prints, and five of "curiosities." The Library Company of Philadelphia was the biggest purchaser, buying so many books that it took twenty-two pages to list them all.

Despite printed assertions to the contrary, there is absolutely no evidence that Charles Willson Peale was either present at the sale, or purchased anything through agents, although some items from Du Simitière's museum may have been donated to him later. He was, however, acquainted with his museum predecessor. In a letter to his son Rembrandt, written in 1812, Peale recalled: "At this time [ca. 1773] I became acquainted with Mr. Simitire a miniature painter, he was fond of collecting objects of natural history, his painting room was ornamented with frames of Butterflies and he had a considerable number of snakes and c. in spirits—he also collected medals & coins. . . . in his latter time, he made a sort of Museum displayed in one or two Rooms—chiefly consisting, with the above, of antic [*sic*] dresses arms & c, he received a small sum for admission."[34]

Peale thus had an acquaintance with Du Simitière and had probably visited the American Museum, for his memory of its contents was quite accurate. There is an unmistakably patronizing air to Peale's description of Du Simitière's effort as "a sort of Museum." Nearly fourteen years later, just before his death, Peale once more mentioned the Swiss: "He . . . collected some few articles of antiquity . . . but he made no attempts to preserve either birds or quadrupeds. He had a few coins, perhaps they were the most valuable part of his collection."[35]

Peale's opinion of Du Simitière seems to have deteriorated during the intervening time. Now Peale accused him of collecting in areas that were not important, and of having paltry collections in general. Far from considering Du Simitière an honored predecessor, Peale thought him a quaint hoarder of marginally interesting material. Clearly Peale felt that he owed nothing in terms of artifacts or of inspiration to his predecessor.

Peale, however, was not being completely honest with himself. Although it is true that he received no artifacts from Du Simitière,

Broadside announcing the sale, at public auction, of the collection from the museum formed by the late Pierre Eugène Du Simitière, Thursday, March 10, 1785 (Courtesy of The Library Company of Philadelphia)

he did garner some direct and indirect examples from his predecessor. He witnessed Du Simitière's transformation of a private cabinet into a public museum, and must have noted with interest that many people were willing to pay to see it. Since he was familiar with Du Simitière's collection, he may have absorbed a few lessons in organization as well. Far from being the "magpie's nest" that Peale's descendant Sellers described, Du Simitière's museum displayed a logical arrangement. Du Simitière despised disorder and bluntly criticized it when confronted with it. For instance, he was disturbed by a visit to the Society of Fort St. David, a fishing club, which met once a week at the Falls of the Schuylkill and which owned a small private cabinet. According to Du Simitière, they kept a house "where in a good number of curiosities natural and artificial are to be Seen, but without choice and in very bad order promiscuously mixt [*sic*] with covers for Dishes, cup boards, China, Pewter & c."[36] Du Simitière's museum was as well organized as the various nature of the collection would allow, and Peale probably observed that fact.

Whatever Peale owed to Du Simitière, he added many innovations of his own, and is justly remembered as a giant in the cradle age of American museums. Du Simitière, however, is another story. With no one to take up his mantle after his premature death, and his collection broken up and sold, it is little wonder that his efforts are largely forgotten today. Yet it was Du Simitière, with no precedents to guide him, who first transformed a private cabinet into a public museum. It was Du Simitière who first mentioned the desirability of forming an American national museum. And it was Du Simitière who first experimented with a forerunner of the American Compromise—a museum simultaneously catering to popular and elite audiences. He failed through a combination of poor management and bad luck, and his ideas were less copied than reinvented by others. Although the trail he blazed has been obliterated by the successive widenings of those who followed him, the credit for being first rightfully belongs to Pierre Eugène Du Simitière.

Charles Willson Peale's Great School of Nature

A well-organized museum is an epitome of the world.[37]

The hammer fell on Du Simitière's collection during the "public vendue" of March 19, 1785, in Philadelphia. On July 7, 1786, Charles Willson Peale, one of America's leading artists, took out the first of a series of advertisements in the *Pennsylvania Packet*, announcing that he would "make a part of his House a Repository for Natural Curiosities—The Public he hopes will thereby be gratified in the sight of many of the Wonderful Works of Nature which are now closeted but seldom seen."[38] Thus, the proper date for the founding of the Philadelphia Museum is 1786, although Peale had engaged in some museum-like activities as early as 1785.

Any consideration of the museum that Charles Willson Peale opened in 1786 and nurtured until his death in 1827 must take into account the studies done by Charles Coleman Sellers. He left a corpus of works on Peale the artist and Peale the curator which ably tell the story of his life and the story of his museum. It would be pointless to duplicate these fine books.[39] Instead, this work will concentrate on the new kind of institution Peale invented, and the cultural imperatives that drove him.

A barrier to a proper understanding of Peale is the sheer length of his life and career. He was born in 1741, came to maturity as a provincial, fought in the Revolutionary War, took part in Pennsylvania politics, then spent the last thirty-two years of his life as the proprietor of a museum. The museum itself survived its founder for another eighteen years. Thus, for a half century, the purposes and motivations behind the "Great School of Nature" developed and changed. These changes were substantive, but usually subtle, so they have often escaped notice of the many scholars who have written about Peale and his museum.

Because his institution endured so long, it went through all or part of four of the six periods delineated in the Prologue, beginning with the Moderate Enlightenment (1780–1800), followed by the Didactic Enlightenment (1800–1820), the Age of Egalitarianism (1820–1840), and the Age of Professionalism (1840–1850).

The changes in Peale's purposes and motivations correspond quite nicely with the model, and all were prompted by the cultural imperatives of those eventful fifty years.

Peale did not, of course, arrive instantly at his understanding of the potential of his new museum. This came about through an evolutionary process which took many years. Like Du Simitière before him, he was driven to create a museum by financial need, for he simply could not make a living as a painter adequate to support his large and growing family. The museum thus had to be a popular institution, one which attracted even the lower orders of society, for only by paid admissions could it be supported. Peale could have made it a freak show, which would have kept the turnstiles busy. Instead, he consulted with three of the most eminent American scientists before he began. David Rittenhouse, the great astronomer and mathematician, thought a natural history museum was a good idea, but feared that it would hinder Peale's career as an artist. Robert Patterson, professor of mathematics at the University of Pennsylvania, was so positive about the plan that he donated the museum's first artifact, a paddlefish. When Dr. Franklin, full of years and scientific honors, returned from France in 1785 and gave his blessing (as well as an angora cat), Peale felt assured of support from the scientific community. He opened his museum to the public in 1786, and just two weeks later was accepted as a member by the American Philosophical Society. This compromise between the popular and the scientific, tenuous as it was, kept the museum both respectable and profitable for more than forty years.

Barely three months after opening his doors to the public, Peale wrote a friend, "I find that I am getting into a much greater field than I first expected or intended, I find it very amusing, and I hope in the end it will be usefull [*sic*]."[40] Peale had been moved to launch his museum enterprise by more than financial need. He was also motivated by factors that were close reflections of American culture after the Revolution. All deserve consideration in detail.

In the cultural constellation of 1786, the five factors that influenced Charles Willson Peale were the Enlightenment, Deism, deference, republicanism, and cultural nationalism. These five imperatives remained strong until the French Revolution, but all save cultural nationalism began to decline thereafter. Before the end of the Moderate Enlightenment period in 1800, these four were so decayed that a new motive joined cultural nationalism as a guiding factor: popular education. These cultural changes are faithfully mirrored in Peale's writings from 1786 to 1800.

The first of the five cultural factors was the Enlightenment. Peale had been from his youth a devotee of what Henry May called the Moderate Enlightenment. Its watchwords were order, moderation, balance, harmony, and tolerance. Peale had read deeply in Rousseau and became his philosophical disciple; he believed fervently in the natural rights of men, the dignity of all people, and the sanctity of liberty.

By 1786, Peale had lived through tumultuous times, but he was confident that Enlightenment precepts would prevail if only men would exercise their powers of reason in order to understand the laws that govern the cosmos. Lillian Miller was quite correct in assessing Peale's life as being "marked by the pursuit of harmony during a period in history unusually troubled by turmoil, social and political upheaval, and violent change."[41] One of the best weapons in this pursuit of harmony, he soon realized, was his museum. It could be made a bulwark against chaos, a place where order reigned supreme. With this idea firmly in mind, he wrote of his first exhibits, "To arrange them classically is absolutely necessary to promote a knowledge of the[ir] qualities to make them useful."[42] Peale carefully arranged his exhibits according to the Linnaean system and initially harbored an artless faith that people could not help but to be inspired by the vista that lay before them.

But what would induce the visitor to come to learn? For Peale it was simple: "the wondrous work." In the early years, he simply could not believe that anyone could fail to be as overwhelmed as he was by the pageant of nature. Today we can only call such thinking naive, but to Peale it seemed reasonable. First in America, then in France, the forces of reason and human dignity had triumphed. The dark ages of despotic kings and parasitic nobility were surely numbered. The Enlightenment appeared to have its own momentum, and people seemed to have an innate thirst for the blessings of rationality the museum could provide. In 1793, when Citizen Genet arrived in Philadelphia as the emissary of the Republic of France, Peale's optimism reached the highwater mark.

But Genet was recalled, reaction rocked France, and a despotism emerged to eclipse the republic. To Peale, as to countless others worldwide, this was a terrible blow. He retained his love for French culture and his admiration for French scientists, but he never regained his blind faith in the efficacy of Enlightenment ideals. No longer would he believe that there was an innate desire to seek reason; he concluded that people must be convinced. After 1795, Peale's writings became less sanguine and more exhortatory. On the other hand, he never lapsed into despair; indeed he remained cautiously optimistic. In 1799, in the second of a course of lectures he was giving on natural history, he declared, "The comfort, happiness, and support of all ranks depend on their knowledge of nature. . . . it is a sourse [*sic*] from which man is taught to *know himself*, whose lessons teach him to *bear with patience*."[43] Natural history was no longer an automatic passport to perfect harmony and rationality, but it still could, if studied properly, give one patience and happiness. And if it was no longer an inevitable key to understanding the cosmos, it was at least a key to self-knowledge. Peale thus adjusted his view of the Enlightenment concepts of reason, rationality, and order, but never abandoned them altogether.

The second factor in the cultural mix that motivated Peale was Deism. He rejected the supernatural doctrines of conventional Christianity, instead positing a Supreme Being whose existence could be rationally probed by the evidence of his creation. Alexander Pope had written:

> All are but parts of one stupendous whole
> Whose body nature is, God the Soul[44]

This might seem a presumptuous claim, but Peale believed that he could prove it by means of his museum. Linnaeus's binomial system of classification would allow him to exhibit animals in ascending order from the humblest slug to the most exalted man. And above man hovered God, the Great First Cause, who had planned this remarkable system, and revealed Himself thereby.

So, by a study of the specimens neatly arranged in Peale's museum, a person could come to understand the perfection of the Creator; the museum was in fact a secular temple. In addition to learning about the nature of God in his temple, one could learn much about human nature. By studying the specimens arranged in the museum, one became aware of how they were all part of "the same chain . . . extended by such small gradations from Animal to Animal throughout the Earth, Sea and Air, and even from animal to vegetable beings and a still further continued series from thence throughout all Nature's productions, manifesting the most perfect *order* in the works of a great *Creator*—who's [*sic*] ways are wisdom, His paths are peace, harmony and Love."[45] Peale did not shrink from the implications of this statement, for several times in his correspondence and writings he referred to his museum as a "temple."

The museum offered the opportunity to emulate the higher virtues and harmonies of God's creation. God spoke to man through His creation, and Peale firmly believed that his museum could amplify the Creator's voice. This temple required no fanatical minister, no speaking in tongues, no laying on of hands—only a quiet communication with nature, and through nature, with nature's God.

The third important cultural influence on Peale in 1786 was the deferential model of society. Later generations would describe the dynamics of deference as a trade-off; the lower orders, such as artisans and mechanics, were expected to submit to the rule of the respectability, those who had property and social standing. In return, members of the respectability would exercise their authority in a benevolent fashion, always acting in the best interest of the lower orders. In short, deference purchased benevolent paternalism.

In his youth Peale had less faith in such ideas. His semi-impoverished beginnings had made him a radical in prerevolutionary Maryland politics and briefly a leader of the very radical "Furious Whigs" in the Pennsylvania legislature in 1779–80. The rancor of such clashes repelled him, however, and he abandoned politics, settling down after the war as a landowner and family man. His experiences in London before the Revolution had led to friendships with Benjamin West and Benjamin Franklin, and during the war he became acquainted with such leaders as Washington, Adams, Jefferson, and Madison. These factors tempered his radicalism; although he remained to the left of center for the times, he came increasingly to adopt the ideas of deference as the proper way to order society. By the end of the 1780s, he was firmly convinced of the necessity of the system of deference.

The Terror and Thermidor profoundly affected Peale. The old buoyant optimism left him, replaced not by pessimism exactly, but certainly by caution. When he looked around him, he saw not deferential lower orders, but rather a potential mob. By 1796, he was moved to hope that his museum would "afford a sourse [*sic*] of entertainment to the mind, the very reverse of [raging?] dissipation and frivolity which seems at present to have seized the inhabitants of this growing City."[46] In a sense, given the danger he feared if society went topsy-turvy, Peale's response was very moderate. Instead of oppression he preferred "giving light and food to the public mind."[47] The museum was the perfect place in which to teach the lower orders a proper respect for rank and gradation. When they observed the system of nature they could see "charming models for every social duty, in order to render man . . . more content in the station where he is placed."[48] The museum was thus a school for civic responsibility, in which a man could learn his place in the social order.

This points up an interesting fact about early American museums. They were not the creatures of the people, certainly, but neither were they the playthings of the aristocracy. They were instead the creations of the respectability, the "upper-middle class" to use the jargon of today. They had to depend on the people to survive, so they could not have been bastions of elitism, even if their owners had wanted them to be. It was a far different story across the water, for European museums "reflected the more socially stratified structure of that society. The European museum was directed toward artists, savants and amateurs of science and art, not toward the populace."[49] Even when Peale was uneasy about the people, he was doing everything he could to draw them in. The museum in America was inevitably a more democratic, open, and boisterous affair than its European counterpart, for the European museum also reflected its native stratified culture.

The model of a deferential society was actually part of a larger cultural whole, which formed the fourth of Peale's motivations. This was the concept of republicanism, which, as Peale and his contemporaries understood it, meant more than a state in which the supreme power resides in the people and in their elected representatives. It included antimonarchism, constitutionalism, a belief in nonaristocratic leadership, an emphasis on the public weal, and a strong emphasis upon the importance of public virtue. Republicanism was a system ideally suited for a small young nation unsullied by widespread poverty nor bedeviled by great diversity. Peale embraced the ideal, but recognized that social cohesion and public virtue alone made it possible, and further understood that such conditions were not automatic. Since only a virtuous, intelligent, and self-sacrificing population was capable of practicing republicanism, such qualities had to be promoted through his museum.

In 1786, Peale was still relatively sanguine about republicanism. The nation was small, the people were virtuous, the future seemed bright. But late in that year, Daniel Shays led the farmers of Massachusetts in revolt against the respectability of seaboard towns. Although Shays's rebellion was crushed the following year, Peale was shaken. In 1794 the twin blows of the French Reaction and the Whiskey Rebellion destroyed Peale's early optimism about republicanism. If it was to survive at all, he decided, the public virtue on which it depended must be inculcated in the people. But how was this lesson in public morality to be delivered?

The answer was to be found in the museum: "The utility of a well-organized repository of Natural History is strikingly obvious in Various points of View, but more particularly important by the instruction it diffuses in the most powerful and pleasing modes.[50] If vice was the enemy of republicanism because it sapped the people's virtue, then the museum was the protector of the public because it offered instruction and what Peale called "rational amusement." Even if the people didn't learn anything at the museum, they would at least be kept away from evil or deleterious pursuits by the good clean fun it offered.

Peale was fond of saying how important the museum was to everybody, but he usually worried most about the lower orders. For instance, in his second lecture of 1799 (he offered forty from 1799 to 1802, in conjunction with the University of Pennsylvania, perhaps the first lectures in America illustrated by museum specimens), he reiterated his intention "to show how important is the knowledge of natural history to every class of citizens. I address the Farmer, the merchant and the Mechanic."[51] Peale knew full well that successful republics of the past had been small; when they grew large, like Rome, the end was near. And here were the lower orders, constantly increasing, threatening to overwhelm the republic by sheer force of numbers. The museum, however, could be of immense service here, for with "the mixture of men at such a rallying point viewing the charming variety of nature, people would become more sociable by being accustomed to see each other frequently in the same pursuits of knowledge"[52] To Peale, his museum was nothing less than a great engine of democracy, teaching people to be responsible, virtuous, and sociable at best, and at the very least, keeping visitors out of trouble. In a system that depended on the intelligence and wisdom of the people for its very survival, the museum was a crucial link in the chain of education. Late in 1799, when Peale was soliciting the representatives of Massachusetts for help in publishing his museum's catalog, he closed by saying that he trusted "it will be unnecessary to . . . state the beneficial tendency of such an Institution in a Republic, to instruct the mind and sow the seeds of virtue."[53]

But of all of the cultural imperatives, the strongest from the beginning was cultural nationalism. A sense of patriotism was implicit in Peale's acceptance of republicanism, and in this feeling he was not alone. Lillian Miller found that the struggle for independence and its victorious conclusion "presented Americans with

Considerable reliance on Miller's work on Peale

a greater and more immediate sense of their responsibility for the moral tone of their country, for its cultural achievements as well as its political well-being and economic success."[54] As an artist who had studied in Great Britain for two and a half years, Peale was keenly aware of America's cultural strengths and weaknesses relative to Europe. Although he thus had a balanced view of the situation, Peale bristled whenever Europeans sneered at the scientific, artistic, or literary achievements of the young nation. It was this sense of cultural inferiority vis-à-vis Europe that drove Peale to establish, both with his pencil and with his museum, that works of quality and value could be produced in America. Although he became a thoroughgoing cultural nationalist, he never became a chauvinist who blindly celebrated America. He looked critically at Europe, adapted that which he deemed useful, and remained in his outlook and actions self-consciously an American.

If there was one area in which the Americans could hope to compare with the Europeans it was science, especially natural history. Here, more than in any other branch of science, Americans were capable of making significant contributions to knowledge. For here was a vast unexplored continent, full of undescribed species of plants and animals. Its geology and topography were equally unknown, and much could be added to man's understanding of the world by anyone who was sufficiently diligent in his research.

Given this bright promise, it was particularly galling to Peale that the Comte de Buffon, one of the world's foremost naturalists, had endorsed the old theory of Western Hemisphere degeneracy in his multivolume *Histoire Naturelle*. This fallacious position, which held that all natural life in the Americas was smaller and weaker than corresponding old world forms, and that species brought to America deteriorated over time, was profoundly annoying to many Americans. Thomas Jefferson had begun his *Notes on the State of Virginia* in 1781 partly to refute this doctrine, and in 1785 he sent the hide and skeleton of a moose to Buffon in order to explode the fallacy. Peale, for his part, spent years correcting Buffon's work on American species, and never quite forgave the Frenchman for accepting the idea of American inferiority, growling uncharacteristically at one point that Buffon must have "either a great *Antipathy to America* or to *Truth*.[55]

Peale felt the stirrings of cultural nationalism within him from the very beginning. Only a few months after he opened his museum, he wrote to Beale Bordley, his closest friend, to inform him of the progress of the new venture. Peale mentioned his hope that his "labours will make a museum that will be considered of more consequence than any [other?] of this sort in America." This was an ambitious goal, for he would have to eclipse cabinets owned by several corporate bodies. But such an institution was vitally necessary for the young nation because it was being denuded of its patrimony: "It is much to be lamented that too many rare and valuable things have already been sent & are still daily sending to the other side of the Atlantic."[56]

Peale's nationalistic mission, however, could hardly be carried out using his own resources alone; he grasped the necessity of making his museum a national institution. Peale would make five separate major attempts to nationalize the museum, and one attempt each to bring it under the patronage of the state of Pennsylvania and the city of Philadelphia. His first effort came in February 1790 in the form of an appeal to all United States citizens, but nothing came of it. This failed essay taught Peale the worthlessness of mere exhortation.

By 1792, the ambitious museum proprietor had developed a plan with more promise of success. He gathered around him twenty-five men of national reputation in various fields, denominated them "a Society of Visitors and Directors" for the museum, and sought to use them to make a truly national institution. It was perhaps the most prestigious board ever to serve an American museum, including such men as Alexander Hamilton, Thomas Jefferson, James Madison, David Rittenhouse, and Robert Morris. Ironically, it also included Du Simitière's executor, Ebenezer Hazard. But Peale found that his high-powered board would show up for meetings only if he nagged them remorselessly, and then only in small numbers. His discouragement turned to despair when he discovered that one of the members, Dr. Benjamin Barton, was stealing specimens from the museum.[57] Peale thereupon stopped calling meetings, and the board simply melted away.

Even though his museum never became a national institution, Peale never ceased to believe it was a national asset. For one thing, it would "present to the American as well as the European World, an evidence of our progress in the department of science, whose successful cultivation has always been a characteristical mark of an advanced civilization."[58] America needed the museum to prove that its people had reached a cultural parity with the proud nations of Europe. Naturally, all of this would redound to the honor of Charles Willson Peale, but it would also be a great boon to the infant republic: "I flatter myself to lay the foundation stone of a stupendious [*sic*] work, which in some future day will become an honor to my country."[59]

Peale, however, was never blinded by his nationalism. The great museums of Europe, he knew, were still far superior: "Although [the museum] cannot for many years hope to come equal [to] many of the Cabinets in Europe in [numbers?] of subjects, yet I hope to see it in as complete order as any of them."[60] A sense of cultural inferiority, coupled with an ambition to remedy it, drove him on: "the hope of laying the foundation of an Institution which in some future day may be an honor to America is too flattering to suffer me to omit any exertion."[61] Some may think that such statements were manufactured for public consumption and not really deeply felt. But in Peale's case they represented genuine emotion. Consider that in 1798, plunged into grief over the death of his son Titian Ramsay Peale I, the stricken father would write in his diary: "Had he lived, in all probability this Museum by his Labours would possess a General Collection in such high preservation as to vie with any in the world. America has case to morn [*sic*] the loss of this promising youth."[62]

As one studies the influence that the Enlightenment, Deism, deference, republicanism, and cultural nationalism exerted on Peale, and how these factors waxed and waned during the Moderate Enlightenment period of museum history from 1780 to 1800, one striking fact emerges: the first four of these imperatives were declining during most of this period. The ideals of the Moderate

Enlightenment were discredited by the aftermath of the French Revolution. Deism was already on its last legs in America by 1786, having been under sustained attack since the beginning of the Great Awakening more than forty years previously. The middle classes were slowly emerging, and with the election of Thomas Jefferson in 1800, bid fair to destroy the deferential system. Republicanism, too, was faltering. As Joseph J. Ellis bluntly put it, "Republicanism idealized the values of a world that was already fading. It was a nostalgic, backward-looking ideology resting on assumptions that were fundamentally antithetical to the market conditions and the liberal mentality emerging in post-Revolutionary America."[63] Only cultural nationalism survived the century as a potent force.

Peale changed with the cultural climate. He tempered his Enlightenment thinking, and altered his opinions regarding deference and republicanism. Even in his Deism, which he never abandoned, he felt compelled to quiet his enthusiasm. The decay of the old deferential, republican model of society, suffused with Enlightenment ideals, was alarming. France had provided grim witness of what happened when a society abandoned moderation and order. To Peale, as to others, the imperative was now to provide a new focus for order in society. He naturally turned to his museum as the instrument, but not in a repressive fashion. Instead, his essential optimism caused him to visualize a great center of popular education in which the people could acquire the means to make correct decisions on their own. This notion of the museum-as-school, fully developed in Peale's mind by 1800, motivated his museum endeavors for the rest of his life.

As early as 1797, Peale spoke of his "labours" to establish a school of Natural history,[64] and he rapidly became more vehement on the subject. By 1799 his chief goal was to "open the eyes of an Ignorant people" to the proper modes of citizenship.[65] To Peale, America was a nation blessed with gifts of freedom and order; the only enemy capable of threatening those blessings was ignorance. In his Introductory Lecture in 1799, he made his view quite explicit: "My friends, if we are not the most *cheerful, pious,* and *happitest* [sic] creatures that inhabit this globe, the fault arises *wholly* from our want of a *proper Education*, and remember, to that end I give my mite towards it, by beginning the Establishment of a *Museum*.[66]

This was more than mere rhetoric, for Peale had a concrete plan. It comprised a two-pronged assault on ignorance, both using the museum collection as a teaching tool. One approach would resemble a university: "Persons should be appointed to deliver courses of Lectures on the several branches of natural History having the real subjects before them; such professors . . . ought to get a sufficient number of Pupils to reward them for their trouble—especially with the addition of Persons who would come from the other states to get the advantage of delightful and powerful instruction."[67]

Such courses would form a higher education in natural history. Students would pay tuition, and the professors would take their earnings from those fees. The benefits would be well worth it, for the "real subjects" of natural history would transcend abstract learning and teach by direct experience.

The lessons of natural history, however, were important to many thousands who were neither serious students nor wealthy enough to pay for a course of lectures. For these people Peale designed a second approach: "And besides these schools [the lectures], a museum in perfect arrangement, with a good Catalogue to give information on each subject, always open to the visitors, would difuse [*sic*] a beneficial taste and knowledge to those who might not be able to attend the courses of lectures [for] the price of admission.[68]

The museum itself was literally a school for everyone. The Linnaean arrangement, illuminated by descriptive labels, was enlightening, but Peale took it a step further, by preparing a catalog that would instruct the visitor even more. He began to publish a comprehensive catalog of his collection in 1795, and by 1800, Peale had fully embraced the mission of popular education in his museum.

The Moderate Enlightenment period ended for Peale even before 1800. The Enlightenment, Deism, deference, republicanism, and cultural nationalism had motivated Peale to launch his museum, but after it was well launched, the first four had faded from the cultural scene. With them disappeared Peale's initial optimism about man and society, which was replaced by a cautious conviction that people were not inherently good and that society was not a self-regulating mechanism. His solution to these problems, however, was essentially an optimistic one: that of educating the people so that they could intelligently take their places as the rulers of the republic. This education, to be sure, was overtly didactic, but that should not obscure the magnitude of his accomplishment. Charles Willson Peale was the first American to grasp the enormous social potential of a museum.

Tammany's Museum and the Remarkable Mr. Baker

Of Andrew of Patrick of David and George
What mighty acheevments [sic] we hear . . .
These hero's [sic] fought only as fancy inspired
As by their own stories we find
Whilst Tamany he sought only to free
From cruel oppression Mankind, my Brave Boys . . . [69]

The Tammany Society or Columbian Order founded a cabinet in New York in 1790 that was destined to endure seventy-eight years and five changes in ownership. Like both Du Simitière and Peale, the Tammany men at first established a private institution open by invitation only. Like both of their predecessors, they discovered that the American cultural climate at the end of the eighteenth century was not hospitable to closed corporations. They were forced to make their cabinet a democratic institution, to open it to the people. The story of Tammany's cabinet from 1790 is one of the decline of the respectability before the democratizing influences of American culture.

The Society of St. Tammany or Columbian Order was a "fraternity of patriots" established in New York in 1786, which formally organized in 1789 with the adoption of its first constitution. The inspiration came from Philadelphia's Sons of King Tammany group, which had named its organization after Tamenend, a once-

famous Delaware Indian chief, who had befriended many early
settlers, most notably William Penn. It was conceived as a cultural,
fraternal, and patriotic organization, replete with pseudo-Indian
costumes, rites, and rituals. The men who joined were by and
large the prosperous merchants and shopkeepers, those who had
risen above the rank and file, but who were not yet on a par
with the old Knickerbocker aristocracy. They were the lower
ranks of the respectability of New York, men who had hoped
to solidify and ratify their social standing by joining this society.

It was one such merchant, John Pintard, who set Tammany
on the road to museum proprietorship. Pintard, a scholar and
philanthropist, was a leader of the organization, with the title
of "Sagamore." He was familiar with the Tammany Society in
Philadelphia, and he had visited Peale's museum. As early as August 1789 he began agitating his fellow members to establish a
museum based on the model of Peale's. Pintard's plan received
unqualified support from the "Wiskinkie" (bearer of the great
standard in processions), Gardiner Baker. Pintard was a man of
many ideas, but he was too shy to advance them effectively.
Baker, however, was a born promoter, and together they were
able to convince the leadership to back Pintard's dream. In June
1790, the "American Museum under the patronage of the Tammany Society or Columbian Order" was established. Although
it was called a museum, it was more accurately a cabinet, for
it was not yet open to the public. The beginning was promising
enough, for the board of trustees included, besides Pintard, such
luminaries as Dr. John R. B. Rodgers, who had been chief of
the medical staff at Valley Forge. The eminent New York physician Samuel Latham Mitchill was an enthusiastic supporter. Baker
was appointed keeper of the collection.[70]

Very few records relating to the founders or the cabinet itself
have survived, so it is difficult to reconstruct their motivations.
It seems reasonable to infer that civic pride and rivalry had something to do with it. Probably many in the Columbian Order felt
it was necessary to provide rational amusement for the rapidly
growing population of the lower orders in New York; at any

rate, Tammany would be the first museum in America to be open to the public gratis.

Ample evidence does exist, however, to suggest that cultural nationalism played an important role in the founding of the cabinet. That sentiment is very clear in the letter of thanks John Pintard wrote to Jeremy Belknap, dated October 11, 1790, when the latter presented the exceedingly rare Eliot Indian Bible to the collection: "I shall deposit it [the Bible] with your permission and in your name in the American Museum laterly [sic] instituted by the St. Tammany Society in this city for the express purpose of collecting and preserving everything related to the natural or political history of America. A small fund is appropriated to that purpose, and should the society exist, this branch of it may arrive to something useful."[71]

It is not surprising, of course, that a patriotic organization should form a cabinet to celebrate America. One has only to read the record of the toasts given at the Tammany banquets around this time to understand the cultural nationalism that suffused them. Such sentiments as "May the flame of Freedom which has been kindled in these United States of America, extend to all mankind" and "Those heros [sic] of France whose patriotic Virtues have Caused the Columbian flame to consume the Gallic yolk of despotism" filled the rooms on these occasions.[72] Pintard was merely reflecting these feelings by limiting the collection to American objects. Such a collection would prove to the world that America was a nation of consequence, and it would provide a rallying point for American pride and unity.

Pintard's sentiments were codified on May 21, 1791, when the society began advertising its museum in the public prints. The advertisements (and the broadsides that followed on June 1) were headed "American Museum Under the Patronage of the Tammany Society." These made it abundantly clear that "the intention of the Tammany Society . . . in establishing an *American Museum* being for the sole purpose of collecting and preserving whatever may relate to the history of our country and serve to perpetuate the same, as also all American curiosities of nature or art."[73]

The cultural nationalism animating this avowal could not be clearer. Although the eight New Yorkers who signed the notice were men of the world, they preferred to emphasize American productions in the museum. They hoped that by exhibiting such articles they could promote among the public such sentiments as patriotism, love for liberty, and independence, all of which the Tammany Society approved. The museum would do more than promote public virtue and national pride, for it would make the Tammany Society and the respectable classes of which it was composed the leaders of that wave of patriotism. The museum was thus another way to cement their leadership status. For all of their ambitious goals, however, they were also realistic; knowing that the collection would lose many curiosities if it were limited to American objects, they quietly admitted, "Every thing, and from whatever line, will be acceptable; for although the funds of the Society are confined to American productions, the doors of the Museum are, nevertheless, open to voluntary contributions from every quarter."[74] This was clearly an attempt to increase variety, but it also meant that the collection was doomed to be a miscellaneous aggregation of curiosities.

There was also some ambivalence as to just how welcome the general public might be. The families of Tammany Society members visited without charge. The first newspaper notice, in the New York *Daily Advertiser* of May 21, 1791, said the museum was "at present open gratis, every Tuesday and Friday afternoons, for the gratification of public curiosity."[75] Apparently this policy was quickly dropped, for the June 1 broadside specifies free admissions only for society members. In so changing, the Tammany Society was bowing to reality, for the cost of maintaining the museum and paying a full-time keeper quickly became an onerous burden. Baker imposed an admission price of two shillings per person, roughly twenty-five cents according to the prevailing exchange rates. This was a reasonable sum, and Baker also offered a yearly ticket for a dollar.[76]

The colorful Wiskinkie, Gardiner Baker, cut an almost comical figure as he scurried about the museum, a "snub-nosed, pock-pitted, bandy-legged, fussy, good-natured body, full of zeal and bustle in his vocation.'"[77] Like so many pioneer museologists, Baker's interests were broad and his enthusiasms many. He was a corresponding member of the Massachusetts Historical Society, studied natural history, meteorology, and astronomy with equal fascination, was a painter and a bibliophile, and loved animals so much that he kept a menagerie. He also had a flare for showmanship that foreshadowed his successor at the American Museum, P. T. Barnum. If any man in New York was qualified to run a museum in 1790, it was Gardiner Baker.

The history of the American Museum is one of initial optimism followed by virtual abandonment. John Pintard's success in convincing the society that they needed a museum was matched by his success in convincing the Common Council that the collection should be housed in the room in City Hall in which Congress had met until they moved to Philadelphia in 1790. By September of that year, the collection had a home. When it was opened to the public the following May and it began to grow, all must have seemed well. Clouds began to gather, however, over the person of John Pintard. The scholarly merchant was becoming alarmed at the direction the society was taking, for by 1792, Tammany was forsaking culture for politics. Pintard was to the right of center politically, but Tammany was moving to the left and embracing the Jeffersonian Republicans. A split was inevitable, and in 1792 Pintard left the society. Shortly afterward a disastrous financial reverse caused him to move to New Jersey, and eventually, from 1797 to 1798, he was imprisoned for debt. Baker, although a Republican, remained fast friends with Pintard, but he had lost the museum's founder and most influential patron.

By 1795, the men of Tammany were more anxious than ever to gain stature among the leaders of the young republic, but after five years of museum proprietorship, they discovered that their collection produced many bills and little tangible power. The American Museum had not made the society the leader of a national surge of pride and patriotism; for these ends, politics seemed to promise more hope of success. The society determined to consolidate its efforts and jettisoned the museum. As political organizations will, it sought to put a brave face on failure, claiming that the museum was to be given as a gift to Baker in recognition of his faithful service, provided that he retain the name, keep the collection intact, and allow Tammany members and their families to visit without charge. Charles Willson Peale heard it differently, perhaps from Baker himself. The museum, said Peale, was given to the keeper in lieu of his wages.[78] Baker now had lost external support and would have to do what Peale had been doing for nearly ten years: make a profit on paid admissions. More importantly, 1795 marked the end of the respectability's control over the museum. Baker and his successors would be neither supported nor limited by association with a private organization. From 1795 until the final demise of the museum seventy-three years later, the proprietors would be totally dependent on the people for their very existence.

It would be wrong, however, to say that the abandonment by Tammany transformed a scholarly institution into a popular one. Baker had tried to maintain a certain intellectual tone; for instance, in one advertisement he had boasted: "The Library consists of upwards of 500 volumes, most of which respect the history of the country. . . . it contains the best history of our country that is collected together. The Proprietor, in order to make this Library really useful to his country requests and privileges every person, who is 21 years of age and upwards, without any expense, to resort to it everyday and read any of the books . . . (for this purpose a room is set apart particularly having no connection with the museum)."[79]

This was an admirable service to scholars, and it satisfied the spirit of militant patriotism of the times, but it obviously did not pay the bills. Charles Willson Peale, who first visited the Tammany Museum on June 6, 1791, found no attempts at scholarship, but he did find "many curious article [*sic*]. One of the most extraordinary was a horn which had grown on the head of the mother of Mr. Cutinous . . . about 5 or 6 inches long of an irregular shape about the thickness of a small finger."[80]

One might expect Peale, as the proprietor of a museum, to be somewhat critical of Baker's efforts. Indeed, others were more appreciative. A visitor named John Drayton came twice to the museum. On the first occasion, when it was still located in City Hall, he found it "shewn to the worst advantage, being but partially exposed, and that in a very small room."[81] By 1793, at the time of Drayton's second visit, Baker had moved the museum to the Exchange Building on Broad Street, a large barnlike structure with a sizable loft, one block from Battery Park. Here Drayton found that the museum "offers a more extensive gratification to the spectator. [The exhibitions] are now placed with an happy taste in a room 60 feet by 30: with an arched ceiling twenty feet high."[82] One of the exhibits that Drayton observed was an elaborate "habitat" for Baker's natural history specimens, replete with an artificial hill and painted walls, all copied from an earlier exhibit by Peale.[83]

Baker rapidly diversified his holdings. He added the wax museum created by Daniel Bowen, and early in 1794 formed a "menage," consisting of five animals and two birds. These he placed into a rudimentary zoo on a lot on Pearl Street near the Battery. On November 25, 1793, Baker published a broadside describing the contents of his museum. With the exception of the horn Peale noted, the broadside omitted mention of the more frivolous items in the collection of natural history specimens. Baker had expanded the museum's hours; it was open Monday through Saturday from 10:00 A.M. until 5:00 P.M. with a break of one hour for lunch. On Tuesday, Thursdays, and Fridays, the museum was open until 9:00 P.M., being illuminated by candlelight. The price was doubled; it was now four shillings for adults and two for children. Thus Baker, by his long hours, sought to make his museum easily accessible to the public. And by energetically adding new exhibits to the museum and new animals to the menagerie, he hoped to keep them coming back.

The divorce from Tammany in 1795 made Baker reach for more extravagant promotions in an effort to increase visitation. Thomas Twining, a traveler who came to New York from Philadelphia, noted in his diary: "I walked to the museum. . . . It was an older and more extensive collection than the similar one at Philadelphia. It consisted principally of shells and fossils and arms and dresses of the Indian tribes. There was also a machine, said to exhibit perpetual motion. It . . . seemed likely to hold out for the time a spectator would stop to observe it."[84]

Twining's statement captured much of the duality of the American Museum. He erred in saying it was older than Peale's, but if it was indeed more extensive, it was because of Baker's indiscriminate collecting. Mixed in with articles of unquestioned value, such as the fossils and Indian artifacts, was the fraudulent perpetual motion machine. By contrast, it is instructive to note that Peale exhibited a similar machine in his museum for the purpose of demonstrating the concealed mechanism that actuated it, and thus denouncing it as a fraud.

Not even perpetual motion, however, could generate large enough crowds. Moreover, there were troubles on other fronts. Some valuable coins were stolen from a museum exhibit case, and the "menage" was closed by the city after several residents complained about the smell that issued therefrom. Baker needed a spectacular stunt, and he found one in the young science of aeronautics. Jean-Pierre Baptiste Blanchard, the dashing French aeronaut with forty-five balloon ascents to his credit, proposed to make his forty-sixth in New York. Baker remembered that three years before, Blanchard had made the first balloon ascent in America before an enormous Philadelphia crowd, which had included George Washington. Baker proposed a partnership to Blanchard; if the aeronaut would take Baker along as a passenger, Baker would promote the event. Blanchard accepted, and the date of the ascension was set for August of 1796.

Baker kept his end of the bargain, for he issued a steady stream of newspaper ads and broadsides, offering subscriptions at one dollar each. In spite of Baker's exertions, the subscriptions lagged. The partners first postponed the launch, but the venture collapsed altogether when the balloon was badly damaged in a storm on September 14. Neither the impecunious Blanchard nor Baker, who had nearly bankrupted himself paying for the publicity, had the money to fix it. Each blamed the other and waged a war of words in the public prints for months afterwards. The balloon fiasco mired Baker in debt and entangled him in a host of lawsuits from which he never fully extricated himself.

Baker, however, remained optimistic in the face of disaster. He still had his museum, and he still felt a strong sense of responsibility to his public. In February 1797 he wrote his old friend John Pintard about his current condition. Baker took pains to assure Pintard, "While my existance [*sic*] is accompanied with any acts of Public utility, I wish to live, and no longer—this is really the sincere wish of my heart, and whenever you can point out to me any object of public utility you will confer the greatest of all the favours of this life."[85]

The promotion of patriotism among the people was, in Baker's opinion, of the greatest public utility. He told Pintard, "The pleasure that [I] feel in being the promoter of this very usefull [*sic*] institution, is the most charming Compensation that the active patriot can receive for public services."[86] Baker believed that in a new nation, which needed unifying factors for its very survival, the promotion of a public museum was a patriotic measure, for it united Americans taking pride in American natural history and American genius.

Baker's high aims, however, did not translate into specific performance. After Charles Willson Peale returned for a series of visits in June 1798, he made a balanced assessment of the efforts of his friendly rival. Writing in his diary, Peale judged, "Mr. Baker has a great deal of merit for his industry and management of his museum for in a confined place he has contrived to make a very considerable desplay [*sic*] of a prodigeous [*sic*] number of Pictures, Prints and Wax Works articles of Curiosity of natural subjects." Peale admitted that he was "much entertained" with the sight of many "Valuable articles of Natural History therein contained," and he mused that "these fine pieces . . . must have cost him a prodigeous [*sic*] sum of money. But Peale also noted, "It is arranged without method, works of art are premiscuously [*sic*] jumbled together, except at one end of the Room was placed a pretty display of a classical arrangement of insects, the labour of Mr. Fenton."[87] "Mr. Fenton" was Jotham Fenton, a self-taught optician. Peale was so impressed that he promptly asked Baker if he could spare Fenton's services. The financially strapped proprietor probably was unable to pay Fenton's wages anyway, so the ingenious optician became Peale's employee and put to use in Philadelphia the experience he had gained in New York.

Fenton, in 1798, was leaving a sinking ship. Baker candidly confessed to Pintard in March of 1798, "I have for the last 18 months been very unsuccessfull [sic] in all my undertakings, and have unavoidably became [sic] indebted, about 2,000 dollars, my experience has taught that the Museum, at best, will not give more than sufficient for my family's support and now and then to make some small addition to the museum."[88] Baker gambled at reversing his fortunes by purchasing Gilbert Stuart's full-length portrait of Washington. He placed it on exhibit in New York for one month, then planned to go on the road, visiting several American cities and even making a foray to Europe. But it was not to be. In late September of 1798, at the tour's first stop in Boston, Baker was abruptly stricken with yellow fever and died.

Baker's death cut short, for a time, the evolution of the Tammany Museum from a bastion of the respectability to a truly popular institution. Baker himself had been moving toward an ever more egalitarian position in his writings. Only a few months before he died, he told John Pintard: "You know my friend my duty and readiness to afford my fellow citizens any communications that may be in anyway pleasing or usefull [sic] if the way is pointed out. . . . I think the results are much simpler and plainer to be understood by all ranks of men."[89]

Baker certainly did not feel that his museum served only a small audience of scholars or dilettantes. It was for the people, all of the people, and its mission was to provide them with useful information and to teach them to love their country. These aims of Baker were congruent to those of Charles Willson Peale, although Peale did add a strong urge toward popular education which Baker lacked. Nevertheless, Baker was well on his way to inventing a museum for the people by 1798, despite being hobbled by financial stringency. He recognized that fact himself, lamenting, "At the time that I am becoming better and better capacitated to render service to my fellow creatures, it seems that my unpleasant pecuniary circumstances will in some measure defeat [me]."[90]

The ultimate defeat came with Baker's death. *The New-York*

Gazette and General Advertiser gave Baker a tribute that he would have enjoyed: "His industry and attention in the selection and arranging of the curiosities of Nature, perhaps, was never excelled. In short, his death may be considered a great public loss."[91] Indeed it was, but perhaps it spared Baker more grief. His optimism and faith in the public was characteristic of the spirit of the Moderate Enlightenment, which by 1798 was rapidly waning. The dawning age of the Didactic Enlightenment, which would be in full swing in 1800, was more at home with pessimism and efforts to keep the public in their place. For the rise of the masses, so clearly foreshadowed in the experience of Peale and Baker before 1800, would become worrisome to the respectability after that time. A new age was dawning.

3

The Didactic Enlightenment, 1800–1820: The Decline of the Respectability

The years from 1800 to 1820 marked in museum history the era of the Didactic Enlightenment. This period witnessed the decline of the authority and power of the respectability and the corresponding rise of the middle classes to political and social influence. The French Revolution had shaken the optimism of the respectability; now they were faced with the deterioration of their position in society and the simultaneous upswelling of power from below. These twin tremors caused them to cling tenaciously to their remaining prerogatives, while at the same time attempting to manage the behavior of the middle classes, to channel it into forms acceptable to the "better sort." The proprietors of museums, who came from the respectable classes, sought to turn their institutions into instruments for social control. Two of the established museums, Peale's and Baker's American Museum, and four museums that were to be founded, those of the New-York Historical Society, the Elgin Botanical Garden, the Academy of Natural Sciences of Philadelphia, and the Western Museum of Cincinnati, met this challenge in varying manners. The American Museum's new proprietors would attempt to guide the interest of the middle class toward the mysteries of natural history. Peale attempted to shape the perceptions and outlook of the rising classes by a program of popular education. The New-York Historical Society would withdraw from the public, harking back to the cabinet "for members only." The Elgin Garden, the Academy of Natural Sciences, and the Western Museum would attempt to avoid close contact with the people by concentrating on science to the exclusion of education. This would allow them to keep the public at arm's length and still plausibly claim that their institutions were useful to the people. All, however, shared a common response in one respect: they refused to accept the new order of things and tried to control the ascending middle classes.

The proprietors hardly could be faulted for resisting change, for the transformation of American society during the two decades from 1800 to 1820 was profound. It was during this time that "America changed from a tenacious traditional society, fearful of innovation . . . to a shifting, reckless and insecure world. . . . that such a shift did take place in the years between the War of 1812 and the time of Jackson is clearly evident."[1] The members of the respectability, however, experienced the changes long before the War of 1812. The French Revolution and the Republican ascendancy beginning in 1800 had been the opening salvos in what promised to be a long struggle to maintain status. At times, the two sides battled over important issues like the franchise, disestablishment of churches, and political contests. More often, however, the conflicts manifested themselves in trivial matters, such as complaints that the wealthier of the common people were dressing above their station and driving carriages. In the first two decades of the nineteenth century, however, "there was nothing to be done about it. In colonial times, laws might be passed prohibiting the lower orders from dressing like their betters, but in . . . America that sort of legislation was no longer possible."[2]

A recent work by a respected scholar provides an interpretive framework for explaining this conflict between the respectability and the middle classes. Robert Wiebe, in his book *The Opening of American Society*, discovered two strains of thought and action in America from the signing of the Constitution in 1789 until the mid 1840s. The first was the traditional approach of what Wiebe calls the "revolutionary gentry." These upper-class leaders attempted to retain their control over society by widening the base of the elite, while simultaneously building a strong government to keep the masses in line with tradition. The emerging middle classes, on the other hand, sought to repudiate tradition and institute what Wiebe calls a "revolution in individual choices." The respectability wanted "comprehensiveness"; the middle classes wanted a new, democratic society. As Wiebe saw it, "Along these two planes . . . two histories had been unfolding contemporaneously."[3]

These two histories were constantly in conflict. Washington and Hamilton had represented the ideal of comprehensiveness; the advent of Jefferson's weaker government in 1800 launched the revolution in individual choices. It was not in the political arena, however, that the respectability met its downfall. Instead, the harsh realities of economics made the middle class triumph inevitable. The mobility made possible by the revolution in transportation, by steamboats, canals, and turnpikes, loosened the grip of the respectability. The advances in transport fueled the industrial revolution, which profoundly altered the social structure, creating both nouveau riche on the one hand and a large working class on the other, and substituted a dynamic market economy for the older agricultural one. The development of the West decentralized American politics and created new opportunities for the middle class to rise to positions of leadership away from the oligarchies controlling politics in the East. The inexorable advance of these impersonal forces, aided and abetted by the political leadership of the middle classes, destroyed the respectability's dreams of comprehensiveness and slowly eroded the upper-class position. As Wiebe put it, "By 1820 these waves of change were washing relentlessly at the foundations beneath a tottering national hierarchy. By the 1840s, no traces remained."[4]

Although extinction was to be their ultimate fate, the respectability from 1800 to 1820 was by no means willing to give up without a fight. Instead of bowing to the new middle-class sensibilities, they attempted through exhortation to change the outlook of the rising class. The optimism of the Moderate Enlightenment faded away; no longer was society to reach a deferential millennium simply by allowing history to unfold. The only hope now was to manage actively the last interests of the respectability in an increasingly egalitarian age.

A Museum for the Masses:
John Scudder's American Museum

Public opinion, as I have already intimated, had become somewhat doubtful as to the wisdom which marked the French Revolution. Many, once seemingly secure in the light of nature alone, now felt themselves led into a delusion, the results of which threatened more than temporal inconvenience. The middle and best classes of society, the responsible citizen, who had at one time fraternized with these apostles of liberty, now foresaw that certain doctrines . . . were more serious than their intent avowed. . . . As the darkness which had shrouded the actual state of things broke away, new light shown upon the conduct of the revolutionists.[5]

These words, written by John W. Francis, physician and member of the New-York Historical Society, typify the reaction of the respectability to the excesses of the French Revolution. As their own social status began to crumble after 1800, members of the respectability became increasingly strident in their criticism of the rising middle classes. They searched for a means to reinforce their position in society, while at the same time attempting to mold the middle class in their own image. In New York, John Scudder opened his museum to the public in order to teach them proper modes of behavior, shifting Baker's emphasis on useful education to didactic education.

Gardiner Baker's death nearly finished the American Museum. His wife had to borrow money to return to New York from Boston, and once back she attempted to carry on the management of the museum. But a combination of her own indiscretion (she carried on an open affair with a French lover, despite public disapproval) and municipal action (the corporation condemned the Exchange Building in 1799) spelled doom for her efforts. The final act in the Baker tragedy was the sudden death of Mrs. Baker early in 1800. She died intestate, leaving four minor children dependent upon her husband's old friends for survival.

Daniel Phoenix, the New York City treasurer, acting as executor of the estate, immediately attempted to sell the museum collection and the lease of the Panorama Building on Greenwich Street, where it had been exhibited since the Exchange was condemned. Phoenix ran an advertisement in the *Commercial Advertiser* from May 12 to June 30, 1800, noting in his offer that the museum would be sold with the restriction that members of the Tammany Society and their families were to be admitted gratis. The buyer was one William I. Waldron, a grocer, who purchased the properties in September 1800 as a speculation and immediately offered them for resale. Since no buyer was readily forthcoming, he opened up the collection to the public as Waldron's Museum. In the early spring of 1802, he moved his operation to 69 Broadway, and leased the Panorama to a tavern-keeper.

Waldron left few clues to his motivation and ideology, but an advertisement in the New York *Mercantile Advertiser* for March 31, 1801, revealed that he was manipulating the newly assertive middle classes. In a manner that foreshadowed P. T. Barnum's methods four decades later, Waldron dared his patrons to judge for themselves: "Have you travelled thro' the pages of the *Natural Historian*? come and satisfy your mind, that he has not deceived you. Come and look nature in the face, and you will be more highly delighted and satisfied than by historic description. Have you, at any time, read of beings whose existence you doubted? call at this repository. Your doubts may vanish, and before you depart your mind may receive impressions emanently [*sic*] conducive to morality and virtue."[6]

Charles Willson Peale and Gardiner Baker had both written of their desire to use their museums to inculcate morality and virtue in the people. Waldron, however, seemed to say that this great aim was incidental to the greater one of letting the people be the sovereign judges. The people need not accept the word of the experts; they may verify for themselves, using their own senses to gather the proof. This foreshadowed the approach that P. T. Barnum would later employ at this very museum. Waldron, however, was not Barnum. The great showman would be content to allow the judgment of the people to stand, whether it was right or wrong. Waldron, by contrast, was not in the vanguard of the middle-class ascendancy. He was still concerned with demonstrating the proper methods of behavior to the middle classes. The grocer maintained that the great desideratum the museum offered was "a species of knowledge that may be found necessary in almost every condition and department of life. Even a slender knowledge of nature removes a certain littleness of mind, protects us from compositions which affected greatness too often attempts on ignorance and credulity, and pulls forth emotions of gratitude to the great Parent of All."[7]

Waldron was hardly a tribune of the people, calling on them to be the final judges. He was merely using his challenge as a lure to draw them to his collection. Once they had paid to enter, he hoped that they would be enlightened, broadened, and rendered less susceptible to the blandishments of intriguers and enthusiasts. Far from being a populist, Waldron was a paternalist, who was trying to exert control over the middle classes. The tone of condescension in his remarks is unmistakable.

During the summer of 1802, a painter by the name of Edward Savage purchased the museum from Waldron. Savage liked to think of himself as a historical artist, but he was in fact an experienced showman. Back in 1794, he had opened the Columbian Gallery of pictures and prints in Boston, and he had also operated a panorama in Philadelphia. Savage opened a second Columbian Gallery in New York in 1801. It was thus a natural step for him to expand into the museum business by purchasing the Tammany collection from Waldron.

Savage proved from the beginning to have a good grasp of the cultural realities of museum proprietorship. He took advantage of a day dear to the hearts of all patriots, the anniversary of the Battle of Bunker Hill, to open his establishment. In one of his first advertisements, on August 21, 1802, he described his museum as an "elegant place of genteel resort . . . replete with objects highly gratifying to Every rank of citizen."[8] Lest anyone suspect that it was too elegant or too genteel to accommodate the common man, Savage was careful to state that it "will form a complete source of amusement for every class."[9] Savage's museum was clearly to be a place in which people could be entertained, while at the same time gaining a veneer of sophistication. This was precisely what the emergent middle classes sought in a museum—a place respectable enough to visit openly but one which dispensed diversions in generous quantities. Savage, in his City Museum at 80 Greenwich Street, never pretended to be running a school or a scientific institution. It was frankly a diversion for anyone with a quarter.

In fact, Savage was mainly an absentee landlord. He remained an artist at heart, and left the actual operation of the museum to his assistants. Savage's first and finest assistant had been working as a foreman in a tobacco company when the painter heard of his skill in mounting animals. He enticed John Scudder, at the age of twenty-six, to become curator of the City Museum. Scudder's enthusiasm for natural history was immense, and his ability as a taxidermist was quickly recognized. Scudder soon chafed at serving an employer who preferred art to natural history. At some point, possibly around 1805, he left Savage's employ and enrolled as a seaman aboard ships trading between New York and various ports in New England. This employment allowed him to augment his capital, and also to purchase curiosities for his private collection, which he hoped someday to turn into a museum of his own.

Scudder soon had his chance. Savage had continued to operate his museum, but his advertisements came less frequently and his heart did not seem to be in it. Finally, in 1809, he sold the contents of his collection to his former assistant. Scudder combined his own collection with that of his mentor, and opened his establishment at 21 Chatham Street in March 1810. Scudder called it the New American Museum, which was technically accurate, since both the Tammany Society and Gardiner Baker had called the collection the American Museum from time to time during the 1790s.

Less than two months later, "A Visitor" wrote to the *Commercial Advertiser* with regard to the American Museum, proclaiming that it "promises to become an honour to this City. The selection, preservation and arrangement of the various subjects of Natural History, do infinite credit to the taste, skill and judgment of Mr. Scudder. . . . Parents will find this Museum an instructive school to teach their Children to behold and admire the marvelous works of creation."[10] Whoever the anonymous visitor (it may have been Scudder himself), the city's scientific elite also praised the American Museum. Samuel Latham Mitchill, the physician, mineralogist, and leader of the New-York Historical Society, lauded Scudder's taxidermy in the *Medical Repository*, the journal Mitchill edited. Mitchill judged, "The collection of insects, zoophytes, vermes and serpents, is already considerable, and is increasing very fast. The shells promise fair to grow to an extensive mass of conchology, and the fossils are extending rapidly to a body of mineralogy."[11]

These testimonials demonstrate that Scudder was too dedicated to natural history to offer merely catchpenny shows in the manner of Savage. His meticulously accurate mountings could serve the naturalists of New York as models of the natural world. Scudder presented lectures illustrated by specimens from the collection, so his museum was in effect a school of natural history. On the other hand, he catered to the popular taste with such attractions as a waxworks starring Sleeping Beauty and her baby. A brutally frank English traveler referred to these as "prodigies of absurdity and bad taste."[12] Like Peale (and perhaps in conscious imitation of the Philadelphia artist) Scudder sought to find a middle ground between the naturalist and the average man, between the student and the pleasure-seeker. He had thus altered the philosophy of the museum, from Savage's position of giving the people what they wanted, to his own of giving the people what he felt they needed. In this sense, he was firmly in line with the Didactic Enlightenment.

But John Scudder had chosen a poor time to open a serious institution. The hard times brought on by the war in Europe hindered his efforts, and soon America was embroiled in the hostilities. America's entry into the war exacerbated the recession, and Scudder barely kept his head above water. He survived only by opening a "Grand Naval Panorama" to exploit the patriotic fervor engendered by Oliver Hazard Perry's victory over the British in the battle of Lake Erie. Few were as happy as Scudder to see the return of peace in 1815.

Eighteen-sixteen was a banner year for Scudder and the museum. The nation's economy was rebounding and the museum found a new home. The corporation of New York owned a building on the north side of City Hall Park, which had been built in 1795 as an alms house. By 1816, however, the paupers had been transferred to Bellevue, and the structure stood empty. The various scientific and literary societies of the city repeatedly petitioned the corporation to deed the alms house to them as a central scientific and cultural headquarters. With the help of many influential backers, including John Pintard, Governor De Witt Clinton, and the celebrated physician David Hosack, the corporation gave in. The scientific and literary societies were to have the premises rent-free for ten years, and thus commenced an experiment in the civic promotion of culture. Scudder's American Museum moved into the west wing of the newly christened New York Institution. Among his neighbors were the American Academy of Fine Arts, the New-York Historical Society, and the Literary and Philosophical Society of New York.

The new arrangement was much admired throughout the United States as a model of civic support for cultural advancement. But to some it seemed ironic that artists and scientists should be living in an alms house. Fitz-Greene Halleck, in his satirical poem *Fanny*, published in 1819, referred to this unusual situation:

> . . . the Corporation took it
> Into their heads to give the rich in brains,
> The worn-out mansion of the poor in pocket,
> Once the old alms house, now a school of wisdom,
> Sacred to Scudder's shells and Dr. Griscom.[13]

Scudder's greatest expense, that of rent, was now obviated. This allowed him to concentrate on improving his collection and to offer more demonstrations in the institution's lecture room and experimental laboratory. He spent freely to arrange his rooms in the institution elegantly. John Pintard noted, in a letter to his daughter, "Scudders [*sic*] museum is a picture & will be ready for exhibition by the 4th of July. He will have expended nearly $8,000 in accommodating his apartments."[14] The result was impressive. Scudder's room measured 94 by 41 feet, with a raised gallery ringing it, and boasted 164 cases containing more than 600 natural history specimens and thousands of shells and butterflies.[15] His best-received innovation was a band that played popular tunes on an outer balcony to attract customers. The band also inspired Halleck:

> And music ceases when it rains
> In Scudder's balcony.[16]

The band was sometimes too successful. On July 4, 1819, John Pintard visited Scudder's museum and discovered, "The crowd was so great and the heat so insufferable, that no gratification could arise from viewing his elegant preparations. The music was very fine, & the Spectators outside had the best of the bargain."[17]

Just before Scudder opened his museum in the New York Institution in early July 1817, he had a distinguished visitor. Charles Willson Peale was on a trip to New York with his third wife, Hannah, and he paid three different visits to the New York Institution. He was embroiled in yet another attempt to establish his Philadelphia Museum as a public institution, this time as a city museum. Peale was growing weary of Philadelphia's indifference to his efforts to establish the museum officially, so he was evaluating his alternatives. He was disappointed to find that Scudder had been given an entire wing of the New York Institution, leaving nothing for him. It was unclear, however, whether Peale seriously contemplated a move to New York, or if his public pronouncements to that effect were aimed as a threat at recalcitrant Philadelphia officials.

Peale gained entrance to Scudder's private apartment (Scudder lived at the institution, as well) and chatted with his counterpart. Scudder clearly attempted to impress his visitor; Peale recorded, "The expense of his establishment . . . is immence. . . . in short,

he says that he don't [*sic*] care for the expense provided that he
can make a handsome display—and he says that he hopes to surprise the public with the novelty of his exhibition in many curious
things of which he possesses in abundance." Scudder backed up
his boasts, for Peale admitted that "he speaks correctly."[18] Peale
also noticed, however, that Scudder had copied many of his innovations, including an imitation of a hill covered with trees that
Peale had built in his first museum, and even the use of the phrase
"A World in Miniature" which Peale had coined years before.

Peale, though, was distracted by other concerns. His next visit
to the institution found him at the New-York Historical Society,
speaking with Dr. David Hosack. The doctor was virtually a one-
man cultural establishment. As the founder of the Elgin Botanical
Garden, a cofounder of the New-York Historical Society, and
a member of the Literary and Philosophical Society, Hosack had
enormous prestige in New York's scientific and historical circles.
Now he hoped to lure Peale's museum to New York. Peale recalled the meeting clearly:

> I paid a visit to Doctr. Hosack, who was anxious to know my
> situation with the corporation of Philada. and when I had stated
> every particular, he urged me to join with Mr. Scudder. I told
> him I could not do that, or make any advances towards obtain-
> ing a change of situation of my museum, at least while the cor-
> poration had my proposition before them, and that the whole
> of the building called the *New York Institution* was not too large
> for an increasing museum. . . . He told me that the academy
> of fine [arts] might be accommodated in another way. . . . I
> told him that it was impossible for me to know at present what
> would be done to secure my Museum to the public.[19]

Hosack's dream of a united Peale-Scudder museum was a bold
initiative, one which would have ratified New York's status as
the emerging center of science in America. Peale may have been
receptive had Hosack been able to offer him an edifice, such as
the New York Institution. The institution, however, was filled
to capacity. Peale, who had had enough of general declarations
of support, held out for specifics. It is intriguing to speculate
about what might have been, but as it was, Hosack and Peale

parted with no agreement, and the contemplated merger came to nothing.

Peale paid one more visit to Scudder's American Museum before returning to Philadelphia. This time, he was far more critical. He found the animals "disposed in such manner as [to] excite [the] admiration of those unacquainted with proper attitudes and would not look for the form of muscles. Everything is disposed to show the beauty of plumage and slickness of skins." In short, Peale accused Scudder of mounting for effect, not for accuracy. The fastidious Peale also complained that "some prints in the case of the Sleeping Beauty . . . savoured too much of nudity."[20] After Peale had finished criticizing, he returned to Philadelphia, ending forever the possibility of a marriage of his scientific acumen with Scudder's showmanship.

Scudder did blend scholarship and popular promotion well enough to prosper as a museum proprietor. With his rent-free status and flair for management, he had no trouble in keeping his museum solvent. Scudder played host to luminaries such as President Monroe and ran a "very progressive" establishment.[21]

How progressive was it? Surely, Scudder was not a champion of the emerging middle classes. He took care to reverse Savage's popular emphasis and provided a solid didactic message in his lectures and exhibits. However, no one could accuse Scudder of being an elitist like his neighbors in the New-York Historical Society, who actively discouraged public participation in their affairs. He made an honest effort to provide New Yorkers with an attractive museum that would provide both entertainment and information in even doses. In this, as in other things, he imitated Charles Willson Peale, who also sought to walk the narrow line between public desires and public needs. Unlike Peale, however, Scudder never embraced popular education as a means toward helping the middle classes prepare for their new position of authority. He was content merely to present didactic lessons.

The pressure of cultural changes may have eventually altered Scudder's approach, but the question is moot. He never had a robust constitution (he had nearly died in 1816), and the constant fatigue of running a museum, combined with frequent exposure

to poisonous taxidermy chemicals, caused his premature death
on August 7, 1821. The Age of Egalitarianism had barely begun
when Scudder left the scene, so one can only speculate whether
he would have moved, as did Peale, increasingly in the direction
of popular education.

John Pintard's tribute to Scudder is very instructive. Writing
to his own daughter, Pintard remarked, "Several scientific charac-
ters paid their last mark of respect [to] his memory & a vast con-
course of all sorts, for he was universally known."[22] John Scudder
had managed to gain the affection of the middle classes without
losing the respect of the respectability. He had neither pandered
to the people nor patronized them, but had honestly attempted
to guide them according to his best understanding of their needs.
Scudder was a worthy disciple of the Philadelphia master, Charles
Willson Peale.

"To Amuse and at the Same Moment to Instruct": The Peale Museums

I have moralized a little which I hope will not be unacceptable. . . . I sermonize the actions of men and know from what
impulse they move, and w[h]ere I can do no good I am silent,
But if I could, I have desired to inform the bulk of my fellow
creatures.[23]

The progressive decay of the respectability, and the concurrent
rise of the middle classes, was becoming ever more apparent by
1800. The very symbol of the respectability, the Federalist Party,
had gone down to defeat in that year before the Jeffersonian Republicans, who seemed to many to represent the vanguard of mob
rule. The old deferential system was breaking down, and the
lower orders were no longer content to let their social betters
guide them in politics or in culture.

To many members of the erstwhile ruling classes, these developments portended the end of a golden era and hence were to
be stubbornly resisted. Charles Willson Peale and his sons were
alarmed as well by the collapse of the old order, but after briefly

fighting a rearguard action against the emerging middle classes, they worked toward an accommodation with them. The corner-stone of the Peales' *modus vivendi* was popular education. Peale, as stated previously, had come to that conclusion as early as 1797, but at that point his conception of education consisted of a didac-tic, moralizing approach, one in which the respectability shaped the conceptions of the masses. During the two decades from 1800 to 1820, however, Peale and his sons overcame their doubts about the middle classes and moved toward a conception of popular education that emphasized the presentation of supposedly objec-tive facts to the people so that they could make their own deci-sions. For those who would not or could not learn, the museum would at least provide "rational amusement" that would reduce the need for frivolous pleasures or vices. The museum would thus be simultaneously a school in which the sovereign people could learn to make wise choices and a place of wholesome diversion for the thoughtless.

This slow return to optimism took nearly two decades to ma-ture. Peale was concerned that the rising middle classes were not capable of wielding power. He worried that they showed a lack of reflection and a strong tendency to be seduced by vices. "I neglect many little contrivances which might serve to catch the Eye of the gaping multitude," Peale wrote one correspondent in 1802, and this was not a solitary note of misgiving about the public.[24] He complained about "people who do not take on them-selves the trouble of thinking, which is very much the case with the bulk of mankind."[25] And the "rude and uncultivated" people who stood on upholstered benches, scratched their names into wooden frames, and fingered the glass were a constant annoyance to Peale.[26]

Annoyance, however, did not lead to exclusion. Despite his frustration with the lower orders, Peale never became an elitist. Exclusionary ideas were suggested to him, including an idea for segregation from, of all people, Thomas Jefferson: "When in a great City, [one] will find persons of every degree of wealth, to jumble all these into a room together I know from experience is very painful to the decent part of them, who . . . revolt at being mixed with pickpockets, chimney sweeps, etc. Set three different divisions of the day therefore at three different prices, selecting for the highest when the *beau monde* can most conveniently attend. The 2nd price when merchants and respectable citizens have most leisure, and the residue for the lower description."[27]

In reply to this suggestion for adopting elitist policies, Peale gently demurred, and instead sketched his idea of a useful institution: "Such a Museum, easy of access, must tend to make all classes of people in some degree learned in the science of nature without even the trouble of study."[28] Despite his reservations about the middle classes, and despite his contempt for the dissipated, Peale never became an elitist who kept the people away from his museum. He was too much imbued with a sense of mission for his museum to even contemplate such a course. The people needed guidance, and he was prepared to provide it.

At the beginning of the nineteenth century, Peale clearly saw himself as the didactic mentor of the people. In the same letter to Jefferson in which he pledged to attract "all classes" of men, Peale revealed his purpose: "Whether a diffused knowledge of this kind may tend to mend their Morals, is a question of some import—furnishing the Idle and disapated [*sic*] with a great and new source of amusement ought to divert them from frivolous and promiscuous entertainments."[29]

The museum's purpose was two-fold: education and entertainment. But as Peale clearly stated, the content of this education was to be moralistic in tone. The middle classes, if left to their own devices, were vulnerable to all sorts of moral pitfalls. The museum would show them the proper course and help them to avoid errors. Peale, in 1802, equated education with a paternalistic urge to mold the middle classes into the form of the respectability. The museum would "save the idle from vicious habits" and be a moral guardian for society.[30] Over the course of two decades, however, Peale's moralism became diluted. The fabric of American society had not been hopelessly shredded as a result of the rise of the middle classes. Peale's optimism slowly returned, and though he would never give up the moralizing entirely, his tone softened. He would continue to complain of "young men in a rattling manner," but he ceased to employ strong pejoratives in describing the rising classes.[31] The fear induced by the aftereffects of the French Revolution was beginning to evaporate.

This pessimism was replaced by a sensible realism. Back in 1786, Peale had believed that his museum could inspire reverence and rationality in all men, that all could benefit equally from its lessons. Since then he had seen a great deal of variety in the people who had come through his establishment. Some had come to learn, but the majority sought only entertainment. Peale had initially belittled the latter attitude, and had tried to inspire the merrymakers with a hunger for learning. Now, in the years following 1800, Peale slowly grasped the fact that a truly useful museum would have to accommodate both the serious and the casual visitor, both the scholar and the person who wished to be diverted. Peale was thus the first to grasp the essential form of the modern American museum: an institution that promotes scholarly research, provides popular education, and offers an acceptable form of entertainment.

Peale did not have this insight all of a piece, but rather groped toward it all during the Didactic Enlightenment period. In 1800, as shown above, Peale's concept of education was essentially a didactic effort to control the lower classes. His first break from that idea came in 1802, when he purchased a small printing press, with the plan of printing the museum's catalog for distribution to all visitors. When this proved too impersonal, he wrote a small pamphlet entitled *A Walk with a Friend through the Philadelphia Museum*. Peale wrote that this pamphlet "is not ment [sic] to be a mere catalogue, but a view of what is most interesting, intending to be amusing as well as useful, and withall to give a comprehensive view of what the museum really contains."[32] Peale, ever the tinkerer, was here cobbling together a new invention.

Americans (and Europeans as well) were used to the cabinet for dilettantes, and accustomed as well to exhibitions for the masses, but no one had ever tried to formulate, in theory or in practice, a museum for everyone. Peale's guide was to be written so as to delight in the process of informing, simultaneously to please both the serious and the casual visitor.

Peale slowly moved toward a workable theory as the years went by. By 1808 he declared, "Some amusements should be mixed with studies,"[33] and by the next year he called the museum "a place of Public resort for amusement and instruction & C."[34] Peale believed that education was crucial to happiness, but he knew from observation that many refused to learn because the process of learning was often tedious. By injecting a leavening of entertainment into the business of learning, Peale hoped to make people enjoy it. His didacticism had largely evaporated, having been replaced by a new sense of faith in the capabilities of the people.

Peale's fullest statement of his new optimism came in an address to the Corporation and Citizens of Philadelphia in July of 1816. He was still engaged in his ongoing search for a means to establish his museum as a public institution, and he defended the worth of his museum with some of his most impassioned rhetoric: "Though man is infinitely superior to all other animals in his intellectual capacity, yet it is principally by education that his superiority becomes apparent. An elevated knowledge of arts, of science and of natural history, diffused through all classes of society . . . is of the highest importance when it continually leads them to a sweet humanity."[35]

Although man had every natural advantage, his full potential could be reached only by assiduously honing his capacities. With knowledge came a wisdom born of maturity, one which could banish narrowness and bigotry. To Peale, the museum made this knowledge available to everyone. For a visitor who was studious, the museum offered a chance to "learn to know himself and by studying his relationship to other beings, know the chain by which the whole is held together."[36] For those who sought only entertainment, "we know that relaxation from labour is often salutary, and we know that amusements will be sought for. [Their] morals . . . by visitations here . . . are certainly improved."[37] Thus at the same time they were teaching the studious, the exhibits were amusing the idle in a rational and informative fashion. The museum was a schoolroom disguised as a funhouse.

Peale's great goal was easily stated: "To form such a school of useful knowledge, to diffuse its usefulness to every class of our country, to amuse and at the same moment to instruct the adult as well as the youth of each sex and age . . . a great school of nature which speaks a language intelligible to all mankind; where all classes of men from the most learned to the most illiterate, from the aged down to the tender youth, all may read and be happily amused, and certainly instructed."[38]

Peale's insight came sooner to him than to any other museum proprietor. His museum was to be the most democratic institution in a democratic country. The scholar was welcome here as he struggled to find new facts. The intelligent visitor, who came to learn about God's wonderful creation, felt very much at home. And the casual visitor, who came to be diverted, found the museum just as congenial as any of the others. All of this happened simultaneously; the museum truly amused in the same moment as it instructed. Charles Willson Peale, in 1816, had invented the democratic museum, and he *understood* that he had invented it.

The elder Peale's museum ideology was transmitted to his sons as well. Three of his sons, Rembrandt, Rubens, and Charles Linnaeus, became museum proprietors, and Peale museums would be founded in Baltimore, New York City, and Utica, New York. It would be wrong to assume that these were branches of the Philadelphia Museum, or that there was a coordinated plan to organize them. They were individual efforts of the various brothers, and although the elder Peale helped them by gifts of specimens and advice, he did not exert any control over them per se.

The first of these ventures was launched by Rembrandt Peale in Baltimore. Young Rembrandt had been groomed to be a painter; his father had arranged for him to study art in Paris. In 1810 he returned to Philadelphia and opened the "Appolodorian Gallery of Paintings," which he expected would make his fortune. Instead, his efforts were largely ignored except when he was falsely accused of displaying a copy as an original composition.

Discouraged by this failure and unwilling to work under his father, in 1812 Rembrandt determined to open a museum of his own in Baltimore. Charles Willson Peale was dubious about his son's prospects and attempted to dissuade him. But Rembrandt persisted, moved to Baltimore, raised sufficient capital, and built a fine new museum building. Young Mr. Peale had managed this fund-raising feat by selling stock, borrowing money, and creating a large ground rent on the property, so he began his career mortgaged to the hilt.

Rembrandt also began at the least auspicious time imaginable, August of 1814, just as Baltimore was placed under siege by the British. He saw the enterprise through the siege, however, and got it off to a fair start. Rembrandt wrote to his father's old friend, Thomas Jefferson, and explained, "The general plan . . . will differ from my father's museum, it being my intention to render it more properly a museum of Arts and Sciences, and, without neglecting any branch of natural history, to bestow my chief attention to the formation of a picture gallery,"[39] Rembrandt's plan was actually much like his father's, for it embraced natural history specimens, a gallery of heroes, and specimens of historical, mechanical, and curiosity value.

Although he was not given to philosophizing as was his father, Rembrandt did remark that his museum was "an institution devoted to the improvement of public taste and the diffusion of science."[40] This echoed his father's goal of amusing while instructing. The museum offered a sensible form of amusement that would improve the quality of public behavior. At the same time it taught the basic principles of science that were so important to the citizens of a rapidly developing nation.

In the heady early years of the museum, Rembrandt stuck closely to this ideal. Although he did display a couple of nude artworks, he concentrated on such valuable activities as philosophical experiments, lectures on the steam engine, an orrery display, and in 1820, an exhibit of the paintings of John Vanderlyn. But Rembrandt's huge debts came back to haunt him; and when his heavy investment in Baltimore's first gas company proved a failure, he was in desperate straits. By 1820, against his better judgment, he turned to more spectacular and less scientific activities in order to keep the museum afloat.

The era of the Didactic Enlightenment for the Peales was marked by a slow revival of optimism. Their fear of the rising middle classes slowly evaporated, and their faith in the efficacy of popular education grew apace. Abandoning their former heavy-handed efforts to control the masses, they instead embraced the concept of "rational amusement" to divert the people's attention from harmful ends. They sought to instruct the middle classes in the important fields of art, science, and history. The great goal was "to amuse and at the same moment to instruct," to combine, in one grand operation, entertainment and education. By so doing, they became the first to arrive at the modern conception of a museum: an institution which equally serves the scholar, the inquisitive visitor, and the pleasure-seeker. In short, the Peales invented the modern American museum: a truly democratic institution, a place for everyone.

The Last Bastion of Elitism: The New-York Historical Society

It is moreover contemplated to . . . lay the basis of a National Institution that will afford infinite advantages for the intellectual improvement and rational amusement of our fellow citizens and reflect honour on our City.[41]

Federalists of our age must be content with the past.[42]

The men who came together to form the New-York Historical Society in 1804 had learned to speak the language of the nineteenth century, but in their hearts they lived in the past. They were all of the Federalist persuasion politically, were anglophiles and francophobes in international relations, and fervently believed in the deferential model of society. By 1804, their respectable world was crumbling. The Federalists had lost the White House in 1800, and with that, their troubles had only begun. There was a massive expansion of popular participation in politics from 1800 to 1816, a revolution which enshrined political parties as a fixture on the American scene, and which eventually insured that the popular will would become the ultimate authority.[43] Hence, the deferential order of society was crumbling. As if these domestic problems were not enough, France seemed poised to crush England.

The Federalists had to decide how to respond to these shocks. The experience of the Order of the Cincinnati, in which a popular reaction had forced Federalists to open the meetings of what they had intended to be a secret hereditary society, had taught them that overt elitism would not be tolerated in the young nation.[44] Instead, they became "masters of the main chance, experts in the art of the possible, spokesmen for a new and covert elitism."[45] The founders of the Historical Society could and did mouth the slogans of the emerging middle class, but their actions were firmly rooted in an idealized deferential past. They celebrated Federalist heroes and holidays, treated the era of exploration and settlement as a golden era, and regarded the revolutionary period as a silver age. Their Historical Society was not intended to be an engine pulling America into a boundless future; rather, it was to be a shrine to the glorious past, or perhaps more accurately, a fortress dedicated to protecting a threatened way of life. It was no accident that they retained the archaic spelling of "New-York" to name their society. Their increasing isolation places them at the reactionary end of the spectrum of American museums during the Didactic Enlightenment period.

The list of founders was headed by John Pintard, who by 1804 had gotten out of debtor's prison and who had long since shaken the dust of the Republican Tammany Society from his boots. Pintard discovered more conservative and thus more congenial company among his cofounders, who included De Witt Clinton, Dr. David Hosack, and the Reverend Samuel Miller. They were among the eleven men who met on November 20, 1804, in the Picture Room of New York's City Hall, to form the New-York Historical Society. The new society was to be housed, thanks to the influence of John Pintard, in City Hall. The founders soon issued an address to the public, with queries on various subjects.

They had formed the New-York Historical Society, they said, "for the purpose of discovering, procuring and preserving whatever may relate to the natural, civil, literary and ecclesiastical history of our country, and particularly of the State of New York."[46] This ambitious program, however, went largely unfulfilled for the first twelve years of the society's history. The cramped space at City Hall, and later at the Government House, from 1809 to 1816, effectively stifled any collecting program, as did a chronic shortage of funds. In addition, the society placed emphasis mainly on building its library, to the exclusion of the collection. The society had only a very small cabinet as late as the year 1816.

Once more, John Pintard was the innovator. In a long letter to his friend and fellow Historical Society member, De Witt Clinton, dated August 28, 1812, he suggested that the American Academy of Fine Arts, the American Museum of John Scudder, the City Library, and the Historical Society be housed in one edifice. He suggested this as a means of "fostering the Arts, Sciences & Literature in this place. . . . by concentering [*sic*] all our resources we may give a greater impulse and elevation to our intellectual character."[47] Moreover, Pintard wished to persuade the city to provide these institutions with a rent-free building. He had his eye on the Alms House, which in 1812 was scheduled to be abandoned in favor of a new facility at Bellevue.

Pintard, with De Witt Clinton's help, flawlessly handled the ensuing delicate negotiations with the corporation, and in 1815, when the Alms House was vacated, the building (now rechristened the New York Institution) was turned over to the Historical Society, the American Academy of Fine Arts, the Lyceum of Natural History, the Literary and Philosophical Society, and John Scudder's American Museum. The Historical Society had four large rooms on the first floor, together with storage space in the basement, all for the "yearly rent of one peppercorn, if lawfully demanded."[48] Here the society had the opportunity to begin collecting in earnest.

So they did, but in a far different way than Charles Willson Peale or John Scudder. According to John Pintard, the American Museum was "eminently calculated to cultivate and diffuse the knowledge of Natural History besides affording a pleasing field for gratifying innocent & laudable curiosity."[49] This sentiment sounds a great deal like that of Charles Willson Peale's idea "to amuse and at the same moment to instruct." As Pintard and his cohorts regarded the cabinet of their own institution, however, they could see no public role for it; indeed, they belittled the public. Even John Pintard, perhaps the most liberal among them, frequently lapsed into elitist statements in his correspondence. Before the Alms House became the New York Institution, for instance, it had briefly been the venue of the New York Court of Sessions. Pintard's dim view of the people can be clearly seen in the letter he wrote to De Witt Clinton on this subject. According to Pintard, "The tried defendants on that court are composed of the vulgar rabble of the city, who will soon wear out the marble staircases, defile the walls & deface the panel & ornamental work—In short, the whole building is contaminated by the intercourse."[50] Pintard and his compatriots surely held a dim view of the very constituency their cabinet would serve if opened to the public.

They did, however, collect, and soon aimed to fill their commodious new quarters with a variety of artifacts. De Witt Clinton was one of the driving forces behind this transformation. As early as 1807, when the Society was still in the constricted quarters of City Hall, Clinton wrote, "The mineralogical cabinet is [precious?] in my view beyond all other arrangements."[51] Now, with the room to keep a collection, Clinton teamed with John Pintard to systematically gather artifacts. On December 31, 1816, Pintard gave notice that at the next meeting of the society, he would propose the formation of five collecting committees: Mineralogical, Natural History, Coins & Medals, Manuscripts, and Books. At the meeting a committee was named to examine the expediency of establishing a mineralogical cabinet, and they reported positively at the conclave of February 11, 1817. At the same meeting, the other four committees Pintard recommended were approved as well.

The motivations behind the formation of this cabinet stand out clearly in the "Report to the Public" prepared for the meeting of March 11, 1817:

> The progress of the science of mineralogy in the United States has been very satisfactory to its friends in this country and the labours of American mineralogists have met with great applause in Europe. . . . to collect these scattered materials of our natural history, to display the riches of the mineral kingdom of each of our states; to inform the scientific traveller and citizen; to encourage the growing taste of this science in our country; to communicate discoveries and invite researches; are objectives so useful; so important, that it would be impossible to doubt of the public favour being shown to this undertaking.[52]

The cultural nationalism that runs through this statement is unmistakable, but the talk about the "useful" and "important" work that the society was doing for the public rings rather hollow. After all, the society proposed to accept donations from the public and then make them available only to society members and "scientific" travellers; in other words, only to certifiable members of the respectability. The sole benefit that the public would receive was a rather nebulous "encouragement" to pursue mineralogy. This inaccessibility and exclusivity are in sharp contrast to Peale's and Scudder's approaches. They too supported researchers and scholars, but did so while remaining accessible to the public.

Although the society meant to build an exclusive cabinet rather than a public museum, at least they went about it in a big way. At that same meeting of March 11, 1817, the society also approved the formation of a cabinet of American zoology and lectureships on zoology, geology, botany, vegetable physiology, mineralogy, chemistry, and natural philosophy. David Hosack further proposed that the society form an herbarium much like the one he had already collected and donated to the New York Hospital. At the meeting of April 8, 1817, Hosack was given permission to go ahead with this project.

The collectors set out with a will to gather specimens. On March 6, 1817, circulars were sent out to potential donors all over the country to solicit artifacts for the mineral cabinet, one of which was sent to Charles Willson Peale. On March 11, Samuel Latham Mitchill sent out a circular for the cabinet of American zoology and geology. And finally, on June 16, 1817, another circular was sent out, again over Mitchill's signature, which requested specimens for all the collections, identifying the society's cabinet as consisting of "Zoology, Botany, Mineralogy, Coins and Medals, & C. & C."[53] In the space of less than six months, the society had transformed itself from a club with only the rudiments of a collection into an organization with an active plan for augmenting its cabinet by comprehensive acquisitions.

It was still very much a cabinet, manifestly not for the use of the people. True, they spoke of the "great public utility" of their collecting,[54] but this hardly meant that the public was welcome in the society's rooms at the New York Institution. Admission would be limited to the learned scholars in natural history, who might therein learn something which may benefit the general public later. The society's members frequently claimed that they could not afford to open the doors to the public. The treasury was always in a state of collapse, and John Pintard had had to personally transport the society's library to the New York Institution, since the society could not afford to hire movers. Fortunately, the rhetoric of public service was free, and the society used it extensively, even though it did not fit the reality.

Some historians have tried to lay the blame for the society's elitist stance solely on the chronic shortage of funds. Clarence S. Brigham, for instance, maintained, "What faults are chargeable to the Society—and they are sins of omission rather than of commission—are imperfections chiefly due to the lack of means."[55] This is unacceptable for two reasons. First, the philosophy of the membership made it highly unlikely that they would have reached out to the public even if they had had ample funds. Second, the membership possessed, as a whole, considerable means, and they were active individually in many charitable endeavors. If they had really been distressed by their isolation from the public, they could have enlarged the endowment themselves, or raised the money for that purpose. Their lethargy in fund-raising strongly suggests that they were content to maintain an exclusive retreat while talking about the importance of public service.

The move to the New York Institution, moreover, provided a convenient excuse for keeping the society inaccessible. With the public always welcome at Scudder's museum and at the public exhibitions of the American Academy of Fine Arts in the same building, it hardly seemed necessary for the Historical Society to welcome them too. In fact, it appeared to be a sensible form of specialization to have the society cater to the scholars while other institutions served the people. However, in an age which was becoming ever more egalitarian, such elitist sentiments were dangerous if spoken aloud. Hence the society's members became quite adept at speaking the language of public utility for public consumption, while speaking an entirely different language of exclusivity in private.

Nothing could illustrate this dual stance better than the reception the society accorded to Charles Willson Peale during his visit to New York on May 23 to June 14, 1817. One might have expected the elitist society members to shun the "populistic" Peale. Instead they lionized him. Peale met with David Hosack, John Pintard, and Samuel Latham Mitchill. Mitchill, in particular, got on well with Peale, a great irony, since the gentle painter and the irascible physician were temperamentally so different. At their first meeting, Mitchill, according to Peale, "received me with great kindness and saluted me as the father of Natural History in America."[56] At their second meeting, Mitchill, speaking of the many organizations in the New York Institution, "considered finally they would become great in their institutions and diffuse much useful knowledge. I told him that it gave me pleasure to see so many gentlemen so zealously united together in their pursuit of knowledge. . . . He paid me many compliments for my industry in the rearing up [of] my museum."[57] Mitchill was full of praise for Peale's museum, which catered to the people, and spoke of his interest in popular education. But none of this admiration would be translated into imitation at the Historical Society.

The society continued to flatter Peale. As already stated, Hosack tried to lure Peale's museum to New York, and the society itself conferred an honorary membership on the venerable Philadelphian at a meeting he attended. Perhaps these attentions tended to blind Peale's normally critical eye, for he had little to say that was negative about the society. He did note the significant fact, however, that the society was "composed of many wealthy members, whose zeal for the objects of their institution lead them to disregard costs."[58] Peale was speaking of the fitting-up of the cases to hold the mineralogical cabinet, but clearly this liberality could have been extended to the society as a whole, had the members cared to do so. Again, it is clear that the society members could have had an accessible museum had they truly wished one.

Although the members of the society envisioned their society and its cabinet as a haven from an increasingly distasteful world, they did not underrate the social value of museums as a didactic force. John Pintard, in a letter to his daughter, clearly spelled out the "proper" social function of the museum in the age of the Didactic Enlightenment:

> To afford innocent amusement to growing opulence is among the duties incumbent on all who regard the morals of Society. Mankind cannot always be praying, nor working. Gross dissipation always [*sic*] prevails where refinement is not cultivated. The vices of polished society tho' pernicious, do not shock by their grossness & as wealth & its consequent indulgences more & more abounds, we must aim at giving a proper direction to young minds, find out new resources for occupation & *killing* time, among wh. Theaters, Operas, Academies of Arts, Museums & C. are to be classed as the means to attract and prevent the growth of vice & immorality. These are among the reasons which operate with me to lay the foundation of institutions wh. I cannot ever expect to arrive at even moderate perfection in my day.[59]

Although obviously written in haste and without revision, this is an excellent summary of the Didactic Enlightenment outlook. The rise of the lower classes in society, the "growing opulence" of Pintard's phraseology, was superseding the old order in which lower classes were controlled by their employer and their church.

Their increased leisure time and their greater means threatened to engulf society in any number of coarse vices such as gambling, drinking, and prostitution. Museums offered an "innocent amusement" which might absorb some of that excess time and money and thus keep it from being funneled into vice. This sounds somewhat like the Peale dictum "to amuse and at the same moment to instruct"; but unlike the essentially optimistic Peale, who believed that the middle classes could be elevated by means of education, Pintard was for the most part pessimistic. His only goal was to mold the people's leisure time as much as possible; in contrast to Peale's educational goals, Pintard sought to "find out new resources for . . . *killing* time."

The history of the New-York Historical Society from 1804 to 1820 is a story of elitism. The members' idealistic statements were mere rhetoric, their poverty, although real, was self-inflicted, and elitism was their guiding creed. The men who made up the society were not looking to the future, as were Peale and Scudder, but rather turning to the past. They were conscious that their ideal society was rapidly passing away, and cheered as their neighbors in the New York Institution sought to mold the new society that was replacing it. Instead of entering the fray, however, they wrapped themselves in the glorious past of their ancestors and the interesting scholarship of the present. They wanted nothing to do with the popular society that surrounded them, but were too much imbued with cultural nationalism to turn to European models. Isolated in the New York Institution, the New-York Historical Society was out of step with even the respectability during the Didactic Enlightenment period.

The Solace of Science: The Elgin Garden, The Academy of Natural Sciences, and The Western Museum of Cincinnati

Under all the vicissitudes and trials of life, after a sincere invocation to Divine Providence, the safest reliance is on the dictates of learning and science; and in the midst of the widest desolation, our exertions for their benefit should never relax.[60]

During the time of the Didactic Enlightenment, the respectability who ran the museums were forced to confront the rise of the middle classes. Peale and Scudder met this challenge by seeking an accommodation of popular education and rational amusement. In contrast to this relatively "popular" approach, the New-York Historical Society turned an elitist face toward the people by disdaining any contact with them whatsoever. In so doing, the society ran the risk of being labeled a closed corporation of no use to the people at large, a heavy charge indeed in an age of popular ascendancy.

In other museums run by the respectability, the proprietors discovered a formula which allowed them to be useful to the public without requiring them to open their doors to all who wished entry. The "scientifics" of the Elgin Garden, the Academy of Natural Sciences of Philadelphia, and the Western Museum of Cincinnati all found their solace in promoting scientific studies. The benefits of their discoveries would make these institutions useful to all people, but the very nature of scientific investigation would require a certain amount of solitude for the investigators. This theme foreshadowed the arguments of later professional scientists, but it did not prove durable as an operating principle; by 1820 the Elgin Garden would be defunct, and the Academy and Western Museum would be yielding to popular pressures.

The Elgin Botanical Garden, 1801–1816

The first of these institutions was properly a botanical garden rather than a museum. But inasmuch as the founder, David Hosack, espoused a philosophy related to that of many museum proprietors, and since the garden contained many museumlike features, such as a permanent collection of living plants and an herbarium, it is proper to consider it as a part of the museum scene. Hosack, a leader of the New-York Historical Society and other New York cultural organizations, moved in the highest circles of New York's society, but he was not a reactionary as were some of his fellow society members. He was a professor of medicine, one of New York's most respected physicians, and also a passionate collector.

These interests united in the matter of a botanical garden. Hosack had taken his medical training in Edinburgh and London; while in London he became intimate with the botanist William Curtis, who was the proprietor of a botanical garden at Brompton. Hosack later recalled, "I visited the botanical garden daily throughout the summer of 1793."[61] Here he became convinced that the only way to teach *materia medica* was by reference to the actual specimens.

After Hosack returned to America, he was named Professor of Botany at Columbia College in 1795, and in the following year he added the Chair in *Materia Medica*. At once he began promoting the notion of a botanical garden as an indispensable teaching tool. Hosack later recalled his motivations:

> I now readily perceived that an abstract account of the principles of these sciences, as taught by books, coloured engravings, or even with the advantages of a *herbarium*, must necessarily be very imperfect and unsatisfactory, when compared with an examination of living plants, growing in their proper soils . . . and that a botanical establishment was indispensably necessary in order to teach this branch of medical science with complete effect . . . affording the medical student an opportunity of practical instruction in this science.[62]

Despite his repeated attempts to interest Columbia College in establishing a botanical garden as an educational tool, Hosack had no success. So he struck out on his own; on September 1, 1801, he bought twenty acres of land three miles to the north of New York's city limits for the sum of $4,807.36. The site (now occupied by Rockefeller Center) was still a wilderness, and Hosack poured his own money and time into its development. He encircled the entire plot with a stone wall, planted a belt of forest trees and shrubs inside the wall, and cleared the rest for planting. He built a large and expensive greenhouse and employed numerous keepers and farmers. This massive outlay produced, after only a few years, an impressive establishment. Hosack used it as an open-air laboratory and classroom for his students and also produced a few cash crops there. As it reached a high state of development, he began to hold an annual strawberry festival for his students and even allowed the general public to walk through gratuitously on certain days.

From an educational standpoint, the garden was a great success. Not only did Hosack teach there, but so did Samuel Latham Mitchill, who brought his classes to Elgin to illuminate his lectures on botany.[63] Naturalists, the medical faculty, and even the general public (when allowed in) were unanimous in their praise. Hosack, however, who had confidently expected Columbia or the corporation to take over Elgin, was going deeply into debt for its upkeep. On March 5, 1805, he asked the legislature for a loan to maintain operations. Despite a personal visit from the governor of New York and his favorable report, the legislature took no action.

Hosack proved that his business acumen did not match his medical ability, for he continued with his ambitious program, and even added another building to the garden. Reality finally set in on April 5, 1808, when Hosack asked the legislature to buy the garden from him. His memorial betrays a significantly different rationale for the project than he initially held. In place of his sole emphasis on the garden as a medical teaching tool, he now added a role as a public educator. He admitted that his goal had been to give medical students "a more accurate knowledge of Plants and their Medicinal qualities," but insisted that he had always desired to render it a "public benefit."[64] Now Hosack envisioned Elgin as being "productive of great advantage to the Public by providing the means of extensive experiments and consequent improvements in agricultural gardening." Finally, it was a popular educator as well, for it brought about "a general diffusion of learning."[65]

It is interesting to note that an institution originally projected as an exclusive reserve for higher education suddenly became, when writing to the legislature, a public benefit and a popular educator. Such claims had some truth, for the people could benefit from new discoveries made at the garden and they could learn about botany while walking through. But these had not been Hosack's main goals in establishing the garden, and, as will be seen, evidence exists to suggest that in reality they never were.

Hosack continued to work for a purchase of Elgin by the state. Finally on March 12, 1810, New York purchased the entire establishment from Hosack, pending an assessment of the value of the land. Hosack had worked hard to effect the purchase, even organizing a letter-writing campaign to sway influential people. One such letter begins, "Doctr. Hosack is much interested in initiating the good will of the legislature . . . inducing them to adopt his Botannic [sic] Garden . . . devoted to the good of the public."[66] After the purchase was secured and the land was assessed, however, Hosack wrote a candid letter to his former pupil, Amos Eaton, revealing his true attitude toward the public. In contrast to the benign rhetoric of the "public good," the doctor spelled out a series of educational goals that were calculatedly paternalistic. Hosack, speaking of the educational value of natural history for young people, told Eaton:

> It has always appeared to me a very absurd practice in our schools to occupy children with studies of an abstract nature and which require faculties to comprehend them which are not yet unfolded. You have adopted, in my opinion, the true system of education, and very properly address yourself to the senses and to the memory instead of the faculties of Judgement and of Reason which are of comparatively slow growth—by this system of instruction their minds will be stored with truths that cannot fail to prove useful.[67]

Hosack here presents a brief for the respectability's attempt to retain control over the lower classes. The purpose of education, in his view, was not to stimulate the desire to learn, but rather to inculcate by rote memory proper precepts of behavior. The clear implication of Hosack's argument is that early education must instill proper ideas in the vast mass of humanity, while they are not yet capable of reasoning for themselves.

Hosack then made his implication explicit, explaining to Eaton: "In proportion as the mind attaches itself to subjects of this sort it is diverted from those vicious propensities and pursuits which otherwise attract attention at this early period of life. Studies of this nature are no less calculated to improve the morals of youth . . . thereby improving their virtue as well as their wisdom."[68]

It is clear that Hosack's primary educational goal was the teaching of his notion of virtue and proper behavior to the lower classes. To his mind, teaching as an intellectual activity was restricted to higher education. The lower orders, with their "natural" tendency toward vice and immorality, must be molded by those who possessed education, taste, and "virtue." When Hosack spoke of the "general diffusion of learning" that the Elgin Garden was effecting, it was this paternalistic, didactic effort he had in mind.

The garden was destined never to fulfill Hosack's program of didactic education. In January of 1811 it formally passed into the custody of the regents of the state of New York, and a sure and steady decline set in. The state hesitated over which of New York's two medical schools, Columbia or the College of Physicians and Surgeons, should be awarded the garden. In the meantime, the regents appointed a caretaker named Michael Dennison, who systematically removed every plant of any value from the collection, while doing little to maintain that which remained. For six years the garden languished, first placed under the nominal jurisdiction of the College of Physicians and Surgeons, then in 1814, under Columbia. During all of this time not a cent was expended on maintenance. Finally, in 1816 Columbia received complete jurisdiction over the site. Hosack attempted to secure the transfer of the garden to the College of Physicians and Surgeons, with which he was connected. His effort was rebuffed, as were subsequent attempts in 1819 and 1824. Columbia had lost all interest in botany, and now looked upon Elgin as a real estate asset with which they were loath to part. The garden soon disappeared entirely.

David Hosack's scheme to use public funds to promote higher education was an idea that would eventually find favor in America, but was premature in 1801. The rising middle classes, such as merchants and substantial farmers, were not yet in a position to see much direct benefit from such an expenditure, and legislatures did not dare to offend their sensibilities. The solace of science comforted David Hosack, but only briefly. Popular pressures made a purely scientific organization an impossibility at this point.

The Academy of Natural Sciences of Philadelphia, 1812–1820

The solace of science seemed particularly attractive to a group of gentlemen who came together in 1812 to form the Academy of Natural Sciences of Philadelphia. The seven men who first met in January of that year were not of the city's first families; no Cadwaladers, Copes, Biddles, or Tilghmans were members.[69] Most were, however, members of the respectability: John Speakman was an apothecary; Jacob Gilliams was a dentist; Gerard Troost was both a physician and a chemist; John Shinn, Jr., manufactured chemicals; Nicholas S. Parmentier was a distiller; and Camillus Macmahon Mann was a physician. The seventh, Thomas Say, was an aspiring naturalist.[70] Like members of the respectability in other cities, they were vulnerable to a loss of status due to the rise of the middle classes; one hedge against this was membership in an exclusive society.

There is abundant proof that the seven sought to build a scientific bulwark against the rising tide of egalitarianism. After Thomas Say died in 1834, George Ord, who later would become president of the academy, blasted the seven in his usual vituperative style: "[The Academy's] founders had anything in view but the advancement of science. Strange as it may appear, it is nevertheless true that the club of humorists which . . . dignified the association through the imposing title of Academy, had its weekly meetings merely for the purpose of amusement."[71]

Some of Ord's hostility can be ascribed to the superiority felt by a quasi-professional scientist toward his amateur predecessors. There is no evidence to suggest that the founders were as flippant as Ord claims; rather, they were very serious men. Ord, however, did have a point in one sense; the records do suggest that social concerns were almost as important as science to the founders.

Only two of the seven, Say and Troost, had any real experience in scientific endeavors, and only Troost had any formal scientific training. A look at the early minutes of their meetings, moreover, proves that the membership occasionally worried about social standing to the exclusion of scientific matters. For instance, the preamble to the minutes of the first gathering, recorded by Camillus Mann, begins, "at a meeting of gentlemen, friends of science and rational disposal of leisure moments . . ."[72]

This slim purpose was elaborated upon at the "foundation meeting" of March 17, 1812, when the founders waxed philosophical: "This institution is conceived for the purposes of rational, [?], literary and scientific conversations, and for the enjoyment of social recreations susceptible of improving intelligent beings in knowledge or in goodness. It is formed for the purpose of affecting the wiser and the better by the more agreeable. . . . we meet to supersede listlessness, to chase away ennui, and to restore the balance of our minds when worn with the cares of life or the fatigues of business."[73]

Such a description sounds suspiciously like a private club whose pretext was science, rather than a scientific society. The general tone of exclusivity it implied was reinforced by such avowals as, "It being irreversibly our intention to permit none but persons of gentlemanly manners 'genteel and gentle,' it cannot enter into our contemplation to suffer the presence or entrance of persons of a contrary deportment."[74] The founders could not have made it clearer that they wished to have nothing to do with the lower classes. The academy was to be a haven for the "right" kind of person. In fact, the minutes even prescribed the proper mode of respectable behavior for academy members, calling for "good humored tones of voice, good humored expressions [and] the manners of honourable and reciprocal deference."[75]

Although it seemed that the founders were living in the past, they did display an understanding of current problems. They noted (echoing John Pintard) that the academy could fill a void for the "right" kind of citizen: "In this large city, the young men generally have few modes of social recreation when their daily business is over except frequenting the theatres at a considerable expense, taverns, gaming houses, dancing rooms, or places of a more degrading atmosphere where they can gain no improvement but are sure to acquire habits injurious to the spirit of a good citizen."[76]

The academy could provide rational amusement for young men of good backgrounds, and thus keep them from the pitfalls of vice. It was to be a gentleman's club, one which felt little responsibility to the community at large. The founders' main goal was not service to the people, or even the discovery of new scientific truths, but rather to use science as a form of "recreative amusement."[77]

Almost as an afterthought, the founders did resolve, at that initial meeting, to "contribute to the formation of a Museum of Natural History . . . and every other desirable appendage . . . for the illustration and advancement of natural knowledge."[78] The first years of the museum were extremely lean ones. The academy had first to find a permanent home and build up a respectable collection before they could have a useful cabinet. A beginning was made in 1813, when the academy purchased a collection of nearly 2,000 minerals from Dr. Adam Seybert, and began soliciting specimens from both members and nonmembers. They began to shed their exclusivity to some extent in 1814 and 1815 when they offered a series of lectures, based on the collection, to anyone with ten dollars to spend. The lectures raised needed capital and brought in new members, but five years after its founding the academy still was a modest venture.

All this began to change in 1817 when William Maclure was elected president to succeed Gerard Troost. Maclure was a remarkable man who had packed a prodigious amount of living into his fifty-four years. He was born in Scotland in 1763, and by 1781 worked in a mercantile house in London. Maclure was an eminently successful businessman and rapidly amassed a large fortune. Like many other British capitalists, he retired from business at the height of his career to devote his life to science and philanthropy. Maclure settled in the United States in 1796, and became so respected that he was sent to France on a diplomatic mission in 1805.

While in Europe, he studied the geology of the Continent and of England, traveling extensively to collect specimens. When he returned to America in 1807, he decided to make the first geological map of the United States. For nearly ten years he roamed between the Atlantic and the Mississippi, usually alone and always at his own expense, crossing and recrossing the Allegheny Mountains fifty times. By 1817, he had published and then revised his results, making him the leading American geologist.

Maclure had picked up another interest in Europe. In 1805, while sojourning in Switzerland, he had visited the school at Yverdon just founded by Johann Heinrich Pestalozzi, the Swiss educational reformer. Maclure was impressed by Pestalozzi, who eschewed rote learning in favor of a method emphasizing concrete experience, structured so as to correspond to the natural order of individual development. Maclure's enthusiasm for Pestalozzian methods would profoundly affect his vision of the academy's museum.

For now, however, Maclure's philanthropy delivered the academy from its tentative early years and launched a period of steady growth. He donated money, specimens from his personal collection, and literally hundreds of books from his library. In addition to insuring the society's survival, Maclure changed its direction. He was completely convinced of the efficacy of education to effect social progress, and sought to make the academy a pedagogical instrument. On February 26, 1817, a committee which Maclure headed recommended that the academy publish a journal.[79] Its purpose was to diffuse knowledge of natural history; to make it as widely interesting as possible, the academy excluded papers on natural philosophy and discouraged contributions of a theoretical nature. After a tentative start, the journal was discontinued until 1821, but a pattern of responsiveness to the rising classes had been established.

By 1820, the academy had broadened its membership and its mission. Two of Charles Willson Peale's sons, Rubens and Titian

Ramsay Peale II, were members (the latter for a time was corresponding secretary) and some of less "respectable" background were also joining. From its origin as a club of gentlemen interested in natural history, it had become, under Maclure's leadership, an association of dedicated amateur scientists who felt an obligation to enlighten the public about natural history. The cabinet of the academy was still too underdeveloped to open to the public, but it was growing apace. With Maclure's influence paramount, the academy was poised to dive into the role of popular educator during the Age of Egalitarianism.

The Western Museum of Cincinnati, 1818–1820

In Cincinnati, as well as in New York and Philadelphia, science provided a haven for the respectability. Cincinnati, the "Queen City" of the West, had experienced phenomenal growth during the first two decades of the nineteenth century. By the end of that period, it was home to more than 9,000 people, was the hub of western trade, and seemed to have an unlimited potential for expansion.

A Cincinnati merchant named William Steele was the first to suggest that a museum be established in the Queen City. But the real credit for its founding belongs to Daniel Drake, a doctor whose accomplishments were so varied that he was nicknamed "the Franklin of the West." Drake's conception of museums had been formed by a long and intimate connection with Philadelphia. He had studied medicine there at the University of Pennsylvania from 1805 to 1806, no doubt visiting Peale's museum in the process. By the time he returned to the City of Brotherly Love in 1815 to complete his studies, Drake's corpus of published works on natural history and medical matters had gained him membership in the American Philosophical Society and the Academy of Natural Sciences. Drake soon had an opportunity to put his experience with museums to practical use after he returned to Cincinnati in 1816.

Drake, Steele, and their three cofounders, President Elijah Slack of Cincinnati College, Editor James Findlay of the newspaper *Lib-*

erty Hall and Cincinnati Gazette, and Land Agent Jesse Embree, met to found the Western Museum in the spring of 1818. These members of the respectability, with the exception of Drake, cared little for popular education. Their goal was to provide a haven for the "right" kind of people. This was apparent in the circular they produced, dated September 15, 1818, which was disseminated to possible donors all over the country. Entitled "An Address to the People of the Western Country," the circular (which was patterned after one Daniel Drake had received the year before from the New-York Historical Society) called for a permanent and comprehensive museum, one which would provide an "exquisite feast" for "zoologists and geologists" and improve the taste of "the lovers and cultivators of the fine arts."[80] Not a word was said, however, abut popular education or public responsibility.

Such an approach struck a chord in the Queen City. The museum was organized as a joint-stock company; $45,000 worth of subscriptions were raised at $50 per share. Drake and his cohorts quickly hired a capable staff; the curator was Robert Best, a talented Englishman, and the taxidermist was a young artist named John James Audubon. In addition, James Griffiths, who for many years had preserved quadrupeds at Peale's museum in Philadelphia, signed onto the staff.[81] At some point between August and December of 1819, the museum opened for business.[82]

At this point, the influence of Peale's museum seems to have asserted itself, and began to guide Daniel Drake's actions. The admission price was pegged at twenty-five cents, like Peale's, and in December of 1819 Drake followed another Peale precedent and offered a pair of public lectures. The inspiration for these may have come directly from Titian Peale, who visited the museum in 1819 along with other members of the Long Expedition, on their way to the West. Drake himself gave one of the lectures, a week before Christmas in 1819. This "Introductory Lecture on the Study of Mineralogy and Zoology" was, according to Frances Mason, one of the doctor's auditors, illustrated by museum specimens (another Peale innovation) but sparsely attended due to its high cost.[83] Still, it was significant that an effort at popular education was being made at all.

The lectures were not a financial success, but they seemed to have inspired Drake to a greater sensitivity toward the public. From this point forward he moved the Western Museum rapidly in the direction of popular education. Drake was not alone in his metamorphosis. The cultural imperatives of the dawning Age of Egalitarianism were everywhere breaking down the last ramparts of the respectability. Science had proven to be only a temporary solace for Hosack, the academy, and Drake. The people were not to be denied; popular education was to be king.

4

The Age of Egalitarianism, 1820–1840: The Ideal of Popular Education

Reform! The word echoed and re-echoed throughout the Age of Egalitarianism. From 1820 to 1840, people seemed determined to remake American society in almost every way imaginable. Millennalism, Millenarianism, spiritualism, Mormonism, and schisms of countless varieties swept through the religious life of the nation. Older causes, such as prison reform and temperance, were joined by newer callings, such as antislavery, women's rights, and popular education. The realm of health did not escape the wave of reform, for homeopathy and Sylvester Graham's system of vegetarian dietetics found many converts. There were even attempts to reinvent society, for a number of communal experiments, the most notable of which was that of Robert Owen at New Harmony, Indiana, flourished, if only briefly.[1]

What common thread, if any, unified this crazy quilt of reform organizations? Ralph Waldo Emerson devoted an essay to the subject, "New England Reformers," and perceptively concluded, "In each of these movements emerges . . . an assertion of the sufficiency of the private man."[2] Emerson's "private man" had emerged by 1820 as a result of the convergence of several factors: the decline of the respectability, the decay of deference, the rise of the middle classes. The reform movements were for the most part a middle-class phenomenon, both a means of struggling for equality and a ratification of their newfound status. The gospel of these newly risen classes was equality, expressed in the simple phrase, "One man is as good as another." Elitism in any form was regarded as a mortal enemy to the good of the republic. Reform was thus also imperative to remove any unfair advantages one might have over another.

To be sure, there were isolated voices of dissent from the gospel of equality and varying degrees of resistance to reform. The most articulate nay-sayer was James Fenimore Cooper, who would write in 1838, "'One man is as good as another' . . . is true in neither nature, revealed morals, nor in political theory."[3] Cooper and others of his ilk were shouted down, or at least ignored. Americans living between 1820 and 1840 believed egalitarianism could be a fact. The finding of some recent historians, notably Edward Pessen, that egalitarianism was in many ways a myth, does not change the fact that Americans from 1820 to 1840 believed that they were living in a land of equality.[4] This belief is illustrated by a keen observer of the American scene during this era, Dr. Thomas Nichols. Dr. Nichols evaluated America as both a detached observer and a knowledgeable participant, for he grew to manhood in England, spent most of his adult life in America, and then returned to England. He stated, "As none were very rich, and none had any need to be poor, and as all were equal in theory, and not very far from it in practice, we all went to the same schools, and were taught by the same schoolmasters."[5] The gap between theory and reality was sufficiently slim to keep people believing that equality was a fact.

Nichols also mentioned the central reform in an age of reforms: education. Americans had long paid lip service to the notion that education was the most important need in a nation in which the people ruled. Now, however, the people really were ruling. The franchise had been extended nearly to the point of universal white male suffrage, and the newly certified voters were no longer electing their social betters to office as a matter of course. The republic was truly in the hands of the man with the ballot, and it was more imperative now than before that he be properly educated so that he might correctly discharge his responsibilities to the commonwealth.

The obvious first step in this mission was to develop and improve local schools, and this was done a thousand times over throughout the country. By the end of the period, Horace Mann was in place as secretary of the Massachusetts Board of Education, building a public school system that would be copied all over the nation. Again and again in lectures and publications, Mann hammered home the message that the unprecedented responsibilities thrust upon American citizens required them to prepare themselves by acquiring the "unexampled wisdom and rectitude" that a public school education had to offer.[6]

In scores of American cities and villages, the people supplemented the public schools by transforming a British invention, the mechanics institute, into the peculiarly American lyceum. Mechanics institutes had been established in Glasgow and London in order to provide practical scientific instruction to laborers. A Connecticut teacher, Josiah Holbrook, seized the idea and adapted it to American conditions. Holbrook had studied at Yale under the great science educator (and later, museum curator) Benjamin Silliman, and recognized a good way to diffuse scientific knowledge when he saw one. In October of 1826, he proposed a few hints for forming "Societies for Mutual Education" in that month's issue of *American Journal of Education*. Holbrook suggested that people interested in learning band together, purchase "books, apparatus for illustrating the sciences, a cabinet of minerals, and other articles," and establish regular series of lectures. Among the officers of the societies were to be five curators, who would care for the objects in the lyceum's collection. The goals of the societies would be "to procure for youths an economical and practical education . . . to diffuse rational and useful information through the community generally . . . and to apply the sciences . . . to all the common purposes of life."[7] Holbrook's "society" sounded very much like a museum, for it was to have a collection and curators, and it was to sponsor lectures. The emphasis on popular education was similar to Peale's approach in Philadelphia.

Holbrook quickly put his idea to the test. Just a month after his article was published in the *American Journal of Education*, he founded the first lyceum at Millbury, Massachusetts. Once established, the idea began to spread with ever-increasing speed. Within two years a lyceum had been founded in Boston (by Daniel Webster, no less) and they swiftly spread over the country. By 1835 it was a miserable village indeed which did not contain a lyceum or some reasonable facsimile. This system of mutual improvement at the grass-roots level was working admirably, with locals organizing their societies and lecturing each other. It was a pure example of the hunger for popular education abroad in the land.

Holbrook's brainchild did much to diffuse the museum idea throughout the country, for it encouraged the collecting of tangible objects. It profoundly affected established museums as well. No longer could they maintain the pretense of public service when in reality they were catering to dilettantes and scholars. If museums were going to survive, they had to respond to the needs of the people in their communities, just as the lyceums were.

American museums responded to the cultural challenge of the Age of Egalitarianism in three ways. The first approach, which was embraced by the Peale museums and the Academy of Natural Sciences, was to meet the demand for popular education while at the same time serving the needs of the scholar. This foreshadowing of the American Compromise was an attempt to tread a middle ground between the needs of the popular and the elite. It was a precarious balance, but one which they managed to maintain throughout the period. The second response, illustrated by the Western Museum and the American Museum, was to cater to the lowest tastes of the public, to become a gaudy and sensational spectacle. Thus began the image of the museum-as-sideshow. Finally, the New-York Historical Society chose a third course, that of isolating itself from the public, giving rise to the notion of the museum-as-elitist-enclave. The Age of Egalitarianism was a critical period in American museum history, for the challenges museums faced, and the responses they chose, have been repeated again and again down to the present.

Struggling for the Middle Ground:
Peale's Museums and the Academy of Natural Sciences, 1820–1840

It is by our being well-informed, by a virtuous education,
that our republican government, and the liberties of the people, will be *secured, maintained* and perpetuated.[8]

Where the general mass rules, the diffusion of knowledge
is positively necessary for the prosperity of the social order,
and the foundation of general happiness.[9]

The rise of the middle classes trivialized the American and Western museums, and provoked the New-York Historical Society
into a reactionary stance. These two extremes, however, do not
exhaust the list of responses to the Age of Egalitarianism. Both
the Peale museums and the Academy of Natural Sciences charted
a course between "buncombe" and elitism, seeking to retain their
respectability while attracting people of all classes to their museums. Their rationale was simple. The common people were now
the sovereigns of the land, no longer deferring to their social betters. It was therefore essential for the continued functioning of
America's democratic system of government that every white
male receive an education that would prepare him for the duties
of citizenship: to read, write, and hold positions of public trust.
In an age when the public schools were not yet fully developed,
museums, like the lyceums, stepped into the vacuum to play a
role in the education of the public. By the end of the period both
the Peale museums and the academy had failed to achieve their
ends, but in their failure were planted the seeds of future success.

The Peale Museums

Charles Willson Peale, as noted earlier, had come to realize by
1817 that his museum could and should be a popular educator.
By 1820 he was beginning to understand that it was not enough
simply to let people read labels or a guidebook; more active mea-

sures were necessary. The 1820s, and to a lesser extent, the 1830s, were marked by experimentation in popular education at all of the Peale museums.

In 1821 Charles Willson Peale decided to make his museum an active educational institution. He named a board of five trustees and charged them with the task of hiring a faculty of professors. The four chosen, Dr. John Godman, physiology; Thomas Say, zoology; Dr. Richard Harlan, comparative anatomy; and Gerard Troost, mineralogy, were all members of the Academy of Natural Sciences. The trustees petitioned the Select Council of Philadelphia for permission to use the lower room of the Statehouse to hold the lectures, explaining that they were "desirous of making the [museum] more extensively useful by procuring Teachers, who by public lectures shall assist by diffusing knowledge and thereby improve and benefit society."[10]

This high educational purpose momentarily seemed fulfilled in the spring of 1821 when Godman and Troost lectured together. Peale was ecstatic after the first effort, by Godman, writing, "Doctor Godman's introductory Lecture on Physiology was highly gratifying to a polite audience, of Ladies as well as gentlemen."[11] Peale dreamed that the lectures "may bring the Museum into some reputation of its usefulness in diffusing Scientific knowledge"[12] It was not to be. The attendance was disappointing, and Godman and Troost, after finishing their courses, did not repeat them. Harlan and Say never gave a single talk, and in 1823, when Peale tried to fill the vacuum himself, his lectures were very sparsely attended. Peale reluctantly abandoned the faculty idea, blaming his failure on the competition: "We have had and still have so many public lectures that it becomes difficult to make numerous visitors to attend the lectures be it what it may."[13]

Peale went beyond lectures in his efforts to promote popular education. As early as 1821, he offered free admission to "Teachers of School, when accompanied by their class of schollars [sic] who pay 12½ cents each."[14] This inducement was one way to make the museum a truly educational institution, for young scholars as well as for old. It was also the first recorded partnership in

America between museums and schools for the purpose of popular education. No record remains, however, to document how Peale promoted this novel idea.

Peale devised one further educational innovation. <u>In 1824 he decided to shift his efforts in popular education from lectures to publications</u>. *The Philadelphia Museum, or Register of Natural History and the Arts* was a little sixteen-page magazine which was meant, as its editor said in a section entitled "To Our Readers," to "diffuse a taste for the study of Natural History, as well as to those delightful arts which contribute so much to the improvement and gratification of the mind."[15] The little journal was aimed squarely at the middle classes; its purpose was to popularize the knowledge obtainable at the museum. Articles on "Natural History" and "Interesting Facts Relative to the Opossum" were intended to be written so "that truth should be presented in her most attractive form."[16] Not only would the journal diffuse knowledge, it would also promote visits to the museum for further education. Peale made a special point of the museum's value for children: "This Museum affords the most excellent means of early initiating . . . children in the words of nature, of instructing them with slight effort in branches of knowledge fitted to expand and enlighten the mind."[17]

Peale left no doubt that the purpose of his little journal was popular education: "As the study of nature, has always been co-existent with the illumination of the human mind, and the advancement of social happiness, we may with greater advantage consider the benefits derivable from an universal diffusion of that knowledge . . . whose first effect is to enlarge the understanding and strengthen the judgement, and whose ultimate tendency is to refine our feeling and elevate our views."[18]

Peale believed that the investment in education for everyone would pay handsome dividends in the stability and happiness of society. Citizens, if their training were broad enough, would be prepared to make correctly the choices that faced them. In short, the demands of democracy required an enlightened citizenry to fulfill them, and the museum and its magazine stood ready to enlighten. Peale and his helpers, however, were hardly attuned to popular tastes in writing. The ponderous prose of the *Philadelphia Museum* did not cause a clamor for a second number, and no more were issued.

This failure was discouraging to the old museum proprietor; moreover, an ominous threat was on the horizon. The museum's constituency was being chipped away from both sides. From the very beginning of the museum, Peale had succeeded in attracting both the serious students of science and the popular audience eager for diversions. As the 1820s progressed, however, those who cultivated science increasingly went to the Academy of Natural Sciences, whose members always welcomed researchers. On the other hand, the popular audiences were being siphoned off by such competitors as the Washington Museum at Second and Market streets. There one could see nude paintings and sensational shows. Even though Rubens Peale had, during his tenure as museum manager from 1810 through 1821, introduced entertainments, they were far too tame for those who had become accustomed to the spectacular offerings at the Washington Museum. Peale's middle ground was progressively narrowing; it was becoming more difficult to compete with the scientific specialist on the one hand and with the popular entertainers on the other.

Added to this difficulty was the increasing infirmity of old age. Peale, during the last three years of his life, which ended in 1827, was mainly a spectator rather than a participant. As his museum came upon increasingly hard times, he could do little to meet the challenge. Despite the difficulties, his faith in popular education never dimmed; he never lost interest in "the progress of diffusing knowledge through a rising generation."[19] Charles Willson Peale died on February 22, 1827, and popular education lost its first and greatest friend in the American museum world. The American Philosophical Society sent a tribute, as did several other organizations and individuals. The patriarch of the Peale museums was gone, but he had left his children to carry on for him.

Peale's sons Rembrandt, Rubens, Titian, Franklin, and Linnaeus carried on the struggle for the middle ground. As the 1830s wore on, the increasing trivialization of their competitors forced them to pander more to the lower levels of popular tastes, and the vision of the elder Peale slowly melted away.

The decline first became apparent in the Baltimore Museum. Rembrandt had plunged himself deeply into debt to start the museum, and the trustees he had once regarded as his salvation proved a contentious nuisance. Rembrandt yearned to escape the museum business and return to painting, and Rubens, who had been managing the Philadelphia Museum since 1810, was anxious to leave Philadelphia after his father had returned from retirement. In 1822, therefore, Rubens bought out Rembrandt and took over the Baltimore Museum.

Rubens made a supreme effort to keep the Baltimore Museum a serious enterprise. He initiated the first of four annual art exhibitions shortly after his arrival, and imported Joseph Lancaster for a series of lectures on education. The receipts lagged, however, and soon Rubens was forced to book "Signior Hellenne," a one-man band who played five instruments simultaneously, and eventually "Mr. Munn and his Learned Dogs." By 1824 Rubens was sick of the debts and the popular flummery. He decided to establish a museum in New York; accordingly, he offered management of the Baltimore concern to first Rembrandt, then Franklin. Both wisely refused. Rubens, in 1825, struck a deal with the trustees to hire a manager to supervise the museum while he left for New York. For the next five years, Rubens oversaw the program via correspondence and visits from New York while William Wood managed the museum on the spot. The museum program continued its inexorable decline under Wood, until by the 1830s, it was little more than a sideshow.

With the opening of Peale's New York Museum in 1825, there were Peale museums operating in three cities. While Philadelphia was quiescent and Baltimore in decay, New York was a new opportunity for Rubens. He was by now a veteran of fifteen years of museum management and had a sharp eye for promotion. Rubens opened the museum on October 26, 1825, the very day that De Witt Clinton opened the Erie Canal for westbound traffic. Here he sought to find the perfect mixture of science and entertainment. The New York Museum was doomed to reenact the experience of the Baltimore: high initial hopes followed by a longer deterioration, resulting in purchase by the showman Phineas Taylor Barnum.

In 1825, however, Rubens got off to a good start. He was assisted by the Lyceum of Natural History, especially by David Hosack.[20] His receipts were handsome and his patrons included Hosack, Samuel Latham Mitchill, John Trumbull, Gullian Verplanck, and De Witt Clinton.[21] Things went so well for a few years that Rubens, in partnership with his brother Linnaeus, opened a short-lived museum in Utica, New York.

Rubens, however, was always alert for another method to simultaneously further his educational goals and increase his income. He never lost sight of the fact that "everything depends on pleasing the visitors, if they are gratified, they gratify us with their money."[22] One way of pleasing the people and educating them had been invented by Charles Willson Peale in 1821: admitting teachers free and charging the students half-price. Rubens expanded on this idea; not only did he cut his price for students, but he also aggressively marketed the plan. On March 5, 1829, he wrote to his brother Franklin:

> You have my printed bill, that was sent to many of the schools to be distributed by the teachers to their schollars [sic]—I found that it had a good effect, I gave the teachers, when they came with their schools, admittance gratis, and the schollars [sic] admitted for 10 cents each—the bills thus distributed are much valued and taken home to their parents. We sent to about 350 schools and delivered about 8,800 bills, it produced a good effect but the excessive cold weather commenced and I desisted sending the remainder, and shall commence next month again.[23]

Rubens considered this the ideal promotion. It achieved popular education for school children, exposing hundreds of them to experiences they would not otherwise have received. At the same time, it advertised his museum extensively to those who might otherwise never have heard of it. It was a large-scale and ultimately effective program, one which realized Charles Willson Peale's goal of "diffusing much useful knowledge."

Not even Rubens, however, could make his mixture of science and showmanship work indefinitely. He did keep the museum solvent until the panic of 1837 blighted his profits, and even then he grimly held on until 1842. Rubens had retained his interest in the Baltimore Museum until 1833 when it was partially destroyed by fire. He withdrew from Utica before 1830.

Meanwhile, back in Philadelphia, the museum that Charles Willson Peale had founded continued to exist. The board of trustees, with Rembrandt its leader, hired Franklin Peale as manager and Titian Peale as curator. The educational purpose of the museum was to remain fixed, for Rembrandt, like his father, was convinced of the necessity of popular education. He wished to make the museum:

> an Encyclopedia of Visible Objects, at once capable of being consulted by the most illiterate and of confirming and extending the knowledge of the best informed . . . by teaching the best systematical classifications [and] by such and useful arrangement . . . as will make them the pleasant means of instruction in every Art and every Science. Such an Institution should not only be a School of universal knowledge, but might and ought to be made the means of rational Amusement, even to the most idle.[24]

Rembrandt, like his father, was still clinging to the middle ground. The museum was primarily an educator, but it was also a place of refined entertainment, a "fashionable lounge" to use the term of the day. Both the scholar and the person seeking diversion were to be at home there; as Rembrandt succinctly put it, the museum should "constitute a place of elegant amusement and universal instruction."[25]

In order to effect "universal instruction," Titian Peale altered his father's plan of free admission for teachers and half-price admissions for students. Titian's system allowed a school admission for all of its students for one year at the price of seven dollars.[26] The program was successful. In 1834 there were fourteen subscribing schools, "more than half of which are for young ladies."[27] Moreover, the educational benefits the museum offered were readily accessible to people of all ages; the museum was open in the evenings, for this would "accommodate the leisure of all classes."[28]

As the 1830s went on, however, it became increasingly difficult to attract all classes. Serious scholars were gravitating toward the Academy of Natural Sciences, and the public was increasingly patronizing the sideshow "museums" that competed with Peale's. The museum's location in the Arcade Building on George Street was away from the central city, and attendance was suffering for it. The panic of 1837 reduced visitation even further, and the museum trustees began "investing recklessly in light entertainment."[29] A steady stream of giants, automatons, and tawdry plays were advertised at the museum by the end of the decade. The middle ground, for which the Peale family had fought so gallantly, had diminished to an alarming extent. The Peale Museum itself had become a sort of adjunct to the collection of Chinese artifacts formed by the Philadelphia merchant Nathan Dunn. The unscrupulous Mr. Dunn had managed to become a power on the Peale Museum board and the owner of a large block of museum stock. By 1840, Charles Willson Peale's creation was essentially Dunn's to use or abuse. The high educational purpose of Charles Willson Peale and his sons was all but forgotten.

The Academy of Natural Sciences

The Academy of Natural Sciences of Philadelphia, like Peale's museum, fought for the middle ground during the Age of Egalitarianism. On the one hand, they did their best to serve the needs of serious scientific investigators; on the other, they sought to provide education in natural history to the general public. Like Peale, the academy's members found the task of balancing the two a very difficult one, indeed. The academy's initial casual interest in science was becoming more systematic, for they were aggressively pursuing specimens that would form important study series. The most significant of these was a collection of fossils from the Mississippi basin formed by Joseph Dorfeuille of the Western Museum of Cincinnati.

Dorfeuille's collection consisted of material he had gathered and specimens donated to the Western Museum. He had long been familiar with Philadelphia (having held a season ticket at Peale's museum in 1808), and when he decided to sell in 1829, it was natural that he should look there for a buyer.[30] A long and complicated series of negotiations, carried on by the academy's Samuel George Morton and Richard Harlan, resulted in one of the academy's "angels," John Price Wetherill, purchasing the collection for the academy.[31] Dorfeuille's specimens were not purchased for purposes of public display, but rather for their scientific importance. It was to be a study collection to aid the researcher interested in paleontology.

At the same time, the academy was attempting to promote popular education. The great driving force behind this effort was their president, William Maclure. Maclure dominated the academy from 1817 to 1840; he was reelected to the presidency every year during this span, despite the fact that he was absent from Philadelphia during nearly the entire time. Maclure was respected for his geological work, but the mainspring of his power was his remarkable generosity; his benefactions built the academy a permanent home, filled the shelves in its library, and turned its cabinet into a museum. Time and again, Maclure's generosity rescued the academy from financial ruin. Hence, when Maclure spoke, the membership listened.

William Maclure believed in popular education in the way that some people believe in God: with a passionate intensity. Moreover, he placed his faith in a specific kind of popular education: the Pestalozzian system. In an article in the *American Journal of Science* in 1826 entitled "An Epitome of the Improved Pestalozzian System of Education . . . " Maclure explained the basis of his educational philosophy. He first gave a primer of the Pestalozzian system, explaining how it stressed concrete experiences over theoretical ones. In practice this meant: "a careful examination and inspection of the objects themselves [is] calculated to demonstrate their properties and bring them within reach of the senses. If these cannot be obtained, then accurate designs, or representations, and books, and descriptions, although imperfect substitutes, are employed; but these are not to be resorted to until every possible means of acquiring the first two has failed."[32]

The Pestalozzian system fairly demanded museum experiences for proper education. Where better to get the firsthand inspection of the actual objects that it envisioned? Teachers need not resort to the "imperfect substitutes" of books when a simple visit to a museum would provide artifacts to study. Best of all, a trip to the museum could be made available to everyone, not just the wealthy. Maclure was adamant that the advantages of the Pestalozzian system should be "applied to the great bulk of mankind; namely, the productive, labouring and useful classes."[33] The Pestalozzian system, aided by museums, could provide an education that would train everyone in society to discharge their duties.

While Maclure was undoubtedly the instigator of the academy's interest in popular education, he was by no means the only member to believe in its importance. Gerard Troost, Thomas Say, Richard Harlan, and John Godman all signed on as lecturers for Peale's museum in 1821. Isaac Lea, another academy member, even wrote an article for the *American Journal of Science* entitled "On the Pleasure and Advantage of Studying Natural History." Lea asserted, "It is a truth much to be regretted, that the study of nature is too much neglected in the usual course of education." To Lea, this subject was not a dry, pedantic pursuit, for "Natural History may be said to entice while it instructs; and the student who once enters the portal, seldom wishes to return."[34] Nor was this a narrow interest. According to Lea, "The investigation of nature cannot fail to be valuable. It engages all of our intellectual Faculties to the greatest extent, and by its ardent pursuit, the general stock of useful information is increased."[35] Clearly Maclure was not alone in feeling the spirit of the age.

As the 1820s progressed, academy members began to feel that their growing cabinet should be opened to the public, but recognized that several hurdles must be cleared before this could be done. The academy was in debt. There was no full-time curator or librarian to arrange the specimens, and the artifacts were not in locked cases. Committees were appointed to find solutions to these problems, and "believing it to be the wish of the Society that their collection should be made as extensively useful as can be done consistently with their preservation, and convinced that the attainment of the latter is of vital importance," they set to work with a will.[36] The debt problem was never fully solved, but within less than three years, the collection had been placed into locked cabinets and "Mr. Wm. Willson who was employed for 17 years in Mr. Peale's Museum" was hired as janitor with the added responsibility of guarding the collection.[37] With the collection growing to a suitable size, and with security against theft, the cabinet could now be opened to the public.

In 1828 a committee whose most notable members were Samuel George Morton, John Price Wetherill, and George Ord considered the possibility of opening the cabinet to the public. Their report, offered on August 5, 1828, left no doubt where they stood: "Your committee are unanimously desirous that . . . the opening of the Museum on certain days of the week to the free admission of strangers and citizens [be instituted]."[38] The committee went on to recommend that the museum be opened two half days of every week "for the gratuitous admission of citizens and strangers," but qualified this by adding that only such persons who could produce tickets of admission signed by academy members could gain entry.[39] By this means the members could control the admission into the museum. Unlike Peale's museum, which anyone with a quarter could visit, entrance into the academy was restricted to friends and relatives of academy members. Still, the members were not compelled to open their cabinet, and by doing so, they were doing more for popular education than any other private scientific organization in America had done. The academy accepted the committee report shortly thereafter, and the recommendations were written into the bylaws.

Thus by 1828, William Maclure had achieved, on a tentative and limited scale, an experiment in the use of a museum for popular education. Maclure considered popular education not merely desirable, but absolutely essential. It fit into his complicated and strongly held views on society, all of which he poured out in a series of letters to Samuel George Morton between 1830 and 1839. These hastily scrawled and sometimes rambling epistles reveal Maclure's passionate belief that the inequalities of the old society could and should be swept away by educating the young, so that they could form a new social order.

Maclure viewed the existing state of society as being characterized by two classes: the oppressive, exploiting kings, nobles, and men of property and wealth on the one hand, and the exploited, productive laboring classes on the other. Given these grim facts, Maclure was convinced, "The equalization of property knowledge and power are the *sine qua non* of human happiness—the first and last are out of the reach of individual exertion. Knowledge is the only one that individual efforts can have any effect on—it is with that view that the remainder of my short existence and property is devoted."[40]

Maclure was convinced that only by providing free education to the productive classes, both children and adults, could the vast inequalities of property and wealth be erased. As Maclure put it, "Raising the mass of industrious producers by the diffusion of useful knowledge [is] the only mode of accomplishing the equality on which the freedom and happiness of our species depends."[41] Maclure felt an urgency about diffusing knowledge: "When I was young there was not as much crime in the union in a year than in the town of New York now in a month because both property and knowledge was more equally divided. . . . I have found vice and crime in the same proportion as the inequality of property and knowledge."[42] Maclure regarded popular education as the solution to a number of interlocking social problems. Not only could it eliminate crime and vice, but it could raise all people to a level of equality; it could make for democracy in fact, rather than in name only.

Maclure's high hopes were destined to be dashed during the 1830s. By restricting visitation to those with tickets only, the academy had rendered impossible the diffusion of knowledge on the broad scale that Maclure had envisioned. By January of 1837 Maclure was complaining to Morton, "On the diffusion of science amongst the working classes . . . you have progressed as far as any in the collection of it though not in diffusion of it."[43] Maclure was the most enthusiastic promoter of popular education at the academy but he did not desire education at the expense of scientific research. Instead, like Peale, he advocated a balance between the popular and the professional: "The academy should have the necessary fixtures buildings and etc. to enable them to be most useful to the dissemination of useful and scientific knowledge and at the same time serve as a model of such establishments from [?] the immense utility a little property can be put to in extending the sphere of knowledge which I consider as synonymous with happiness may tempt others to follow the example."[44]

These words are reminiscent of the insight that Charles Willson Peale had had twenty years before: a vision of a democratic museum, one which would serve the needs of the scholar, the interested layman, and the casual visitor. Unfortunately, by 1837 the tide of popular education was beginning to ebb. The members of the academy were more and more interested in increasing scientific knowledge, rather than diffusing it. Resistance to Maclure's ideas had begun early, but the opposition did not dare cross him openly. George Ord had written off Maclure in 1825 when the latter left Philadelphia, in the company of Gerard Troost and Thomas Say, to settle in New Harmony. Maclure spent the rest of his life at the Indiana experiment in communal living founded by Robert Owen. Thereafter Ord's letters mentioning Maclure turned into diatribes on the subject of "that stupid establishment, called New Harmony."[45] Ord, never one to love the working classes, mostly despised Maclure's efforts for popular education. Richard Harlan was another early dissenter. In a letter to John James Audubon written in 1828, Harlan interrupted an attack on New Harmony long enough to complain, "The members of the Acad. here are doing little in the way of scientific publication at present, but they are arranging in complete order their collection in their new building."[46]

However, the 1820s were not the time to challenge Maclure. The full force of the cultural tide was behind him, and his past benefactions made it foolish to oppose his will. Morton, who himself preferred scientific research to popular education, was no doubt mindful of these facts when he wrote to a foreign correspondent, "Mr. Maclure has done more for Science than any other man in America. This is but one of many acts of munificence which he has performed for our institution."[47] As the 1830s wore on, however, Maclure's continued absence tended to reduce his authority to some extent. More importantly, the national ardor for popular education was diminishing. At the same time, in scientific circles, amateurism was being purged, to be replaced by a nascent professionalism. To academy members eager to pursue science as a calling rather than an avocation, the gratuitous admission of the public was at best superfluous and at worst a hindrance. As the 1830s wore on, these members became increasingly numerous and increasingly restive.

The conflict finally broke into the open in 1839. Maclure, by now an ill man, sent the academy a letter from his winter home in Mexico with suggestions regarding public access which caused great consternation among the membership. Maclure specified that the library and museum should be opened to the public gratis for as many as five days per week. This must have come as a surprise to those who thought twice a week was too much, but the really explosive part of Maclure's letter was the single sentence in which he asserted "the necessity of some legal instrument specifying the liberality of the Academy in gratuitously giving access to all classes."[48] Maclure probably feared that after his death the academy would abandon his commitment to popular education, and he sought to assure its continuance.

The members who sought to promote science to the exclusion of education were in a quandary. Maclure, the greatest benefactor of science in America, was ill and probably close to death. To offend him by a refusal might bring an end to his philanthropy and might also exclude the academy from his will. On the other hand, to accede to Maclure's suggestion would mean an institutionalization of the public access that they disliked. After debate, the membership decided that they could not afford to reject Maclure's point of view altogether. Accordingly, on August 27, 1839, they amended the bylaws so as to partially grant Maclure's request. The library was to be open for more days per week, but only at the convenience of the librarian, and only to those whom he chose to admit.

The members, however, would not accept Maclure's legal instrument to guarantee public access in even an adulterated form. The debate on that proposal continued for months, and finally culminated in an official answer dated November 21, 1839. The reply was mainly the work of Morton, who was careful to occupy the first half of it with grateful thanks to Maclure for his past benefactions. Morton finally told Maclure that the academy felt compelled to eschew the legal instrument because "doubts exist as to our power to bind all persons who may hereafter become members of the corporation by regulations which we may adopt on this subject."[49] This was a reasonable reservation. But Morton then pushed the argument beyond logical bounds: "Anxious as we are and have been to follow any advice you give us, we cannot consent to bind ourselves by the adoption of permanent and unchangeable regulations, which would go far to destroy our present usefulness and deprive us of the support of the public generally."[50]

Morton never explained just how opening the museum and library for the free admission of the public would destroy the academy's usefulness, although he may have feared that it could turn the museum into a sideshow. Moreover the statement that such a policy of gratuitous admission would forfeit public support is absurd on the face of it. Morton apparently was grasping at straws in order to attack a proposition which he feared, but could not adequately refute. So strong, however, was the proresearch, antieducation mood of the academy in 1839 that Morton's draft was accepted without amendment. Maclure's attempt to guarantee the future of popular education at the academy had come to nothing.

By the time Maclure received a reply to his letter of June 23, he had only a few more weeks to live. The academy was remembered in his will. His passing in 1840 marked the end of the Age of Egalitarianism for American museums. The middle ground had narrowed, but it had not yet disappeared. The era of professional science would have its day, but popular education had gained a niche in American museums, one it would never lose.

However, the eventual apotheosis of education in museums was not obvious in the late 1830s. Museums seemed to be dividing

into two camps, those which promoted scholarship and professional science on the one hand, and on the other, those which
served up hokum in heaping quantities. But Charles Willson Peale
and William Maclure, those two great champions of popular education, had planted their seeds well. After the Age of Egalitarianism, American museums could no longer afford to ignore popular
education entirely. The idea became submerged during the next
decade, but it surfaced again from 1850 to 1870 to take a place
in the museum world it has never relinquished.

"Oblations to Buncombe": The Western Museum and the American Museum, 1820–1840

It will probably be found necessary to make a few oblations
to Buncombe.[51]

Although Joseph Henry wrote these words in 1847, he may
well have been speaking of the Western Museum and the American Museum in the 1820s. When these institutions found they
could not make a go of it on the strength of their serious exhibitions, they decided to sensationalize their cabinets to attract customers. As a result, they remained solvent but vitiated their intellectual content and made a mockery of the high purposes of their
founders.

The Western Museum, 1820–1840

The Western Museum was launched, at least, to serve high purposes. On the occasion of its official opening on June 10, 1820,
Daniel Drake delivered an "Anniversary Discourse on the State
and Prospects of The Western Museum Society." Its prospects
must have seemed bright, for the collection was growing, the
staff was capable, and the patronage seemed adequate. Drake was
in an expansive mood and spoke of how the museum could be
used as a social instrument. First, it could be a weapon of cultural
nationalism. Drake held, "A dependence on Europe is equally
disastrous and degrading. . . . a simple enumeration of our . . .

dependencies on Europe would make a long and frightful catalogue. . . . to lessen their numbers should be the unceasing aim
of . . . every member of the republic."[52]

The museum could be used as a sword to cut these humiliating
foreign bonds. Lectures, based on the objects in the collection,
should be delivered to teach Americans the skills necessary to gain
full independence from Europe. As Drake put it, "Popular courses
. . . delivered from time to time, as the means of illustration became adequate . . . could not fail to multiply the benefits which
(the Museum) is expected to confer."[53] The museum could be used
as an educational tool to raise all classes to personal dignity. "To
what shall we attribute the greater respectability and dignity of
character which belong to the middle and lower ranks of our people, but the more general diffusion of information?"[54] Drake truly
believed that "in the increase of useful knowledge is the true secret
of our permanent happiness,"[55] and he sought to make the Western
Museum a veritable dynamo of popular education.

It was not to be. Income was the immediate problem; Cincinna-
tians and visitors simply did not patronize the scientific exhibitions being offered. By October 12, 1820, John James Audubon
had left the museum's employ, and indeed Cincinnati, tartly noting "that the Museum managers were splendid promisers and very
bad paymasters."[56]

A graver problem was brewing at the top levels of the institution. Drake and his museum cohort, Elijah Slack, had been
among the founders of the Medical College of Ohio in 1818, and
both were professors at that institution. Slack joined with the
other professors of the college in an intrigue designed to oust
Drake as president, which scheme they accomplished on March
7, 1822. The conspirators reinstated Drake when the decision produced public outrage, but he resigned and left Cincinnati for Lexington, Kentucky. His departure left an unfillable void in the
Western Museum.

In the short run, however, Slack was too happy in his triumph
over Drake to fear for the future. The museum held a party on
June 10, 1822, to celebrate its second year, at which a long piece
of doggerel called "An Ode to Science" was read. Science, how-

ever, was not paying the bills. In 1823, the trustees put the collection up for sale and found no takers. Their solution to this crisis was to do exactly what the Tammany Society had done twenty-eight years before—give it to a curator, reserving the right to free admission for stockholders and their families.

The curator was one Joseph Dorfeuille, who may or may not have been a Frenchman, but was certainly a person of varied background. Little is known of his early life except that he resided in St. Louis from 1817 to 1818 and that he arrived in Cincinnati in 1820 to work at Letton's Museum, a commercial competitor of the Western Museum that had been opened in 1819.[57] He joined the Western Museum at some point between the time of Audubon's and Drake's departures. Dorfeuille seems to have been a scientist at heart, for a European who visited early in his tenure remembered: "The Museum at Cincinnati, though small, is very interesting to a lover of natural history. All the specimens are very neatly arranged. . . . Mr. D'Orfeuil, one of the proprietors of the Museum, has been engaged in some researches on Parasitical insects. He possesses a most powerful microscope, and has made a vast number of most beautiful coloured drawings; I never indeed had seen insects so well painted."[58]

Evidence also exists that Dorfeuille tried initially to attract the respectability to the museum. A poem by "P." (probably Dorfeuille) was published in the March 13, 1824, number of the Cincinnati *Literary Gazette*, which began: "Wend hither ye members of polished society—Ye who the bright phantoms of pleasure pursue—To see of strange objects the endless variety Monsieur Dorfeuille will expose to your view."[59]

The members of polished society, however, did not wend their way into the museum in sufficient numbers to turn an adequate profit for Dorfeuille. Letton's Museum was offering spectacles and wax exhibitions; Dorfeuille was forced to follow suit to keep the turnstiles moving.

Dorfeuille soon moved the museum to the rough and ready area near the public landing, and began plotting spectacular exhibitions of his own. Late in 1827, a shipment of wax figures arrived broken, and Dorfeuille hired an ingenious sculptor named Hiram

Powers to fix them. The repaired figures went on exhibit in January of 1828. By that time, the long descent of the Western Museum had clearly begun; in order to survive, Dorfeuille was pandering to the lowest tastes of the populace.

The arrival of an English immigrant in February of 1828 would make that descent literally a trip to hell. Frances Trollope is remembered today as the acerbic critic of the society of the United States in her book, *Domestic Manners of the Americans*. But in 1828, she was another immigrant hoping to make her fortune in America. In *Domestic Manners*, she coyly mentioned that Dorfeuille, "a man of taste and science," had "constructed a pandaemonium in an upper story of his museum, in which he has congregated all the images of horror that his fertile fancy can devise." In fact, it was Mrs. Trollope herself who was responsible for setting up "Dorfeuille's Hell" or the "Infernal Regions."[60]

The "Regions" consisted of an attic room twelve feet deep by twenty feet long. Mrs. Trollope, inspired by Dante's *Divine Comedy*, saw to it that Hiram Powers populated that room with a wax-figure tableau depicting Lucifer surrounded by a court of demons. A painter named Auguste Hervieu backed the room with transparencies of purgatory and paradise. The exhibition featured, thanks to the genius of Powers, a frozen lake, a fountain of flame, and columns of icicles. He automated the larger wax figures and planted employees in the wings to shriek and groan when the lights were dimmed. On July 4, 1828, the "Regions," complete with movable eyeballs for Lucifer and the bodies of condemned children at his feet, opened for business.

"Dorfeuille's Hell" proved an astonishing success, running continuously for thirty-nine years. People poured into the museum, ministers debated whether it was impious or promoted piety, and Powers kept making his machinery more diabolical. The patrons crowded so tightly into the grate walling off the exhibit that Powers electrified it. The resulting shocks often traveled through several people and panicked the rustics who had come to gape at it. All agreed that "Dorfeuille's Hell" was the best show in Cincinnati.

The success of the "Regions" doomed the Western Museum

as a serious institution. Mrs. Trollope left town in 1831 and Powers departed as well in 1834, but "Dorfeuille's Hell" remained as the museum's chief attraction. Not even the "Regions," however, could attract enough customers by the mid-1830s. Powers's replacement, Linden Ryder, wrote Powers (who was by then a celebrated sculptor living in Italy) many letters complaining of Dorfeuille's laggardness in paying wages. In one, he mentioned yet another tasteless exhibit contemplated by Dorfeuille: "Old Oyster Shell . . . has secured the hatchet with which Cowan [a local murderer] destroyed his wife & children and expects to make a good sum of money by exhibiting it."[61] Nevertheless, the returns on Dorfeuille's investment continued to diminish. As early as March 1837, he began to consider selling the museum.[62] Finally in 1839, Dorfeuille sold the collection for $6,500 to a group of Cincinnati investors. He retained some of the more spectacular curiosities, including the "Regions" figures, and moved to New York where he opened a museum on Broadway in a building once used by Peale's New York Museum. Within a year, the building was destroyed by fire, and on July 23, 1840, Dorfeuille died.[63]

By this time the Western Museum was dead as well, at least as anything but a sideshow. The vision of Daniel Drake and its promising start had been utterly squandered in order to offer crowd-pleasing spectacles. The last word on the subject may belong to Charles Augustus Murray, a European traveler who visited Cincinnati in 1835: "The Museum contains little worthy of notice; moreover, its contents, mean as they are, are miserably deficient in order and arrangement. I was surprised and disappointed, as I had heard of the valuable collection to be seen in this establishment."[64]

The American Museum, 1820–1840

The Age of Egalitarianism exerted cultural pressures on the American Museum in New York, causing it to go through a disintegration which paralleled that of the Western Museum. John Scudder's death in 1821 had left a void at the museum; his son John, Jr., and his four daughters were too young to take over its management. According to the terms of Scudder's will, five trustees, led by the attorney Cornelius Bogert and including John Pintard, assumed the museum's management.

For a time, the trustees kept the museum's aims in line with the cultural imperative of popular education. In 1823, they published "A Companion to The American Museum," a guidebook to the museum's collection, which included "Notes and Explanations" by John Scudder, Jr.[65] The purpose of the booklet was to make the museum's exhibits a means of teaching the populace natural history. Later that year when young Gideon Welles, who would later be a prime mover in the founding of the Wadsworth Atheneum, visited the museum, he was impressed by its educational potential. Welles concluded, "Many things are shown that would excite an interest in almost every individual."[66]

In 1825, as the Western Museum slipped downhill in Cincinnati, the New York museum world began to pall as well. First John Scudder, Jr., quarreled with his sisters and the museum trustees. On July 1, 1825, he opened a rival institution, "Scudder's New York Spectaculum," and began offering tawdry entertainments. Then on October 26, Rubens Peale opened "Peale's New York Museum" on Broadway. New York in the late 1820s was the largest city in America, and constantly growing, but it could not support three proprietary museums. Moreover, many an entertainment dollar was spent organizing and attending lyceums after 1826. Remembering this era, Dr. Thomas Nichols stated emphatically, "The mutual improvement and debating societies . . . became a national and prevading institution."[67] This superfluity of entertainment options led inevitably to competition for patrons and just as inevitably to a cheapening of the product. Soon the "lecture halls" of all three museums featured one-man bands, learned dogs, ventriloquists, and freaks of nature.

The rest of the story is very melancholy, indeed. The mutually ruinous contest in self-debasement continued for ten years. In 1830 the American Museum lost its competitive advantage when the corporation evicted every organization from the New York Institution. The trustees lamented their loss of rent-free space and leased a five-story building at Broadway and Ann streets. The trustees then gambled by giving John Scudder, Jr., the management of the museum. In five years on his own, young Scudder had deteriorated into an unreliable and unpleasant alcoholic, who had run up enormous debts in the course of losing his Spectaculum. Nonethless, he was a clever showman, and he put the museum back into the black, mainly by forsaking any remaining educational value it had. He alienated his sisters so thoroughly that they brought a lawsuit against the trustees on the grounds that the appointment of their brother constituted "senile incompetence" among the board members. Young Scudder resolved the issue by getting into a drunken brawl in January of 1831, thereby giving the trustees a pretext for firing him. Thus cleared of the lawsuit, four of the five trustees resigned, including John Pintard, ending his association with the museum he had founded forty-one years before.

The downhill course continued. Later that year Alexis de Tocqueville and Gustave de Beaumont visited the museum. Beaumont recorded that he and Tocqueville "laughed like the blessed" when they saw the sideshow reality behind the imposing title of the "American Museum."[68] The cholera outbreak of 1832 eroded the museum's financial position, and the great New York fire of 1835 caused further financial decay. The depression following the panic of 1837 destroyed Peale's museum, and drove the American to the brink of extinction. In desperation, the Scudder daughters brought back their despised brother as manager. John, Jr.'s gift for showmanship and the dearth of effective competition caused a revival of sorts, but by 1841 the entire Scudder family was ready to sell. The purchaser was the greatest showman of them all: P. T. Barnum.

The Western Museum and the American Museum were prime examples of the ideals of the Age of Egalitarianism carried past the point of absurdity. Under the guise of giving the people the education they needed, the museum proprietors gave them exploitative entertainment. The social potential of the museum as a school for every man was shamefully and cynically wasted. "The

Regions" provides an apt metaphor for the fall of these two museums in the period from 1820 through 1840.

The Public Be Damned: The New-York Historical Society, 1820–1840

Be assured that I feel more mortification at these cabals than
I have power to express.[69]

The "cabals" to which John Pintard referred nearly destroyed the New-York Historical Society during the first ten years of the Age of Egalitarianism. They pitted the friends of the collections— the library and museum—against those who would divest the society of them, leaving nothing but an exclusive gentlemen's club. The decade-long struggle from 1819 to 1829 so consumed the members' energy that they made no efforts to respond to the need for popular education during that era. In fact, due to the anticollection faction, the society limped through the period with its museum collection gutted, and its elitist barriers to popular use intact. While other museums responded to the cultural imperatives of the Age of Egalitarianism, the Historical Society remained aloof.

The trouble began on January 12, 1819, at the annual meeting. De Witt Clinton, the society's president, was absent. Also missing was David Hosack, first vice-president, and as such, Clinton's presumptive heir. Samuel Latham Mitchill, who had long carried on a personal and professional rivalry with Hosack, was present, however, and managed to get elected in place of Hosack, thus getting in line for the presidency. This maneuver split the society into two camps. Mitchill's group was composed mainly of physicians. Rallying behind Hosack was a varied group which included John Pintard, Pintard's long-time associate, Dr. John W. Francis, and the venerable John Trumbull. The latter group shortly gained the upper hand, for Hosack was elected president of the society in 1820.[70]

This initial squabbling revolved not around ideas but rather around the personalities of Mitchell and Hosack. The war of personalities so effectively consumed the energy of the society that it precluded any possibility of responding to the national hunger for popular education. Soon, however, an issue arose which transcended personalities and made the conflict an ideological one.

The matter in question was the indebtedness of the society. Late in 1823 several members became concerned about the extent of the society's obligations, and a special committee was formed to determine the precise amount. Their findings, presented on March 9, 1824, revealed that the society owed various creditors over $18,000, including $9,000 to Dr. John W. Francis, $3,000 to John Pintard, and $1,500 to the Washington Insurance Company.[71] The committee admitted that they had no suggestions for solving the debt problem, so another committee was established to form a plan. At the two subsequent meetings in April and May, this committee presented a number of austerity measures. Both Dr. Francis and Pintard agreed to forgive $1,000 of the amount owed them. A debt of $500 owed the society by the Lyceum of Natural History must be collected. The post of sub-librarian should be abolished. Dues should be increased, and further revenue could be raised by selling books that were not directly germane to the objects of the society.

This report caused an immediate polarization along ideological lines. The Hosack camp embraced the notion of progressively reducing the debt by increasing revenues. The other camp, now led by Charles King rather than Mitchill, expanded on the committee's last idea, and advocated selling as much of the library and museum collection as necessary to balance the budget. The Hosack camp, on the other hand, believed that the Society's books and artifacts were its very raison d'être.[72]

While Hosack and his supporters did not advocate general admission or popular education, they did feel that scholars and other respectable people should have access to the collections, that indeed the society would be useless if it were not for its stewardship of these treasures. The King faction was contemptuous of any talk of responsibility to the public; no doubt they felt that selling the collection would rid the society of vexatious visitors and allow them to enjoy the sequestered existence of the English private clubs they so admired.

The first open clash between the two factions came at the special meeting called on May 18, 1825, to consider the best way to eliminate the debt. A member of the King camp moved that the committee charged with solutions to the problem "have full powers to dispose of the property of the Historical Society for such a sum as shall be adequate to the liquidation of the debts due by the Society, provided that the purchasers bind themselves to preserve whole and entire the Library and collections and to deposit them permanently with some Literary or Scientific Institution in this City."[73]

The resolution, by stipulating that the collections would remain intact in New York, cleverly answered a major objection of the Hosack camp, that the value of the collections would be destroyed if they were scattered. A new champion, Frederic De Peyster, Jr., rose to frustrate this move. A twenty-nine-year-old attorney who came of an old New York family, De Peyster had been drawn into the society by his association with De Witt Clinton, on whose staff he had briefly served. He had a deep appreciation for museums. During an 1817 visit to Peale's Philadelphia Museum, he had written, "The Museum affords an agreeable resort for a Morning [it promotes] a spirit of public taste . . . in this city."[74] He would later become a patron of Scudder's American Museum, and a warm supporter of educational causes.[75]

Now De Peyster offered an amendment exempting from sale any items which had come to the society as gifts. This would effectively negate the resolution, for the vast majority of the society's books and artifacts had been donated. After a spirited debate, De Peyster's amendment squeaked by, fifteen votes to thirteen. William Gracie, King's chief lieutenant, immediately resigned from the committee on the debts, and De Peyster was appointed to replace him.

Hosack's men, however, could not long savor their victory. Less than a month after the first clash, at a regular meeting on June 14, 1825, John Trumbull of the Hosack faction rose to move that nonessential books be sold in order to pay off the Washington

Insurance Company, and to begin to pay Francis and Pintard. After debate, his motion was defeated. Charles King then offered the same resolution that De Peyster's amendment had derailed a month before. Gracie seconded the motion, and David Hosack, thoroughly disgusted with this unexpected power grab, resigned the presidency on the spot.

Despite Hosack's dramatic move, and the acrimonious debate which followed, King's motion carried by ten votes to six. John Trumbull, who had taken the chair after Hosack stepped down, thereupon resigned, and together with Hosack left the room. Now completely in charge of the "rump" meeting, the King faction elevated one of its number, Gullian C. Verplanck, to the chair, and promptly passed a resolution to pack the committee with three of their own members.[76]

This unexpected coup almost destroyed the society. The regular monthly meetings were suspended until March 14, 1826, nearly nine months later. The minutes at that point began again without a word of explanation, which suggests that the ensuing controversy was so fundamental that it could not even be mentioned with safety. The only solid evidence of the bitter struggle is a letter dated June 15, 1825, from John Trumbull to John B. Beck, the recording secretary of the society. Trumbull protested the actions of King's group on three counts: first, that the judgment of a special meeting called specifically to consider the debt question had been reversed by a regular meeting not called for that purpose; second, that nine of the ten men in King's faction were members of the New York Athenaeum, which was interested in buying the society's books, hence a conflict of interest was apparent; third, that it was illegal for the society to sell items it had received as gifts held in trust. In a postscript, Trumbull added that Hosack had joined him in his protest.[77]

By the time the dust had settled in March of 1826, Hosack was back in the chair, Trumbull at his side, and their faction back in control, if precariously. In the meantime, De Witt Clinton, now the governor of New York, had secured a renewal of the society's charter, which gave it continued legal standing, but no financial support. Hosack sent De Peyster to Albany to lobby the state legislature for relief. On March 1, 1827, De Peyster brought home a $5,000 grant, which covered all but $2,500 of the remaining debt. The society finally retired its debt by writing off $1,400 owed to John Pintard for which he could not produce vouchers, a rather shabby way of thanking the society's earliest and best patron.

The anticollection faction swallowed its defeat and remained quiet for the next two years, probably because they expected the completion of the Erie Canal to cause unprecedented prosperity, both for New York and for the society. As De Witt Clinton predicted to John Pintard in 1821, when the canal "is finished, there will be no limits to our financial prosperity: and then the fountains of public benevolence and public spirit will be opened, and enrich all our institutions with copious streams of munificence."[78] The conventional wisdom, however, did not prove correct; no streams of munificence flowed to the society. By 1829, the anticollection faction struck back.

Practically no records remain to substantiate the reason why, in 1829, the society divested itself of the natural history and mineralogy specimens it had begun collecting so assiduously in 1817. The immediate reason was that the corporation, in 1830, had evicted all tenants from the New York Institution. The society, however, could have moved its specimens to its new home had they chosen to do so. Not a word about the reason for the transfer is included in the minutes, but Robert Hendre Kelby, the society's first "official" historian, provides a clue. According to Kelby, "The growth [of the natural history and mineralogy collections] became so large, and predominated over the real purposes of the Society to such an extent, that in 1829 it was decided to present the collection to the Lyceum of Natural History."[79] The anticollection faction must have argued that historical research, hence the library, was the "real purpose" of the society. Hosack's group acquiesced, perhaps reasoning that by conceding the scientific wing of the society, they would be in a stronger position to save the library and the historical artifacts from the cabinet. Moreover, since Hosack was a member of the Lyceum of Natural History, the blow must have been easier to take.

The New-York Historical Society was not alone in divesting

itself of its natural history collection at this time, for the Massachusetts Historical Society shed theirs, and the American Antiquarian Society ceased collecting in this area, both around 1830. Still, it gutted the collection, for the great majority of the artifacts were minerals or natural history specimens. It also rendered meaningless any question of opening the cabinet for public inspection, for there was little left to see.

The internecine warfare at the society left it exhausted and unable to achieve anything of significance during the balance of the Age of Egalitarianism. The members understood cultural imperatives of that era very clearly, but were either hostile or indifferent to them. Although De Witt Clinton would exclaim, "A good education [is] better than a great estate," he did nothing in the society to promote popular education.[80] When speaking for public consumption, the members solemnly agreed upon the urgent need for "the extensive diffusion of knowledge to all classes and ranks" and the necessity of "promoting all popular means of diffusing knowledge."[81] When acting within their own hall, however, they allowed an important means of disseminating knowledge, their collection, to be severely reduced and their library to remain inaccessible.

The society illustrates the reactionary end of the spectrum of American museums in the Age of Egalitarianism. Its members paid lip service to the ideal of the equality of the common man, but despised it in practice. To them, the society was a haven in a "common" world. The last decade of this period was a sad one. They were finally forced out of the New York Institution in 1832, two years after having been asked to vacate the premises, and had to move again in 1837. The necessity of paying rent almost destroyed the society; no meetings were held between June 11, 1833, and January 13, 1836, and the balance in the treasury stood at $4.68. The panic of 1837 would have finished the society entirely had they not cashed in on the craze for lectures. Seven public lectures in 1838 and 1839 put the society back into the black.[82] Ironically, the people, with their hunger for popular education, came to the rescue of the elitist New-York Historical Society.

The action of the N-Y HS may be an example of specialization and "professionalization".

5

The Age of Professionalism, 1840–1850: The Scientists Lead the Way

In 1840, as the Age of Egalitarianism for museums passed away, a new standard was rising to replace it. Professionalization would be the dominant ideal in American museums throughout the decade of the 1840s. It was strongest in those museums which catered to science, for scientists were ahead of historians or artists in professionalizing, but it affected every museum. As a result, popular education was shunted to the background and museums emphasized their role as research centers for scholars. The apotheosis of professionalism in American museums came quickly, but it did not last for long. By 1850, the pendulum was beginning to swing back toward a synthesis between the popular and the professional in the museum world.

Until about 1820, science in America was dominated by the amateur. He made his living in another trade and pursued science as an avocation. Despite his part-time status, he could become part of the brotherhood, for the body of knowledge that was science was easily understood by any intelligent person. More than that, he could contribute his mite, for new discoveries were within the reach of all.

Around 1820, however, the structure of science began to change dramatically. The bodies of knowledge that made up the sciences were becoming esoteric; that is, what was once a part of the general knowledge of all educated people was now becoming the specific domain of a small group. In natural history, for instance, the Linnaean system of classification was replaced by the natural system, and in mineralogy, physical classification was replaced by chemical analysis. It was becoming progressively more difficult to become one of the brotherhood unless one took specific training to do so. Increasingly, those who pursued science as an avocation began to fall away, replaced by those who made their living by being scientists. Indeed, the very name of the pursuit changed to reflect the new status of these nascent professionals; from about 1840, they were no longer "natural philosophers," but rather "scientists."[1] The beginning of the 1820s also marked a changing of the guard in American science. The first generation of American scientists—learned amateurs such as Benjamin Rush and Caspar Wistar—were dying off, to be replaced by men whose training was more systematic, and whose outlook was more single-mindedly scientific.[2]

Professionalization in science was the result of a series of individual occurrences, but there were institutional manifestations as well. Among the first was the United States Exploring Expedition, initially contemplated during Jackson's second administration, and finally launched in August of 1838, after Joel Roberts Poinsett, Van Buren's secretary of war, assumed de facto authority over the project. The United States had sponsored scientific expeditions before, of course, but never on such a large scale, or at such a high level of scientific sophistication. One of the "scientifics" on that voyage was Titian Peale, and during the nearly four years that the five-boat squadron circumnavigated the globe, he and his compatriots collected literally thousands of natural history specimens. When they returned to port in June of 1842, they had not only given a boost to American science, but had also in effect begun a national museum collection, one which would be absorbed by the Smithsonian Institution in 1857.[3]

While the Exploring Expedition was gone, other evidences of institutional professionalization were becoming evident. In 1838, Edward Hitchcock, a professor at Amherst College, suggested that American geologists form a professional association devoted to furthering the science. After two years of discussion, the Association of American Geologists and Naturalists was founded in 1840, although in a much more limited form than Hitchcock had wanted. This same deliberateness plagued the group for years, so it was not until 1848, when they reorganized as the American Association for the Advancement of Science, that they became truly an active force for professionalization. It is significant, however, that they began in 1840.[4]

The year 1840 was important for yet another institutional manifestation of professionalization in science. Joel Roberts Poinsett was once again the leader, this time of a group formed for the purpose of laying hands on James Smithson's bequest to the United States. Smithson, the natural son of the duke of Northumberland, had died in 1829, bequeathing all of his considerable fortune to the United States of America in order to found at Washington an institution for the "increase and diffusion of knowledge among men." The Smithson bequest, amounting to more than half a million dollars, finally arrived in America in 1838. Meanwhile, the government could not decide what to do with it. Should it be used to found a national university, a library, a museum, an observatory, or something else entirely? Poinsett and his friends had an answer.

The National Institute for the Promotion of Science was organized by Poinsett in May of 1840. His timing was brilliant and his plan was elegant in its simplicity. If the institute could gather a large cabinet before the Exploring Expedition returned, it would become the logical place to deposit the collections that the expedition brought back. If that were achieved, then the institute could approach Congress with a ready-made solution for the question of what to do with the Smithson bequest. Poinsett would hand Congress a *fait accompli*; since a museum would already exist, they would have to find a way to support it.

For a time, the plan seemed to be working. The National Institute absorbed the collection of the Columbian Institution for the Promotion of the Arts and Sciences, a pioneer literary and philosophical society in the nation's capital, whose twenty-year charter from Congress had fortuitously expired in 1838. In 1840, the National Institute purchased, for $1,500, the collection of John Varden, who had been the proprietor of the Washington City Museum.[5] In 1841 the institute was named the repository for the Exploring Expedition collections, and in 1842 it was given a twenty-year charter by Congress.

All was not well, however, with the National Institute. When Poinsett left his position as secretary of war in March of 1841 and retired to South Carolina, the members of the institute were not able to find another man of his stature to lead them. An even greater obstacle came from an unlikely source: professional scientists. These men, having only recently achieved their status as professionals, were extremely sensitive on several points. They had an unholy fear of quackery and demanded sound research and reproducible results. They also disliked being part of scientific organizations led by amateurs. The National Institute, led by politicians and with such a wide roster of membership that it was inevitable that some charlatans were included, was no place for a self-respecting professional.[6] The National Institute was thus top-heavy with amateurs and dilettantes, and lacked the crucial support of respected American scientists. Deprived of Poinsett and the scientists, the National Institute was never able to move decisively toward its goal of capturing the Smithson bequest. Attempts in Congress to do so were tabled, and the beginning of the end came in 1844, when an open rift developed between the institute and the Association of American Geologists and Naturalists.[7] The formation of the Smithsonian in 1846 devastated the institute. It survived on paper until the end of its charter in 1862, after which its collections were absorbed by the Smithsonian.

The experience of the National Institute revealed the basic problem of the new professionals. Everywhere they looked in the America of the 1830s they saw trends toward popularization: the efforts directed toward popular education in museums, the demands for public schools, the lyceum movement. This was good so long as its effect was to diffuse general knowledge. In the view of the professionals, however, all too often the effect was harmful, for such institutions tended to delude ordinary people into the belief that they fully understood complex subjects that only the professional could grasp. The professional's dilemma lay in attempting to limit membership in scientific societies and authorship in technical publications to the few who were capable while at the same time trying to avoid charges of elitism that would have been fatal in antebellum America.[8]

The professionals were exposed to criticism on several fronts. First there were the old scientists, whose work was being superseded. In addition, there were the young amateurs in lyceums and museums whose work was inferior. The clergy could easily become offended if the findings of science diverged too far from Scripture, and the general public would quickly turn on any group it perceived to be a monopolistic "closed corporation." These factors prevented the professionals from moving as far or as fast as they wished.

The year 1840, however, offered what a later age would call a "window of opportunity" for the professionals. The panic of 1837 and the lingering depression that followed claimed as a victim not only Martin Van Buren and the Democrats, but also the ardor of Jacksonian egalitarianism. It did not kill egalitarianism entirely but it did sap its vitality. This allowed the professionals to assert themselves in the museum world, to temporarily deemphasize popular education and stress instead original research, increasing knowledge instead of diffusing it.

An interesting parallel change occurred in the lyceum movement. During the 1820s and the 1830s, the lyceum system had been characterized by mutual self-improvement at the grass-roots level, with townsmen lecturing each other. But its character changed rapidly beginning around 1840. The practice of mutual self-improvement began to disappear; the lyceum was reduced to a lecture circuit serviced by itinerant speakers. By 1846, according to Carl Bode, the lectures "were apt to be smooth professional jobs by trained performers."[9] The well-meaning, but amateurish townsfolk had been vanquished by the "knights of the platform," Emerson, Bayard Taylor, and Henry Ward Beecher among them. Like the museum, the lyceum had been captured by the professionals.

The reign of the professional in the museum world was destined to be short: only ten years. It was, however, an eventful revolution, and like all revolutions, it provoked some fervent reactions before passing away.

The Ideal of Professionalism:
The Academy of Natural Sciences, the Wadsworth Atheneum, and the Smithsonian Institution

William Maclure died in 1840, and an era in the Academy's history came to an end. In the following years, the trend toward professionalism that first emerged in the 1830s continued and became stronger.[10]

During the Age of Professionalism, from 1840 to 1850, one old and two new institutions pursued avidly the ideal of professionalism. The Academy of Natural Sciences and the newly founded Smithsonian Institution both made their museums cater to professional scientists, who could discover new scientific truths, then disseminate them. The new Wadsworth Atheneum was devoted purely to art and its founders sought to serve the connoisseur and the artist. In all three institutions, popular education was secondary to the needs of the professionals.

The Academy of Natural Sciences

The death of William Maclure on March 23, 1840, indeed marked the end of an era in the academy's history. Even before Maclure's demise, the academy had been moving away from popular education toward the professional ideal; now they accelerated their conversion. By October 27, 1840, efforts were underway to exclude visitors from the anatomical rooms; after December 29, the library was closed to the public on days when the collection was open, and by April of 1841, the hall was closed to children under the age of sixteen. At the same time, the use of the hall, at no charge, was offered to the meeting of the Association of American Geologists and Naturalists.[11]

The nascent professional scientists were gaining the upper hand in the academy, and by the middle of the decade were clearly in control. The last stand of the amateurs came in the Speakman affair of 1845. It was a battle the professionals would have avoided if they could have found a way, for John Speakman was a charter member of the academy; in fact, the first meeting of the academy had been held at Speakman's apothecary shop. Moreover, he had been a good friend of William Maclure, and like the late president of the academy, believed "that lack of knowledge of the laws of nature is the source of all social ills."[12] Despite his status as a founding member and his association with Maclure, Speakman, with his amateur's view of science and his continued faith in popular education, was out of step with his fellows.

It was the elderly Quaker apothecary who initiated and ultimately forced the battle with the professionals. On January 21, 1845, he offered a paper for the academy's consideration, entitled "My Views on the Operation of Nature." As was the academy's practice, a committee of three was appointed to judge whether it was worthy of publication in the academy's journal. The document they read was a rambling treatise on force, energy, gravity, and mass, one which was produced without benefit of research or experimentation. Instead, Speakman relied on deductions from mechanical laws to attempt to prove that all of the operations of nature are based on mechanical principles. The committee immediately rejected the article as unfit for publication.

Speakman was stung, and wrote an appeal for help to John Price Wetherill, a generous patron of the academy. In it, he reaffirmed his belief "that there is [not] anything important, or true, that is beyond our comprehension," and declared, "I am still willing to become a martyr to those *views* which I think one day will relieve suffering humanity from its present deplorable condition."[13] The nascent professionals, however, were coming to realize that not even science could reveal everything that was "important or true." Moreover, they were pursuing science for the sake of science, not to ameliorate the condition of mankind. Speakman received no satisfaction from Wetherill.

Speakman made a final effort to sway his fellows in an appeal to the entire membership dated November 4, 1845. In it he complained that his views on the nature of matter had not "been formed independent of the results of modern chemistry," as the review committee had charged. In any case, the issue was not science, but democracy. Speakman believed that the professionals had formed a clique which squelched opposing views; hence his paper had been rejected because it displayed a spirit of "thinking for oneself which sometimes disturbs the equanimity of the monopolist."[14] In his outlook and his rhetoric, Speakman was an amateur of the egalitarian mold, but the Egalitarian Age had passed. The academy rejected the appeal of its venerable cofounder. Professionalism had finally triumphed.

Having defeated the amateurs, the professionals had no one left with whom to squabble but themselves. The biggest argument came in 1847, when Joseph Leidy, a paleontologist and a physician, was proposed as chairman of the curators. A bitter struggle ensued. As Leidy commented in a letter to S. S. Haldeman: "I suspect you have learned sometime since that I succeeded in obtaining the office of Chairman of the Curators in the ANS. It was against a very violent opposition supported principally by Dr. Morton, which he honestly owned to me and gave for the reason that he was comprised in the matter toward Mr. Gambel."[15]

Leidy was elected despite the controversy. However, it seems possible that Morton's opposition stemmed from deeper causes than merely his support for a competing candidate. Morton, after all, had been Maclure's right-hand man, and although he was a nascent professional himself, he still felt that it was important that the academy serve to some extent as a popular educator. Morton made this sentiment clear in an address delivered at the first meeting held in the refurbished library. He sounded almost like Maclure as he admonished the academy: "Let us continue our exertions to make this Institution a practical school of Natural History, by throwing open our doors to all who seek knowledge. . . . let us redouble our zeal to unfold and diffuse the truths of science."[16]

Morton's plea for some attention to popular education left Joseph Leidy unmoved, for Leidy was the closest thing to a real professional at the academy in the 1840s. Although he made a living as a physician, and thus could not be called a true professional scientist, Leidy spent every spare moment working on his paleontological researches. He was so concerned with his research and writing that he had little interest in promoting public access to the collection. In fact, as Edward Nolan pointed out, Leidy could barely be distracted long enough to care for the collection itself: "He was often so absorbed in his work that it was perhaps only a divided attention he could give to the cleaning of windows, the supplying of coal or the repair of the roof."[17]

Given the single-minded devotion to research on the part of the chairman of the curators, there is little wonder that popular education received little encouragement at the academy during the 1840s. In fact, under Leidy the curators of the museum were reduced to the status of guards rather than teachers. At a meeting of the academy on March 28, 1848, it was resolved that at least two members be appointed to be present on days which the museum was open to maintain "order and decorum in the Hall, and in protecting the property of the Society from injury."[18] Instead of instructing the people, the members were to protect the collection from the people.

Even as they were holding the public at arm's length, the members were promoting the ideal of professionalism. As Patsy Gerstner put it, "Not only had it become desirable to keep the public away from the collections, it was now considered advisable to give the scientific community greater access to the material."[19] To this end, the academy allowed scientists, whether members or not, to borrow actual specimens from the museum (previously they had only allowed casts to be made), and they extended their hospitality to meetings of scientific groups, such as the 1848 meeting of the American Association for the Advancement of Science.

It is significant, however, that even in the midst of this professional activity at the academy, popular education was never abandoned entirely. The museum remained open to the public, at no charge, two days per week. The academy could have chosen to repudiate popular education entirely, but they did not. The era of professionalism overshadowed, but did not destroy, the ideal of the museum as an educator.

The Wadsworth Atheneum

The idea for one of the first public museums in America devoted entirely to art, the Trumbull Gallery at Yale University, came from the venerable artist, John Trumbull. Another, the Wadsorth Atheneum, which opened in 1844, two years after Trumbull died, was brought into being by the vision and generosity of Trumbull's nephew, Daniel Wadsworth, a man of wealth who lived near Hartford, Connecticut, where the atheneum was built. Wadsworth's vision in planning the institution was a broad one, embracing many fields of knowledge. The portion of the atheneum devoted solely to the gallery of art was to be a means of raising the level of taste in Hartford, and a training school for serious artists. Popular education was never considered as a goal for the art gallery from 1844 to 1850.

The story of the atheneum properly starts with John Trumbull. Like Charles Willson Peale, Trumbull had served in the Continental Army during the Revolution, and had studied painting in England under the renowned Benjamin West. Like Peale, too, Trumbull was very conscious of the historical importance of the personalities and events of the Revolution, and sought to immortalize them in his art. Trumbull settled in New York in 1804, shortly thereafter joined the New-York Historical Society, and became intimate with David Hosack, De Witt Clinton, and other important members of the society. He was a natural choice to become the president of the American Academy of Fine Arts, which honor he accepted in January 1817. The AAFA had been founded as the New York Academy of the Fine Arts in 1802 by New York Mayor Edward Livingston, thus making it the second organization in America for the promotion of the arts (Charles Willson Peale had helped to organize the first, the Columbianum, in Philadelphia in 1794). When the organization incorporated in 1808, it took the name of American Academy of Fine Arts. The

AAFA accomplished little until it moved to the New York Institution in 1816.

Trumbull's nineteen-year tenure as the president of the AAFA was a study in controversy. He had been in office less than a year when he was accused (unfairly, as it turned out) of stealing thirty-two works of art from the academy. The most fundamental difficulty, however, arose over issues of professionalism. Trumbull conceived the academy as a multifaceted institution, which would both assist artists in their studies and diffuse a taste for art among the general public. Younger artists, who were trying to make their art a paying career, saw the academy solely as an art school in which they could hone their talents. Trumbull believed that public lectures in a library accessible to the people were necessities; to the young artists, they were superfluities. Trumbull was inflexible, insisting that his positions be adopted. He was totally unsympathetic to the needs of the nascent professional artists, and he had the backing of the board, which consisted mainly of patrons rather than artists.[20] Finally, in 1826, the younger artists, led by Samuel F. B. Morse, seceded to form the National Academy of Design. The loss of the young blood crippled the academy, and the requirement to abandon the New York Institution by 1832 virtually ended its useful life. It continued to exist in name a few years longer, in a building that David Hosack had erected for its use. Trumbull resigned the presidency in 1836 (he was succeeded by Rembrandt Peale), just before disastrous fires in 1837 and 1839 destroyed large portions of the collection and for all intents and purposes terminated the academy's existence.

Trumbull, by now old and poor, had no assets except for his paintings and his nephews-in-law. His nephew in New Haven was the celebrated chemist and Yale University professor, Benjamin Silliman. Professor Silliman and Trumbull worked out an ingenious and mutually beneficial plan whereby Trumbull would donate his pictures to Yale and reserve the income generated by their exhibition to assist poor students in obtaining an education. In return, Yale would guarantee Trumbull an annuity of $1,000 for life. Yale accepted the plan, Silliman secured $7,000 from the state legislature to fund a building, and Yale's trustees prided themselves on having made a sharp bargain. They were certain that at 76, Trumbull would live for no more than six years; in fact he lived for eleven, and the trustees came to rue the day they had assented to the deal.[21]

The Trumbull Gallery thus became one of America's first museums devoted solely to art. The tendencies toward professionalization in the wider culture insured that such a thing would eventually come to pass, but neither the people nor the institution were yet ready for such specialization. Visitors could not be enticed to come back repeatedly to see the same paintings. Silliman became the first curator, and given his onerous professional responsibilities and his editorship of the *American Journal of Science and Art*, he had little time left to care for the gallery. Under his administration it was, for the most part, a drawing school for budding artists. In 1843 Silliman honored Trumbull's last request and buried the artist in the gallery. The symbolism, though certainly unintended, was all too apt. The Trumbull Gallery was, by 1843, a more or less dead institution.

Before his death, however, Trumbull was able to launch another museum, once again with the invaluable assistance of a nephew-in-law, Daniel Wadsworth. Daniel was the son of Jeremiah Wadsworth, who had made a considerable sum serving as the commissary to the Continental Army during the Revolution and turned that into a fortune marketing French goods in the United States after the war. Daniel inherited Jeremiah's money, but not his business acumen. Delicate health and a retiring disposition prevented him from engaging in trade, but he used his inherited wealth wisely. Very early in life, Daniel's interests turned to art. He was a better draftsman than drawer, however, for he dabbled extensively in architecture. Wadsworth also became one of America's first patrons of the arts, supporting the work of both Thomas Cole and Thomas Sully.

Young Daniel seized every opportunity to expand his artistic horizons. He became a museum-goer, visiting both Scudder's American Museum and Peale's museum in Philadelphia.[22] He formed a respectable collection of American and European paintings, and housed them in a country place that was itself a work of art: Monte Video. Located on a small mountain five miles from Hartford, Monte Video, designed by Wadsworth himself, was one of the first Gothic Revival buildings in New England.

It was natural that Wadsworth would become involved in the negotiations for the establishment of the Trumbull Gallery at Yale. He had hoped that Trumbull's collection could be divided between New Haven and Hartford, or at least routed between them from time to time. Trumbull vetoed this idea, fearing for the safety of the pictures in transit, and everything went to New Haven. Nonetheless, Wadsworth made a generous contribution to the cause.[23]

Now, in the 1840s, several factors converged to make Wadsworth try to found an art museum in Hartford. Uncle John Trumbull remained in financial straits, and the Yale trustees were in no mood to help him further. Daniel was approaching his seventieth birthday, and may have been feeling the need to leave a memorial to himself.[24] Perhaps the most important reason lay in the demise, in 1840, of the Hartford Gallery of Arts. This institution had begun life in 1797 as the museum of the painter Joseph Steward, and Wadsworth had been its patron since 1801.[25] Now its passing left Hartford without even the semblance of an art museum. Perhaps Daniel had read the comments of such foreign critics as Frances Grund, writing in 1837: "There exists, as yet, no public art gallery in any of the large cities of the United States, to which a young painter could have free access, or where his tastes might be formed. There is not even a school for painting, or any other public institution of a more elevated nature, to foster or develop talents of this kind."[26]

Words of this sort must have stung a good patriot like Wadsworth, but it was all too true that the student of art had no place to turn in Hartford. Nor was there any way of diffusing a taste for art among the ordinary people. This must also have disturbed a man who was celebrated for showing "a kind interest in any school whenever an opportunity presented."[27]

Family loyalty, a sense of his own mortality, cultural nationalism, and the need to provide Hartford with a museum to educate artists and elevate the public taste all converged to make Wadsworth decide to fund the atheneum. Wadsworth gathered around him a remarkable group of people to become cofounders. There was Alfred Smith, Wadsworth's own attorney and a leading light of the Hartford bar; Calvin Day, a wholesaler who was active in politics; James B. Hosmer, who had retired from his dry goods business in 1833 to devote his time to charitable projects; Henry Barnard, an attorney who was making a reputation as an educational reformer; David Watkinson, another retired wholesaler, with a long line of philanthropies to his credit; and Gideon Welles, a newspaperman who eventually became Lincoln's secretary of the navy. Wadsworth could hardly have been better supported.

To galvanize the group into action, Wadsworth, in the summer of 1841, suggested a site for the museum: the property under his ancestral home on Main Street in Hartford. In response to this offer, a public meeting was held on September 24, 1841, to plan a fund-raising campaign. David Watkinson was elected chairman, and nearly $32,000 was subscribed for the building fund. Eventually, $39,000 was raised, of which $9,000 came from Wadsworth, over and above the gift of land valued at $16,200.[28]

With the money in hand, the scheme was expanded. The building would house not only a gallery of art, but also, "the plan was enlarged so as to embrace the Connecticut Historical Society and the Young Men's Institute. . . . In addition . . . a room in the proposed building was appropriated to the Natural History Society."[29] The immediate reason for this move, of course, was that all three of these organizations needed permanent homes. It was also a clever political stroke, for a gallery devoted exclusively to artists and art lovers may have seemed too elitist to some. By adding the other organizations, especially the Young Men's Institute, essentially a lyceum which sponsored popular lectures, the atheneum would be rendered immune from charges of exclusivity. The art gallery could now cater mainly to artists and patrons.

The novelty of the "professional" approach was reinforced by the method of housing the institution. Typically, museums of the past had found lodging in an existing edifice; the atheneum would build a new structure specifically for its needs. The new direction was made explicit by its form. Unlike the Trumbull Gallery at Yale, which the artist himself had designed as a chaste neoclassical box, the atheneum's architects, Ithiel Town and Alexander Davis, created a turreted fortress, a Gothic Revival castle of the arts. Divided within to reflect its tripartite function, the building was virtually a statement of art for the sake of art. The northern section housed the Young Men's Institute, the southern held the historical society, while the central section was home to the atheneum. The Natural History Society occupied the lower level.[30]

Wadsworth and company quickly set out to find artworks with which to fill the building. Alfred Smith, Wadsworth's lawyer, was the chief negotiator for the atheneum in its purchases of art, but Wadsworth usually put up the money. In 1844 Wadsworth, James Hosmer, David Watkinson, and others purchased approximately fifty paintings from the collection of the defunct American Academy of Fine Arts and placed them on deposit in the atheneum. In the meantime, Smith had been negotiating with John Trumbull, and after the artist's death in 1843, with his executor, Benjamin Silliman. Finally in August of 1844, Smith succeeded in purchasing the residue of Trumbull's estate for $4,053.33.[31] Wadsworth added several other works to the collection until his death in 1848.

On July 31, 1844, the Wadsworth Atheneum opened its doors to the public. There were eighty-two works of art in its collection, and the admission, probably patterned after that of Peale's museum, was reasonable: twenty-five cents for adults, half-price for children, an annual ticket for one dollar. This would not be surprising, for both Wadsworth and Gideon Welles had visited Peale's museum.[32] The hours of opening, however, were not as extensive as Peale's: weekdays from 8:00 A.M. to 12:00 noon and 1:00 to 6:00 P.M., with no evening or weekend hours.[33] The catalogue of the collection was a twenty-eight-page pamphlet offering lengthy descriptions of works on exhibit. Since the majority of these were American historical canvases, the descriptions tended to emphasize history rather than aesthetics. Still, it was obviously intended to be a scholarly document, one which would enhance the understanding of people of taste. It was simply too sophisticated to be useful for popular education. [34]

Daniel Wadsworth and his compatriots had created a gallery as a monument to their own tastes, as a school for artists, and as a place where the genteel could hone their aesthetic appreciation. They hoped that the gallery would raise the level of public taste, but they did nothing actively to support popular education. The curator, Edward Sheffield Bartholomew, a sculptor appointed in 1845, had only one duty, that of taking tickets, and he found this task did not often interfere with his sculpting. Once more, people proved that they would not pay again and again to see the same pictures. Just as the people were tolerated, but not encouraged at the Academy of Natural Sciences, so they were allowed to enter the atheneum, as long as they remembered that it was a shrine of the muses, not a palace for the people.

The Smithsonian Institution

Before James Smithson died in 1829, he had willed his personal fortune of more than a half million dollars to the United States for "the increase and diffusion of knowledge among men." Given such vague instructions, an institution created to fulfill the bequest might take virtually any form, and indeed, for the succeeding seventeen years nearly every conceivable legitimate use was seriously considered. Among the proposals were an observatory, a national teacher's college, a national library, a national museum, a laboratory, and a gallery of art. That the Smithsonian eventually became an amalgamation of most of these things was due to a combination of individual wills, coincidence, and popular and scientific pressures. Joseph Henry, the first secretary of the institution, was responsible for much of the shaping of the Smithsonian; it was his insistence on supporting professional science that made the institution a center of scientific research. A museum was not a part of Henry's "research center" concept, and he initially fought vigorously the notion of establishing one under the aegis of the Smithsonian. It would take nearly a decade before Henry finally resigned himself to the fact of a Smithsonian museum. By the

Joseph Henry, ca. 1850, the first secretary of the Smithsonian
Institution (Courtesy of Smithsonian Institution Archives, RU 95,
Neg. #SA-59)

end of the 1840s, it became clear that a museum would be imposed upon the Smithsonian; but Henry struggled to keep it solely a study collection for scholarly research, not a museum open to the public.

Although Smithson died in 1829, various legal tangles prevented the endowment from arriving in America until 1838. In the meantime, beginning in 1836, John Quincy Adams led the fight in Congress, first to accept the donation, and second, to use it to build an observatory.[35] The struggle began to heat up late in 1844, and culminated on August 10, 1846, with the passage of the act establishing the Smithsonian. As Wilcomb Washburn attested, "The Act was a grab bag reflecting varying interests and influences that had been brought to bear on the subject."[36] No mention was made in the act of supporting original research. Congress specifically ordered that a museum, library, gallery of art, and lecture room be part of the institution, earmarked half the institution's income for these purposes, and gave it custody of the government's collection of curiosities. It placed the institution under a board of regents consisting of members from all three branches of government and private citizens. And it made provision for the hiring of a secretary to have charge of the day-to-day operations of the institution.

It was clear that Congress meant to emphasize the "diffusion" of knowledge rather than the "increase," as set forth by Smithson. The regents, however, promptly hired a man as secretary whose priorities were exactly reversed. Moreover, they did this knowingly. While still being considered for the post, Henry drew up a "Programme" for the operation of the institution. The pertinent sections were purely professional:

> To Increase Knowledge. It is proposed—
> 1. To stimulate men of talent to make original researches, by offering suitable rewards for memoirs containing new truths; and,
> 2. To appropriate annually a portion of the income for particular researches, under the direction of suitable persons.
> To Diffuse Knowledge. It is proposed—

1. To publish a series of periodical reports on the progress of the different branches of knowledge; and,

2. To publish occasionally separate treatises on subjects of general interest.[37]

Henry quite simply ignored the museum, library, gallery of art, and lecture hall mandated by Congress. Instead, he envisioned a small office that would expend the great majority of its income in promoting original researches by professional scientists, and then publishing the results. Although Henry was thus undoubtedly an "increase" man, he was head and shoulders above all other candidates, and was chosen secretary in December of 1846.

As if Henry's conflict with Congress and certain of the regents were not enough, he soon had another opponent; in 1847 the board of regents appointed Charles Coffin Jewett assistant secretary in charge of the library. Jewett, one of the most innovative librarians of his day, was determined to transform the Smithsonian into the national library, and he had plenty of support from the board of regents. The battle lines were thus drawn early: increase versus diffusion, library and museum versus research center.

Joseph Henry was a formidable adversary. He had been orphaned early in his life and he had known poverty. In 1819 he entered the Albany Academy and soon fell in love with science. The young man quickly distinguished himself by his incessant quest for knowledge, and by 1826 he became the professor of mathematics and natural history at his alma mater. His particular research interest was magnetism, an area in which he rapidly attained eminence, especially after he joined the faculty at Princeton University in 1832. Joseph Henry had risen to his position of respect by dint of genius and unswerving determination; he became accustomed to having things his way.

Among the institutions aiding Henry in his research were the Peale museums. This association began just as his career was being launched, for in 1826 he visited Rubens Peale's New York Museum and was impressed by the caliber of the experiments on hydrogen and oxygen which he witnessed there: "The experi-

ments wher [sic] very neatly performed on a small scale in operating [sic] with the compound blow pipe. . . . the wand produced
a light too intense for the eye to look upon (this is a beautiful
experiment). His method of exploding hydrogen was also peculiarly neat."[38]

In Peale's Philadelphia Museum, Henry did more than witness
experiments, he conducted them. In early May of 1835 he noted
in his "Record of Experiments": "Exp. in Philadelphia with the
large magnet of Mr. Peal."[39] Later in life, during the centennial
celebrations in 1876, Henry made an "Address on Charles Willson
Peale" in Philadelphia in which he paid tribute to Peale's influence
on his life: "The author of this sketch born in a distant city almost
from childhood conceived a desire to visit Philadelphia especially
that he might see Peale's Museum and the impression which the
sight of this interesting collection made upon his youthful mind
is still retained with a vividness which will be among the last
to be obliterated by advancing years."[40]

Although Henry had known and admired the Peale museum
balance of education and support of science (he referred to it as
"the first scientific Institution of the kind in this country, and
. . . of national importance as an educational establishment"), he
had no intention of duplicating the Peale model at the Smithsonian.[41] He based his plans entirely on the will of James Smithson,
as he understood it. To Henry, the "increase and diffusion" of
knowledge were not synonymous, but rather represented two
radically different terms. To "increase" was to discover new
truths, to "diffuse" was to make old truths generally known.
Even before accepting the secretaryship, Joseph Henry made this
distinction clear:

> The object of the institution is the increase and diffusion of
> knowledge. The increase of knowledge is much more difficult
> and . . . much more important than the diffusion of knowledge.
> There are at this time thousands of institutions actively engaged
> in the diffusion of knowledge in our country, but not a single
> one which gives direct support to its increase. . . . There is no
> civilized country in the world in which less encouragement is
> given than in our own to original investigations, and conse-

quently no country of the same means has done and is doing so little in this line.[42]

Henry believed that the nation's network of schools, colleges, libraries, lyceums, and museums was adequate to diffuse most kinds of knowledge. He meant the Smithsonian to support the quest for new facts and new discoveries in science. These new truths could then be diffused through Smithsonian publications, but that would be a secondary function. As Henry put it: "The most prominent idea in my mind is that of stimulating the talent of our country to original research—in which it has been most lamentably deficient—to pour fresh material on the apex of the pyramid of science and thus to enlarge its base. . . . Practical science will always meet with encouragement in a country like ours it is the higher principles that require to be increased and diffused."[43]

There were, however, many distractions from the "higher principles." The law incorporating the institution demanded a library, museum, and gallery of art. Charles Coffin Jewett meant to carry out one portion of that charge by building a great national library. There was talk that the collection of the moribund National Institute for the Promotion of Science would be given to the Smithsonian. Many in the government were grumbling that the Smithsonian had not yet taken charge of the national collection of curiosities. Henry managed to occupy Jewett's attention for a time by ordering him to form a general catalog of all the important libraries in the United States, but given Jewett's energy, this diversion would not last for long. In the meantime Henry tried to fend off the gift of the National Institute and government collections.

The story of Henry's long struggle to avert a national museum at the Smithsonian has been told elsewhere.[44] He managed to become vice-president of the National Institute, largely to guard against any attempt to transfer its collection. The depth of his aversion to such an eventuality is clearly evident in a memorial sent by the National Institute to Congress in 1848, requesting full authority over the Exploring Expedition materials and appropriations to properly store and exhibit their collection. Two of the memorial's passages were sharply critical of the Smithsonian: the first asserted that it was "funded by . . . a foreigner and intended to increase the fame and perpetuate the name of a private individual"; and the second accused the Smithsonian of being "a private establishment, intending to perpetuate only the name of a single individual."[45] Only a strong antipathy to a national museum at the Smithsonian could have compelled Henry to sign a document which implied that the Smithsonian was merely a private monument to a foreigner. In order to realize his vision of an institution to advance professional science, Joseph Henry was willing to go to great lengths.

Henry's lost no opportunity to hammer home his point that a museum or library would sap the income that could otherwise be used to promote science. In his annual report for 1849, Henry once more stated his position:

> The formation of a museum of objects of nature and art requires much caution. With a given income to be appropriated to the purpose, a time must come when the costs of keeping the objects will just equal the amount of the appropriation. . . . Also, the tendency of an Institution of this kind, unless guarded against, will be to expend funds on a heterogeneous collection of objects of mere curiosity [not] complete definitive collections arranged for scientific purposes.[46]

Henry's rear-guard action against the museum brought mixed results. He had succeeded, at least for the time being, in thwarting the reception of the National Institute and government collections. But the regents prevailed upon him to carry out the terms of the act by forming a small museum and hiring an assistant secretary to run it. Henry grudgingly consented, with the proviso that "instead of attempting to form a miscellaneous collection of objects of nature and art, it is proposed to collect only those which will yield a harvest of new results."[47] If the Smithsonian must have a museum, Henry would see to it that it promoted professional science.

Henry arrived at his position because of his support for professional science, not because he harbored any animosity toward libraries or museums per se. Indeed, as previously noted, the Peale museums were a central influence in his life. He was certain, however, that a national library or museum under the aegis of the Smithsonian would ruin his plans for the support of science. Both institutions, by their very natures, grow rapidly; to accommodate their growth it would be necessary to erect costly buildings and hire large staffs. This would soon eat up the endowment funds, force the Smithsonian to ask Congress for appropriations, and thus subject the institution to political control. Henry wished to avoid this at all costs. Henry's caution was evident in his choice of assistant secretary. He had managed to wrest from the regents the right to choose his subordinates, subject to board approval. Now that he must fill the post of assistant secretary in charge of the National Museum, he pondered the two leading candidates. One was Titian Peale, by now an examiner in the Patent Office, since all the Peale museums were defunct. The other was Spencer Fullerton Baird, a familiar face at the Academy of Natural Sciences and a naturalist at Dickinson College.

The two candidates presented stark alternatives. They were of different generations; in fact, they had literally been born in different centuries: Peale in 1799, Baird in 1823. Peale had gone on his first scientific expedition, with such Academy of Natural Sciences notables as William Maclure, George Ord, and Thomas Say, five years before Baird was born. Peale's training as a naturalist had been in the field; Baird's was mainly academic. Peale's scientific work had always shared time with other jobs; Baird's scientific work was systematic and was his vocation. In short, Peale was, at best, a proto-professional; Baird was a professional. For that reason alone, Peale had little chance against Baird.

There were, however, other reasons to choose Baird. His facility with languages and his editorial skills (both of which Peale lacked) would make him a competent chief of publications at the Smithsonian. He had powerful backing from George Perkins Marsh, a representative from Vermont and regent of the institution. Moreover Baird had skillfully managed to present himself as a professional scientist on the one hand, and as a naive, almost

Spencer Fullerton Baird, ca. 1865, the first assistant secretary of the
Smithsonian Institution in charge of the National Museum and the
second secretary of the Smithsonian Institution (Courtesy of
Smithsonian Institution Archives, RU 95, Neg. #46853)

fulsome admirer of the secretary on the other.[48] All these factors combined to make Baird Henry's choice in July 1850.

If Henry felt that he had guaranteed himself a loyal subordinate by choosing the young and effusive Baird, he was mistaken. Smithsonian employees and regents were resolving themselves by the late 1840s into two camps. Henry was the leader of the first camp, which may be labeled the "active operations" group, to borrow one of his phrases. This group eschewed all functions except support of original research and publication of the results. The second group, which rallied around Jewett and included regents such as Marsh and Rufus Choate, believed that the Smithsonian should be the locus for a national library and museum. Since Marsh had championed Baird's cause from the beginning, the new assistant secretary owed the regent a great deal and naturally must have been receptive to his opinions.

In fact Baird was also obligated to the library-museum group. Jewett had apparently rendered some inside assistance, for in a letter in June 1849, Marsh had promised Baird that "Jewett will do all he can" to get him hired.[49] There was apparently a quid pro quo expected, for shortly after Baird began work, Marsh wrote him, "You will be great aid and comfort to Jewett and will find him a most efficient and able auxilary [sic]."[50]

Baird thus found himself in the middle of a fundamental struggle at the Smithsonian between professional science and popular education, one which would shake the institution to its very foundations in the decade to come. For now, however, Joseph Henry was firmly in control, and charted a course directly toward the pole star of professional science. The "active operations" were to be the only operations at the Smithsonian during the 1840s.

The Academy of Natural Sciences, the Wadsworth Atheneum, and the Smithsonian Institution all pursued the ideal of professionalism during the 1840s. They sought to serve the scholar and the specialist while placing popular education in a secondary position. As the situation at the Smithsonian illustrates, however, the forces of popular education were never wholly vanquished, and by 1850 they were poised to strike back. During the turbulent decades of the 1850s and 1860s they would reassert themselves, and the resulting synthesis of popular education and professionalism would determine the form of the modern American museum.

The Fall of the Older Order:
Peale's Museum and the Western Museum of Cincinnati

Titian had returned to find his own institution in sorry straits. The entertainment program had failed utterly, and neglect of natural history had brought daily attendance down to the lowest on record.[51]

The Western Museum of Cincinnati . . . stumbled, through catering to popular interests, into the category of a sideshow. Its decline reminds us of the perils of even a few oblations to bunkum and provides convincing proof that wax works constitute the beginning of the descent to hell.[52]

Peale's Museum, 1840–1850

Titian Peale returned to Philadelphia from the United States Exploring Expedition in June of 1842, and indeed found Peale's museum in sorry straits. The lingering depression following the panic of 1837 had forced the proprietors to deemphasize science and embrace ever more tawdry entertainments. Not even this expedient worked, however, and by 1840 the museum was deeply in debt, owing Nathan Dunn alone more than $11,000.[53] Dunn, who never let sentiment stand in the way of profit, nearly destroyed the museum during the following year. On July 12, 1841, Dunn announced his intention to sell the museum's building at Ninth and George streets, and to take his own Chinese Museum on tour to Britain. Deprived of its biggest draw and threatened by the loss of its building, the museum hovered on the brink of complete collapse.

This was the grim situation to which Titian returned. The trustees, hoping that he could revive the institution, quickly named him manager of the museum. The choice was a good one, for no one knew better than Titian how the demand for professionalization was sweeping through the sciences. After all, he had just spent four years in the vanguard of that impetus, on the scientific staff of the Exploring Expedition. Yet he returned to an institution which had spurned serious scientific work in order to offer popular amusements. Presumably Titian educated his trustees on the importance of catering to scientists, for a Committee of Investigation led by Rembrandt Peale made an extraordinarily candid public admission of errors to the museum's stockholders:

> At the time the present Board came into office the Institution was still suffering under the injurious effects resulting from the morbid excitement produced by a series of entertainments catered to the public taste in 1839 & 1840 & at a period continued in. . . . Public opinion at all times & under all circumstances Omnipotent has decided that the departure from the legitimate objects of the Company could not be sustained and the converting into a concert room of a receptacle for the works of Nature and Art and for which purpose alone it was reared & nurtured by its illustrious founder, was sufficient cause for the withdrawal of the patronage formerly so liberally bestowed by our most influential Citizens.[54]

The committee forthrightly admitted that the museum had abandoned science and art in order to offer popular entertainments. They recognized, however, that public opinion had turned against them, and that only by restoring the place of science could they expect to regain the public's respect. In Titian they saw their only hope to do so:

> Amidst all this gloom and despondency your Board take unfeigned satisfaction in announcing the reinstatement of Mr. Titian R. Peale as Manager. . . . of the talents & high attainments of this gentleman & his perfect knowledge and experience in the well conducting and improving of a scientific collection it is useless to enlarge: Your Board have full confidence that under his direction the resuscitation of the Institution may confidently be hoped for.[55]

The committee clearly felt that a return to the promotion of science was the cure for all of the museum's ills. Not a word was said about popular education; just as clearly, the Age of Egalitarianism had been replaced by an Age of Professional Science.

Titian, however, inherited a hopeless task. During most of Charles Willson Peale's life, the needs of science and the needs of his museum had matched each other fairly closely. These requirements had begun to diverge about a decade before his death, when he had decided to make his museum primarily an instrument of popular education. By 1827, the gaps in his scientific collection were glaring:

> Peale had almost no herbarium and his collection of minerals was meagre. His arrangement of animals according to the Linnaean system had become outdated. Peale kept only one representative of each species (or a male and female if they differed externally) rather than several for comparison. Moreover, there was no provision for taking specimens out of the cases for examination. The lower animals were grossly neglected. Of the invertebrates, Peale kept insects, shells and pieces of sponges and corals, animals that made a fine display. But what interest would the public have in rows of mollusks or worms in bottles of alcohol?[56]

What interest indeed? The needs of science had become so specialized that a general museum could not hope to fulfill all of them. The times had changed, for "when Peale began his Museum of Natural History, a museum might be *both* a popular attraction which served to enrich the proprietor *and* an institution for the promotion of science." By "1841 this was no longer true. . . . the needs of science had wholly diverged from those of scientific popularizers."[57] The rigor demanded by the professionals simply left the amateurs—and particularly the general public—behind. Peale's museum completely lost touch with serious science in the 1830s as entertainment became its primary function. Titian was attempting to revive the dead when he assumed the manager's position.

The museum staggered on for less than a year and one-half after the penitential new year's resolution by the Committee of Investigation. On May 1, 1843, the building was sold to a Philadelphia businessman named Isaac Brown Parker; then on November 8, 1845, Charles Willson Peale's grandson, Edmund Peale, purchased the collection. Finally, in the summer of 1849, the great showman Phineas Taylor Barnum purchased both building and collection, only to sell both to a businessman named Clapp Spooner, who lost nearly everything in a disastrous fire on December 30, 1851.

The last eight years of Peale's museum presented a pitiful shadow of its earlier existence. No longer useful as a popular educator or as a scientific laboratory, it simply degenerated into a sideshow. The fire only completed the destruction that failure to keep pace with changes in American culture had so ably begun.

The Western Museum of Cincinnati

The decay had also eaten deeply into the foundations of the Western Museum by 1840. Its former proprietor, Joseph Dorfeuille, had sold out and tried to start a museum in New York City, but only a few months later, on July 23, 1840, Dorfeuille died. He had become a showman by necessity in Cincinnati and remained a showman by necessity in New York, but at heart he was a scientist. The spirit of professional science was evidently moving within him, for he was working on a volume covering the antiquities of North America when he died. Dorfeuille's widow, no doubt remembering that the Academy of Natural Sciences had earlier purchased his collection of fossils, asked the academy's Samuel George Morton to help bring the book to publication, but this was not accomplished.[58]

There was nothing of the scientist, however, about Dorfeuille's successors in Cincinnati. Dorfeuille had taken the finest of Hiram Powers's automated figures from the "Infernal Regions" when he left for New York. The new proprietors promptly restocked the "Regions" with poor imitations of Powers's figures, and abandoned all vestiges of serious exhibitions. Lewis Leonard Tucker's judgment on the results cannot be questioned: "The final years of the Western Museum can be summarized quickly. From 1839 to 1867 when it dissolved, the Museum languished as the center of hokum under a number of owners."[59]

Like Peale's museum in its last days, the Western Museum simply became irrelevant. It neither served science nor educated; it was merely a place for cheap and gaudy entertainment. The mixture of solid science and popular education that both Charles Willson Peale and Daniel Drake had envisioned had long since passed away at both institutions by 1840. The auction of the Western Museum's contents in 1867 merely turned the final page in a book whose story had effectively ended long before. The future of museums in American belonged to those which could support research without snobbery and educate without trivializing.

New York's Two Dissenters: The New-York Historical Society and the American Museum of P. T. Barnum

During the Gallatin Administration the Society really got into its stride.[60]

The wave of professionalism, especially in the sciences, that burst over the American museum world during the 1840s immersed most institutions, but not two New York City museums: that of the New-York Historical Society and the American Museum of P. T. Barnum. These two rejected the cultural imperatives for very different reasons: the society because this period marked the last hurrah of its "old Federalist" hierarchy, Barnum because he was exploiting the gullibility of the masses to build a center of popular entertainment. These represent the extremes of the reaction to the rise of professionalism.

The New-York Historical Society

In many ways the 1840s were a time of triumph for the New-York Historical Society. The bitter divisions of the 1820s were a fading memory, and the near bankruptcy of the 1830s had been replaced by relative prosperity fueled by the proceeds from lectures and dues from new members, more than 1,000 of whom joined during this decade. In 1841, the society moved to spacious quarters at the New York University Library. The university provided storage for the library and cabinet and space for meetings and lectures, all "on the most liberal terms which the University could afford to any association or individuals."[61] So by 1841, the comparative prosperity of the society was assured.

The internecine warfare of the 1820s and the financial crisis of the 1830s had so absorbed the society's energies as to preclude any initiatives for popular education, even if they had cared to make them. With these obstacles removed by 1841, the society could have made an effort to promote the new cultural imperative, professionalism. Instead, they did next to nothing. The old guard of unreconstructed federalists who had controlled the society from its inception were, by the century's fifth decade, less receptive than ever to the needs of the people outside the society, and blocked any notion of responding to them. The old order was passing, with the deaths of David Hosack in 1835, John Pintard in 1844, and Chancellor James Kent, the society's fifth president, in 1847, but this only made the remaining veteran members more inflexible. As a result, no effort was made during the entire decade to render the cabinet accessible to the public, or to scholars. The collection sat perched on the gallery level of the New York University Library, invisible to nonmembers. Once again, the members understood the cultural needs, but resisted them. Their only concession to the demand to support scholars came in 1843, when the society library regularized its erratic days and times of opening, and extended its open hours to six per day. This skimpy effort was virtually the only one the society made to support the burgeoning interest in American history in the 1840s. This was ironic, considering that the great American historian George Bancroft was a member of the society during this time.

The members' conservatism was reflected in the society's choice of leadership. In 1843, upon the retirement of the society's eighth president, Peter Augustus Jay, son of the Federalist statesman John Jay, the society chose Albert Gallatin to succeed him. Gallatin had been the secretary of the treasury under Jefferson and Madison, and there had been a time when the old guard would have considered him too radical for the job. However, at eighty-two years of age, Gallatin had become conservative enough to be considered "safe."

The new president's experience with museums dated back to their beginnings in America. He had been personally acquainted with Pierre Eugène Du Simitière and Charles Willson Peale, and had corresponded with both.[62] However, even if Gallatin had learned any lessons from Peale, he was far too infirm to implement them by 1843. His illnesses kept him from attending all but a handful of meetings during his tenure, and those six years may best be characterized as a time of prosperous inertia. Gallatin was too weak to change the status quo even if he had cared to do so, and the old Federalists were content with the old ways. Until his death in 1849, Gallatin was essentially a roadblock to responsiveness in the society.

Although the society did virtually nothing to promote science or foster education during the decade of the 1840s, they were capable of paying lip service to such goals. In 1846, threatened with a proposed duty on imported books, the society fired off a memorial to Congress. The first draft averred that "the security and permanency of all free institutions rest mainly upon the intelligence of a well-informed people,"[63] and the final draft concluded that it was necessary to "foster in every way the widest diffusion of knowledge and information among all classes of the community."[64]

The members of the society were clearly aware of the cultural imperatives, and could even pretend to agree with them when necessary, but they adamantly refused to put these tenets into practice. The cabinet, and to a lesser extent the library, remained inaccessible throughout the decade. By the end of the 1840s, however, the old guard was losing its grip. A younger and more flexible group of leaders would then begin to nudge the society toward responsiveness.

The American Museum of P. T. Barnum, 1840–1850

Across town from the Historical Society stood the first herald of the resurgence of the masses that was yet to come. The moribund American Museum of the Scudder family had been purchased by a small-time showman named Phineas Taylor Barnum, whose gift for promotion soon turned it into a thriving enterprise. Barnum rejected professionalism as did the Historical Society, but not for reasons of elitism. Instead, he intended to build a museum for everyman.

Barnum's accomplishments with the American Museum from 1841 to 1868 remain a subject of controversy to this day. There can be no question but that he was successful; over forty-one million visitors trooped through the museum during his period of ownership.[65] Both contemporary critics and later scholars, however, frequently accused Barnum of having sacrificed scholarship and quality for the sake of sensationalism. For instance, Henry Tappan, who later became president of the University of Michigan, complained after an 1851 visit that the American Museum was a place "for the exhibition of monsters, and for vulgar dramatic performances—a mere place of popular amusement."[66] Among later scholars, Charles Coleman Sellers was not usual in concluding that Barnum prospered due to "the sheer weight of gaudy and tawdry fantastics."[67] For years, the American Museum, and the old Peale museums in Baltimore, Philadelphia, and New York, which Barnum had purchased, were simply dismissed as sideshows having no redeeming value.

Recently, however, scholars have begun to question the validity of this uniformly negative interpretation. These "revisionists" do not deny that Barnum offered the public a steady stream of hokum, but they also acknowledge his accomplishments. According to John Rickards Betts, a pioneer of this dissenting viewpoint, Barnum "did more than any other one person to popularize the museum idea."[68] Neil Harris agreed that "as the collection grew, Barnum emphasized its comprehensiveness and scientific value."[69] Edward Alexander approved of the museum's "serious collections of shells, fish, animals, minerals, and geological specimens."[70]

These scholars all recognize that Barnum's motives were complex and many faceted, and not explicable by means of a simplistic interpretation.

Barnum's critics were blind to his innovations and accomplishments in the museum world because, ironically, they had been humbugged by the great showman. His 1855 autobiography had been conceived and written as a publicity tool, in which he gloatingly told the public how he had defrauded them: how he had passed off an old black slave as the nurse of George Washington, how he had continued a "wooly horse" for the credulous, how he had contrived a "mermaid" that actually consisted of a monkey's head attached to a fish's body. The book was meant to promote public interest in Barnum's future exploits, and it succeeded so completely that it "confirmed his claim to the title 'Prince of Humbugs.'"[71] By the time Barnum came out with a revised second edition in 1869, entitled *Struggles and Triumphs*, he had become so successful that he no longer had need of extravagant promotions, and he toned down mentions of his humbugs considerably. By then, however, the damage had been done. "Those who have written about Barnum have all been indebted to the autobiography, and a number of these authors have consulted little else."[72] Hence was born the interpretation of Barnum as a brash and shameless huckster with no ideals and no interest in anything except the art of money-getting.

There is enough truth in this view to explain the persistence with which it is held. Barnum *was* a hustler who occasionally defrauded his customers with exaggerated or outright false claims. He was also, however, a man with strong moral convictions who passionately fought for women's rights, the Union side during the Civil War, and the cause of antimonopoly afterwards. Another long-held conviction was temperance. In a letter to his friend and confidant, Moses Kimball of the Boston Museum, Barnum explained, "I am going the Teetotal & Sons Temperance *strong* & believe it the most glorious cause on earth."[73] Barnum was, in fact, during his entire life, a curious mixture of cynicism and idealism, amorality and moralism.

To complicate the picture, there were two different Barnums.

Throughout his career, he was a man on the make, but as time passed and he grew more successful and respectable, he became more conservative. He was always a hustler with certain moral convictions, but in his early days he was too consumed by the profit motive to be scrupulous. This impulse was paramount in his career until mid-century, and then gradually faded away during the 1850s, until it more or less disappeared during the 1860s. Slowly rising to replace it "from around 1850 on, was the more solid, respectable image he wished to project to his fellow citizens."[74] He was still enough of a huckster to promote himself as the "Prince of Humbugs" in his 1855 autobiography, but this became rarer as time went on. Barnum matured as he grew wealthy; he longed for respect commensurate with his success and fretted about his place in history. It is, ironically, the earlier Barnum, and only his worst features at that, that most people remember today. The contempt for the showman has extended to his museums. It seems only logical that the "Prince of Humbugs" should have run a gaudy sideshow. To be sure, there were elements of the sideshow in every Barnum museum, but there was also much to applaud and admire. Like the man, the museums required revision.

During the decade from 1840 to 1850, Barnum transformed the anemic museum of the Scudder family into the foremost place of entertainment in America. He did it by dint of audacity, hard work, a flair for promotion, and an eye for quality. The audacity was necessary at the beginning, for when the museum was put up for sale in 1841, he had virtually no capital with which to buy it. A company of speculators which had earlier purchased Peale's New York Museum had gained an option on the American Museum as well, with the plan of selling stock in both, realizing large profits, then withdrawing to let the investors hold the bag. Barnum exposed their scheme in the papers. The investors, hoping that the resulting furor would blow over, allowed their deadline to pass without excercising their option. Barnum then convinced the agent for the Scudder heirs to sell him the museum for $12,000. Adding insult to injury, Barnum, by the beginning of 1843, ran the Peale museum out of business and purchased it for himself.

In 1841, however, that triumph was by no means certain. The American Museum had been in decline for more than a decade, and it was extremely threadbare by 1841. Barnum inherited several dilapidated exhibits and a series of entertainments of dubious value. The showman began spending a series of eighteen-hour days at his museum, seeking some method to draw crowds. And draw crowds he must, for having no capital, he had to make his payments from his proceeds.

Barnum successfully attracted patrons by means of a three-pronged program of action. The triad consisted of didactic theater, spectacular entertainments, and awe-inspiring exhibits. The first was the easiest to achieve. New York was a city of boarders, for few owned their own homes. These lodgers were always in need of diversions for their idle hours, and they had their choice of activities both respectable and not. Lectures led the list of respectable entertainments, but theaters were still considered beyond the pale. The general view of the clergy was that theaters were places which offered lewd plays, with ruffians waiting within and prostitutes without. "Museum lecture rooms, on the other hand, were not theaters but could do what theaters did: mount dramatic entertainments or present variety acts under the guise of education and public enlightenment."[75] Using this extremely transparent fiction, Barnum began presenting melodramas and farces in the museum's "lecture room." He carefully walked the fine line of respectability, giving just enough titillation to assure high attendance, but always delivering moralistic messages and good triumphing over evil. By 1850, the temperance play *The Drunkard,* which displayed the depravities of addiction and the joys of redemption, became the first play in New York to chalk up one hundred uninterrupted performances, and all were on the stage of the American Museum.[76]

Sharing the stage with legitimate theatricals were spectacular and often fraudulent entertainments. There was, for instance, "the great model of Niagara Falls with real water!" which Barnum advertised so effectively that the Board of Croton Water Commissioners feared he would dry up the city's water supply. This was highly unlikely, for the model was eighteen inches tall and used only a barrel of water per season.[77] Barnum and Moses Kimball in Boston shared the spectacular freaks each exhibited, and in their private correspondence made no pretense that most of their entertainments had any redeeming value. For instance, on January 30, 1843, Barnum wrote Kimball, "I *must* have the fat boy or the other monster [or] something new *in the course of this week.*"[78] A steady stream of midgets, bearded ladies, and the like drew visitors to the museum in droves. Barnum's greatest fraud, however, was the previously mentioned "Feejee Mermaid." In 1842 Moses Kimball purchased the "mermaid" from a sailor, and Barnum promptly leased it from his friend, offering to share the profits of exhibiting it. The great showman revealed his new exhibit to a naturalist, who pronounced it a fraud. Undeterred, Barnum prepared a media blitz of epic proportions. The mermaid immediately tripled his patronage. Eventually it was denounced as a fake by leading naturalists, but to their befuddlement, this only made Barnum's turnstiles busier, for people returned to see how they had been duped. In *Struggles and Triumphs*, Barnum claimed to have believed in the authenticity of the mermaid himself. But in a letter to Moses Kimball, Barnum revealed his true feelings on the subject: "That spouting on the *Feejee Mermaid* is rich. *I* get all the curses for humbugging the public with that critter. How *bad* I feel about it!"[79]

Barnum's third course of action, the gathering of awe-inspiring exhibits, was largely overshadowed by the theatricals and the frauds. In the 1840s, despite the cultural imperative toward professional science, Barnum made no pretense of collecting for the sake of science or even for the sake of education. He collected in order to amaze his visitors. Still, in some fields, and particularly in natural history, Barnum's gathering resulted in a collection, if not suitable for the advance of science, at least valuable for popular education. Barnum himself felt that the collection was of serious value, for he wrote, "My permanent collection of curiosities is, without doubt, abundantly worth the uniform charge of admission to all the entertainments of the establishment, and I can therefore afford to be accused of 'humbug' when I add such transient novelties as increase its attractions."[80]

This was Barnum's intellectual rationale for the turgid plays and outright frauds he offered; they only served to attract people to visit the valuable and instructive collections he exhibited. "Humbug" thus served the cause of science and education!

The reality of the 1840s at the American Museum, however, was not humbug serving science and education. Barnum grasped the cultural imperatives and quickly exploited them; humbug was served by popular education and professional science. In 1840, despite the upsurge in professional science, there was still a strong undercurrent of belief in popular education. More specifically, there was a strong feeling that each person was a sovereign individual, who need not accept the word of the expert as final. Each person in this democratic country had the right and the obligation to examine the evidence and decide for himself on any question, great or small. This feeling was extremely vulnerable to exploitation, and Barnum did not miss his opportunity. As Neil Harris points out, Barnum appealed to the vanities and conceits of the creed of the sovereign individual, glorifying doubt and celebrating individual judgment.[81] The prime example of this exploitation was the celebrated "What Is It?" Barnum took a trip to Europe in 1846 to exhibit Tom Thumb, who was long his most lucrative attraction. While there, Barnum displayed a dwarf named Harvey Leach as a "missing link" in a show at London's Egyptian Hall. As Barnum wrote to Kimball: "I half fear that it will not only be exposed, but that *I* should be *found out* in the matter, however, I go it, live or die. The thing is not to be called *anything* by the exhibitor. We know not & therefore do not assert whether it is human or animal. We leave that all to the sagacious public to decide."[82]

The "sagacious public" was all too eager to decide such questions, and Barnum soon discovered he could not lose. If he hoaxed the public, so much the better; if the hoax was exposed, the skeptics would congratulate themselves on their sharpness and the gullible would return to discover how they had been duped.

Professional science, too, was placed into the service of humbug. Barnum delighted in printing fabricated testimonials from imaginary professors "authenticating" a curiosity, then, when such a promotion had run its course, distributing another bogus letter from a different "scientist" denouncing the thing as fraud. He would then be able to call upon the people to settle the dispute between "experts."

The evidence is thus absolutely overwhelming that during the 1840s Barnum duped the masses in order to build a palace of popular entertainment. It does not follow from this fact, however, that the museum was utterly worthless. Barnum knew the cultural imperatives too well to offer a simple *omnium gatherum* of trash. In public statements he spoke of his desire to "combine sufficient *amusement* with instruction, to please all proper tastes."[83] In both amusement and instruction, he sought quality. In a letter to Moses Kimball, he dreamed of building "a five thousand person Lecture Room overhead. *That* would hold such an audience that we could *afford* to put in a show of some merit."[84] He also sought veracity in the presentation of his exhibits. Barnum always had a qualified naturalist in his employ, and when he purchased the Philadelphia Museum from the Peale family in 1849, he implored Moses Kimball, "Do you know a good *naturalist* or two you could send me to help Guilledeau get the thing ready to open here? Also, do you know a man of *taste* who understands the arrangement of cases & C. and who can superintend the fitting up of this whole concern?"[85] Barnum's museums clearly were not merely a tasteless presentation of worthless items.

For those who were willing to ignore the frauds and concentrate on the collection, Barnum's museums had much to offer. The German amateur naturalist Dr. Albert C. Koch had this to say about a visit to the American Museum in July of 1844: "I visited the local American Museum, a fairly good collection of natural history objects. . . . I made the discovery that we in America have, besides the hitherto-known mammoth . . . still another species of the primeval elephant, unknown until now."[86]

If in 1844 Dr. Koch could recognize the merits of the American Museum, it may seem strange that recent scholars have failed to do the same. In fact, however, it was much easier for a contemporary to fairly judge the museum than for later viewers. In 1844 the autobiography, many of the humbugs, and the circus, the things that have distorted history's view of Barnum, were still in the future. Neither did Koch allow the freaks and frauds Barnum exhibited to blind him to the many valuable specimens there to be seen.

By the end of the 1840s, Barnum's outlook had undergone an important change. His tours with Tom Thumb, in which he had rubbed shoulders with royalty, made him long for respectability. By 1850 the museum had made him a wealthy man, so he no longer had as much need of humbug. In that year he ratified his evolution toward high-quality entertainment by managing the singing tour of the "Swedish Nightingale," Jenny Lind. He was poised for the responsiveness of the 1850s.

P. T. Barnum rejected the Age of Professionalism as did the New-York Historical Society. Unlike the society, however, which did so for reasons of elitism, Barnum rejected it to build a giant museum for the masses. The excesses he committed to reach prosperity were many and spectacular, but they should not be allowed to obscure the solid exhibits and occasional high-quality theatricals he presented. The American Museum, gaudy though it was, was also an instrument of some scientific and educational value by 1850.

6 The American Compromise, 1850–1870: The Synthesis of Popular Education and Professionalism

> In the United States . . . the 1850s witnessed a
> subsidence of the radical hopes and reactionary
> fears of the early nineteenth century, and the
> formation of a more stable, more disciplined,
> less adventurous culture.[1]

During the 1850s and 1860s, the earlier enthusiasms for popular education and the later movement for professionalization achieved a balance in the American museum world. This balance, which may be labeled "the American Compromise," has proved dynamic, with swings in both directions, but has also proved stable enough to last down to the present. The synthesis of popular education and professionalism came about during this era for a complex series of reasons. Among them were a general retreat of the professions before the egalitarianism of American life, the scientists' fear of alienating religious opinion, the increased emphasis on the importance of popular education as a result of the "free labor" ideology, the desire to preserve the American past, the popularization of the museum idea stemming from the international expositions of the era, and the effects of the Civil War in mobilizing public opinion. All these factors tended to reduce the ardor for professionalism of the 1840s and revive the enthusiasm for popular education.

The period from about 1839 to 1849 had well served the budding professions in general and the sciences in particular. The lingering hard times precipitated by the panic of 1837 had dampened the "egalitarian celebration of the self-made man" that had been so pervasive during the 1820s and 1830s.[2] Prosperity was finally returning by the late 1840s, and with it came a resurgence of egalitarianism, with its corollary antimonopoly and antiprofessional sentiments. The evolving professions had long run counter to these currents, but by 1850 they began to pull back. One perceptive student of professionalism in America noted that during the 1840s, practitioners sought ever greater professionalization. Then, "about 1850, the professions suddenly appear headed in the opposite direction, recoiling before the great Jacksonian attacks on aristocracy and privilege, falling in with the democratic trend toward conformity. . . . the learned professions were retreating toward mediocrity."[3] In a democratic, relatively egalitarian society, the professionals could not afford to be labeled monopolists or aristocrats; hence they arrested their own progress for the time being.

The sciences were in the forefront of this general tactical withdrawal among the professions. They were in an especially delicate position, for many of their findings were coming into conflict with the teachings of religion. It would have been bad enough if scientists were to lose public support as a result of being perceived as monopolists; it would have been disastrous if they were considered to be godless or anti-Christian as well. As George Daniels pointed out, "Therefore it was necessary that the very appearance of conflict be avoided; and the burden of avoiding it was on the new professionals."[4] Most scientists, therefore, quite simply slowed the pace of their professionalization, and attempted, whenever possible, to emphasize how their results confirmed the wisdom of God's plan. Daniels added, "Scientists continued to justify their work . . . in the dangerous terms of religious value, until late in the nineteenth century. From this position of security, they were later able to rid themselves, almost, from external controls and push their claims of autonomy."[5] So the fever for professional science was prudently cooled by its own practitioners, to avoid both charges of monopoly and appearances of godless tendencies.

The retreat of the professionals left a void that others were eager to fill. Antislavery forces, which were beginning to coalesce in the early 1850s, shared the ideology of free labor, which held that in America there was a great race of life, in which any individual could rise from the humblest station to the highest by dint of hard work. In this open competition, any advantage that could make a man a better competitor would be a great boon. And what greater advantage could there be than a good education? Increasingly during the 1850s, the need for popular education was emphasized by the men who formed the Republican party.[6]

This ideological boost for education was fortuitously coupled with a popular interest in American history during this period. The deaths of the last of the revolutionary-era heroes during the previous decade, such as John Quincy Adams in 1848 and Albert Gallatin in 1849, made Americans conscious that their past was slipping away from them, and inspired efforts to preserve it. John Higham neatly summed up the feeling and the response:

> A disturbing sense of remoteness from the heroic age of the Revolution infiltrated American minds in the middle of the 19th century. To counteract the malaise and rebuild continuity with the past, a movement got underway for preserving and creating historic landmarks. In 1848 the cornerstone of the Washington National Monument was laid, and two years later New York State acquired the Hasbrouck House in Newburgh because of its Washington associations. In the mid-50s, the Mount Vernon Ladies Association rescued Washington's home from neglect, while Philadelphians began the restoration of Independence Hall.[7]

The preservation movement spawned museums all across the country, and the need to preserve and transmit the American heritage to the rising generation gave another boost to the resurgence of popular education in museums. The most famous of these preservation efforts, the struggle to save Mount Vernon, was a classical case of popular involvement in museum-making. Ann Pamela Cunningham, a thirty-seven-year-old invalid from South Carolina, in 1853 took on the task of saving the dilapidated home of George Washington. Miss Cunningham set up a nationwide organization called the Mount Vernon Ladies Association. Headed by a vice regent in every state, the association reached out to the people in its fund drive. Soldiers, fraternal organizations, fire companies, private and public schools, and even newsboys were among those the association tapped for funds. This grass-roots organization managed to raise the purchase price of $200,000 and part of the endowment goal of $150,000. By participating in the fund drive, the public became attached to the institution in a way they never had to proprietary or academy-owned museums. In return, the historic preservation movement tended to stress popular education rather than professionalism in its operations, and brought the museum experience to smaller towns, like Newburgh, throughout the republic.[8]

Another influence diffusing the museum idea in the fifties was the vogue for international expositions, which started with the Great Exposition of the Industry of All Nations in London in 1851. The "Crystal Palace," as it was popularly known, brought together the arts, manufactures, and curiosities of countries from all over the world, and was a smashing success. By 1853, an American imitation had opened in New York, which copied its English predecessor both in its name and in its architecture. The affair was so poorly managed, however, that not even P. T. Barnum, who eventually was called in to save the exposition, could coax a profit from it. Nonetheless, the New York Crystal Palace Exposition did attract the patronage of many who had never entered a museum, and thus popularized the museum idea.[9]

By the late 1850s, the ideal of the museum as an institution that both educated the public and aided the scholar was coming into sharper focus. Peter Cooper, an inventor who had made a fortune in the railroad and telegraph industries, quite thoroughly understood this balance when he was planning his Cooper Union, which opened in New York in 1859. Cooper envisioned his union as a school of the widest possible scope. Here both men and women, both rich and poor, both young and old, would be able to find instruction in a wide variety of subjects. Although the union was primarily aimed at the working man, Cooper took pains to point out that it was a school for everyone.

Peter Cooper had been profoundly influenced throughout his life by the American Museum in New York. He had first visited it before 1810, when Edward Savage was the proprietor. Cooper became a good friend of John Scudder, and continued to patronize the museum after Scudder died in 1821. P. T. Barnum's purchase of the American Museum in 1841 made no difference to Cooper, for he was still a loyal patron in 1859. He was fascinated by virtually everything he saw at the American Museum, but he was particularly enchanted by the mechanical devices and the cosmorama, an exhibition of pictures viewed through peepholes to allow for special effects of perspective and lighting. He was determined to include many of these elements in his union.[10]

Cooper's final plan resembled the American Museum writ large. The basement of the building was to be occupied by a cavernous lecture room. The first and second floors were to be taken up by laboratories and classrooms. The third floor would hold a reading room, art gallery, and scientific collections; the fourth would be a museum and cosmorama. Science could be promoted by the use of the labs and the scientific collection, popular education effected through the classes, museum, and reading room. Cooper was especially interested in the educational possibilities of the museum, for which he bought a stuffed white whale as a central exhibit. His plans included a series of dioramas arranged so that it would illustrate, a step at a time, the building of a ship or the development of a human.

Cooper's plans, unfortunately, were never realized. The art gallery existed for but a few years, and the museum and cosmorama were never established at all. The laboratories proved useful for popular demonstrations, but not for professional work. By 1869, Cooper's chief assistant would admit that the union "makes no pretense to be an institution for any but the working classes, hence it has no reputation and deserves none as a school of science."[11] Peter Cooper, in trying to combine a laboratory, a school, a gallery, a museum, and a library under one roof, had simply been too ambitious. Yet the fact that he tried to make an institution for both scholars and the public reveals the extent to which the American Compromise had been accepted by 1859.

Cooper's efforts were echoed to the north at Harvard's Museum of Comparative Zoology. The guiding genius behind this institution, which was established in 1859 and dedicated during the next year, was the great Louis Agassiz. Born in Switzerland, educated at the University of Zurich, at Heidelberg, and at the University of Munich, he worked closely with such giants of European science as the naturalists Baron Georges Cuvier and Alexander von Humboldt. He was only twenty-five in 1832 when he became a professor and museum director at the College of Neuchatel in Switzerland. For the next fourteen years he accomplished prodigious feats of scholarship in natural history, with special concentration on fossil fishes and glaciation. His work brought him to the attention of the scientific world far beyond his small Swiss town. Benjamin Silliman corresponded with Agassiz as early as 1835, and the Swiss was elected as a corresponding member of the Academy of Natural Sciences in 1837.[12] In 1846 Agassiz journeyed to America, ostensibly only for two years, on a grant from the King of Prussia to collect American specimens of natural history.

Agassiz quickly took the American world of science by storm. In order to keep him, Harvard established a "School of Instruction in Theoretical and Practical Science," and placed the Swiss scientist at its head. Besides his Harvard professorship, Agassiz was a star attraction on the lyceum circuit and, as mentioned earlier, was the inspiration for the revival of the Charleston Museum. As early as 1848 he began planning for a geological museum to be located at Harvard, but other projects interfered. Throughout the 1850s, however, Agassiz collected such a vast aggregation of natural history specimens that it became inevitable that a museum would have to be built someday.

At last, early in 1859, a public subscription was mounted to build the "Agassiz Museum." Agassiz skillfully manipulated the heartfelt American patriotism by issuing such statements as, "my great object is to have a museum founded here which will equal the great museums of the Old World."[13] The Museum of Comparative Zoology, as it was officially known, was clearly meant to teach and conduct research in science, for it was to have a faculty of eight professors and fifteen resident student-scholars conducting research.[14] At the same time, however, it was designed to be a popular educator to a large extent, for there were to be public visits, exhibitions, and in a pioneering outreach effort, classes specifically designed for public school teachers.[15]

The Museum of Comparative Zoology would, in later years, develop more as a science museum and less as a popular educator. This does not detract, however, from the beginning ideals of Louis Agassiz, who though he was not born in America, certainly aimed to create a museum that fit the pattern of the American Compromise.

The Civil War and its aftermath placed the final touches on the American Compromise. Like every other resource, museums had to be pressed into service for the war effort. It would never do to have institutions that could reach so many people obsessed with esoteric research; instead they must exhort and otherwise serve the cause. The war effort, taking inspiration from the international expositions, also spawned a final museum popularizer: the sanitary fair. The United States Sanitary Commission, which had been established in June of 1861 to provide for the health and comfort of Union soldiers, held a series of exhibitions in 1863 and 1864 to raise money for their cause. These sanitary fairs were held in cities as large as New York and Philadelphia, and as small as Kalamazoo, Michigan. They combined features of revivals, lyceums, estate sales, and museums, with many of the wealthy in the communities giving prized possessions for sale, which were exhibited and then auctioned. The sanitary fairs directly affected thousands who might otherwise never have considered visiting a museum.

So the Civil War, with its emphasis on exhortation and its sanitary fairs, promoted popular education in museums. It also, however, boosted professionalism. The young veterans released at the war's end had tasted the strong discipline and systematic organization of military life, and many transferred this discipline to their civilian careers. "Driven by a growing faith in science and the war-born desire to be 'useful citizens,' they hastened to offer themselves as candidates for the scientific elite."[16] The war, in its ultimate effects, promoted the balance between popular education and professionalism.

The resurgence of popular education during the period from

1850 to 1870 led to a synthesis between it and professionalism in museums. The American Compromise has been dynamic, swinging toward professionalism during the Victorian era, and surging toward popular education during the 1960s, but the compromise has proved an enduring reality for American museums. Thus it was during this period that the distinctive form of the modern American museum, as an institution that simultaneously promotes professional studies while conducting popular education, was fully determined.

Responding to the Public: The Academy of Natural Sciences, the Wadsworth Atheneum, and the Smithsonian Institution

I find educational matters more eagerly discussed than ever. . . . the people will do without Latin and Greek, but will have science and modern literature. . . . At New York and Philadelphia I heard precisely the same declaration. It is evidently a crisis.[17]

Perhaps Sir Charles Lyell was exaggerating when he spoke of an educational crisis in the United States in 1853. He was certainly correct, however, in noting the revival of a cultural emphasis on popular education. This revival did not escape the attention of the Academy of Natural Sciences, the Wadsworth Atheneum, and the Smithsonian Institution. All three responded to the cultural needs, slowly giving way from their mainly professional stances of the 1840s, making more and more allowances for popular education.

The Academy of Natural Sciences

The 1850s and 1860s were boom years for the Academy of Natural Sciences in terms of collection growth, but not in terms of prosperity. Both the library and museum collections were expanding by leaps and bounds, but the balance sheet of the academy was always precarious. In fact, the growth of the collections contributed to the poverty of the institution. The irascible old George

Ord, by now the president of the academy, explicitly noted that connection in a letter to Titian Peale, saying, "After your long experience of the expense of maintaining a Museum, I feel assured that you can form a just opinion of the situation of the Academy. . . . God grant that this noble institution may not be crushed beneath the weight of its own riches!"[18]

The growing collections required increasingly larger buildings to house them, and the academy's members knew that they would have to make public appeals for funds for every building project. Therefore, they could not afford to alienate the people of Philadelphia. Around the year 1850, the academy's membership, mindful of this fact, began to cut back on their strictly professional activities while simultaneously taking measures to make their museum more accessible to the public. This is not to say that the academy abandoned professionalism altogether. As Patsy Gerstner has noted, "In the years after 1850 the move toward professionalism continued, but the Academy as a professional society was to some extent eclipsed . . . by its renewed interest in pursuing a public role in the Philadelphia community through its Museum."[19] She went on to speculate, "The tendency after 1850 to emphasize the Museum at the Academy suggests that the Museum may have been looked upon as the road to long-term survival and security."[20] Gerstner's insight is valid. The change in the cultural climate, resulting in a new demand for popular education, led to a decided change in attitude at the academy. If the people must be courted, the most effective way to do it was by offering the free education they craved, at least to the best of the academy's ability to do so.

The members moved quickly to make the museum the centerpiece of the academy. Within the space of less than three months in 1851, they substantially relaxed the entrance requirements for the museum. They extended to widows and families of deceased members the right to issue tickets for the museum; they allowed medical students to visit at all times; and donors to the museum could visit freely for six months.[21] The members were always eager to garner free publicity for the museum from the Philadelphia press. When the Philadelphia *Inquirer* lamented the sale of the last of the artifacts from Peale's museum in 1854 and called for a new museum to be built in Philadelphia to provide entertainment for the populace, academy member William S. Vaux was quick to respond.[22] In a letter to William S. W. Ruschenberger, a leading member of the academy who later became its president, Vaux suggested immediate action: "The enclosed I cut from the *Inquirer* of Saturday—how would it do to make some reply, to bring the Academy a little more into notice! of course, we are not a museum as in the communication intended, but still some capital might be made of it."[23]

The academy's efforts to be accessible and useful to the public bore fruit, for Philadelphians responded favorably to the academy's many requests for funds during this era. Indeed, their problem was not public indifference to the museum, but rather too much interest in it. Although formal records of attendance were not kept until 1866, there is evidence that the public was eager to get in. In 1855, a new set of regulations was issued to address the problems of overcrowding in the museum. These regulations banned children under the age of twelve at the museum unless accompanied by an adult, and limited school tours to groups of no more than ten at one time, always accompanied by a teacher. The third rule was italicized for emphasis and read, "On other days of the week [other than the normal 'open' days, Tuesdays and Fridays] visitors will not be admitted, unless accompanied by a member."[24] The explanation offered for this rule was that too frequent visitation damaged the collection and disturbed the study of members. This negative evidence suggests that the academy's museum was a popular and indeed sought-after place of resort in Philadelphia by 1854. It is tempting to speculate that the instigation for allowing school tours may have come from academy member Titian Peale, but this cannot be proved.

The success of the academy's efforts to be accessible raised a divisive issue. If the academy were not accommodating enough, they could lose public support. If the members were too accommodating, they could become so inundated by visitors as to bankrupt their treasury. In 1859, the conflict flared up briefly when a resolution was offered to open the museum more frequently, and to extend to nonmembers the right of issuing tickets of admission. Both suggestions were defeated by the opposition of Joseph Leidy, the museum's curator.[25] This was consistent with Leidy's general pattern of opposition to liberalized admission policies for the museum.

Not even Leidy, however, dared return to the days of nearly pure professionalism that the academy had known during the 1840s, especially after the advent of the Civil War in 1861. With the nation gripped in a struggle for its very existence, a struggle whose success depended on public support for the war effort, it would have been unpatriotic to close off the museum from both the battle-weary soldiers and a war-weary populace. The academy got up, for the first time, a booklet to serve as a guide to the collection, and published it in 1862. The booklet reveals that the academy was attempting to make its exhibits as intelligible as possible to the average visitor, for:

> the labels attached to the specimens are bordered with various colors. They designate the portions of the globe from which they were obtained, and as far as practicable follow the color of the inhabitants. Thus—
> Red . . . . American
> Brown . . . Europe
> Black . . . Africa
> Yellow . . . Asia
> Green . . . Polynesia

The handbook also advised the public that the museum was an educational tool for their benefit: "It should be remembered that *no pecuniary profit* accrues from the labor and pains bestowed in arranging and labeling the many thousands of objects which have been brought together here for the sole purpose of diffusing knowledge among our fellow citizens."[26] Nor did the members consider it enough merely to extend the accessibility of the museum during wartime. On special occasions, such as the Philadelphia Sanitary Fair, the academy hastened to open the museum to the general public, and several schools and conventions were invited to visit gratuitously.[27] The academy members were swimming with the tide of the educational revival.

The academy's success posed a series of new problems. By 1865 Joseph Leidy declared that owing to the increase of both the collection and visitors to it, it was no longer possible for "volunteers or amateur curators, or members to give that degree of attention, which is required for the preservation of destructible collections."[28] From that point forward, the academy began to pay its curatorial staff. By 1866, the attempt to extend the open hours of the museum, which Leidy had squelched in 1859, was revived and accepted in a limited form, as an experiment. From April through June of 1866, the museum was to be open weekdays from 1:00 P.M. until sunset, the changed hours were to be announced in at least three daily newspapers, and an as-

Benjamin Waterhouse Hawkins and the reconstructed skeleton of *Hadrosaurus foulki*. After the dinosaur had been identified by Joseph Leidy, Hawkins reconstructed the skeleton in a bipedal stance for exhibit in 1868 at the Academy of Natural Sciences, where it was a popular attraction. After later studies revealed that *H. foulki* was a quadruped, the skeleton's stance was altered. (Courtesy of The Academy of Natural Sciences)

sistant doorkeeper would be hired to handle the increased visitation.[29] The result was extremely gratifying, for the curators were able to report in mid-June, "The number of visitors during April [w]as 4090, during May 5056, and that the average number per day during April, May and June [was] 220."[30] The large number of visitors was at least partly attributable to the fact that later hours allowed working people to visit. The museum obviously was filling a need as an educational institution in Philadelphia.

Increasing the hours of opening was also a strategic move to build support for the academy in the Philadelphia community. The academy's building was far too small for their needs; they were searching for a new home, and needed to launch another public fund drive to finance it. Another reason for the academy's desire to move sprang from the facade of their old home, which scandalized contemporary tastes in architecture. An editorial writer for the Philadelphia *American and Gazette*, for instance, could hardly restrain himself as he referred to the academy's building as "hideous in aspect," completely "repulsive to good taste," without doubt "a positive disgrace to both the institution and the city," and as a "miracle of ugliness."[31]

The academy needed to launch a fund drive, that is, unless the contemplated "Penn Squares" project came to pass. This scheme was the brainchild of an informal consortium of Philadelphia cultural institutions: the American Philosophical Society, the Library Company of Philadelphia, the Franklin Institute, the Academy of Fine Arts, and the Academy of Natural Sciences. Early in 1867, these institutions asked the city of Philadelphia to appropriate for their use the vacant squares at the intersection of Broad and Market streets, which had been reserved for the erection of public buildings. Their proposal envisioned a series of buildings, put up at pubic expense, which would consolidate all of the city's cultural organizations in that one area of town. The academy immediately went on record as supporting the Penn Squares idea, and with a wetted finger to the cultural wind, accorded popular education a place of equality with professional science as their raison d'être:

The established policy of the Academy of Natural Sciences of Philadelphia is to employ all its means to facilitate scientific investigations by its members and others, and at the same time contribute to the diffusion of acquired knowledge freely among the people. With this view it has opened its Museum gratuitously to the public, two days of the week, since the year 1828, and when it shall be arranged in a new hall it is not improbable that the number of days will be increased. During the year 1866, 34,500 persons visited the Museum, and since the commencement of the present year about 4,500 visitors have been admitted every month.[32]

This is a perfect summation of the synthesis between professional science and popular education that would characterize the American museum world by 1870. The academy's museum was now more than a locus of scientific investigation; it was also the dispenser of education to the people. The academy was anxious to make the point that the museum was effective as an educator in fact as well as in theory, and attendance figures proved that it was a truly popular center of education. Due to the academy's past reputation as a research center, however, the members thought it best to underscore their devotion to education: "The Institution is conducted with a view to popular usefulness in extending, so far as its means will permit, knowledge of the natural sciences to all, and for this reason it may be classed among the free educational establishments of this city."[33]

The press and the public generally agreed with this assessment and supported the Penn Squares Project. The Philadelphia *American and Gazette* lamented that Peale's museum, once "the greatest of its kind in the republic," was no more, and called for such replacement "as shall blend the useful with the curious, the scientific with the ornate, and give at once employment for the attention and interest of all classes."[34] The *Sunday Dispatch* echoed in applauding "the rational recreation it will afford to the thousands," but the main reason for their support was that such a museum would "be the means of creating and fostering, among the most ignorant people in the community, a desire to learn."[35] Although the press often emphasized education more than research, they mainly understood the nature of the synthesis. One editorial page author grasped this duality clearly when he wrote: "Since the year 1828 the Academy has opened it [their museum] to the public, without charge, two days of the week; and through this liberality alone, it has founded a claim to the kindly consideration by the City Government whenever it may be deemed expedient to assist institutions whose exclusive aim it is to acquire knowledge and diffuse it freely to all who are willing to accept it."[36]

The Penn Squares project never came to pass, and the academy was forced to fund a new building by their independent efforts. The attempt to establish the Penn Squares idea, however, was significant for the light it shed on the change in the academy's attitude toward popular education. In 1847, just two decades before, most members of the academy had conceived of it as an institution for the advancement of science, and only in a very secondary sense as a place of public education. By 1867, the majority of members saw the academy in a very different light. Certainly the pursuit of scientific knowledge was still the primary goal, but it no longer eclipsed every other consideration. The democratic forces demanding popular education had persuaded the academy, in order to stay in the good graces of the public, to elevate popular education to nearly a level of parity with original research. The academy, for its part, attempted to prosecute both agendas simultaneously, and to a considerable extent they succeeded, as evidenced by the favorable editorials in the popular press.

Thus, by 1870, the Academy of Natural Sciences had embraced the American Compromise. They realized that the mission of a museum in a democratic land was to sponsor original research, and to educate the public regarding the current state of knowledge. They had too high a purpose to merely amuse the public; but on the other hand they realized that the public would never support an institution that did not directly benefit them. The American Compromise allowed for a single institution to both facilitate research and foster education, to avoid triviality on the one hand and elitism on the other. Thus, by 1870, the academy had finally fulfilled the vision of William Maclure: the scientific institution as popular educator.

The Wadsworth Atheneum

In our country, the term "Public Institution" ought to stand for something broader, freer and more expansive than the same expression used in any other land. Here, if anywhere, founders of institutions for the promotion of learning and the arts may be expected to cherish the most enlarged views, and to make endowments for the benefit of posterity from a sense of duty to their kind, and to fulfill a great mission for the diffusion of light and knowledge among men. Any attempt to restrict the benefits of such institutions to the few, does injustice to the masses, and stands in the way of the accomplishments of the intentions of their founders.[37]

These words, written by a former employee of the Wadsworth Atheneum less than fifteen years after it had first opened its doors, caught its directors flat-footed. The atheneum had not kept pace with the times, for in the 1850s it was still espousing the ideal of professionalism and paying scant attention to popular education. The directors soon found, however, that any course of action placed them squarely on the horns of a dilemma; on the one hand, the public would not return to see the same old pictures, but on the other, the money to buy new works had to come largely from admission fees. Any attempt to raise the cost of entry, however, would only discourage further visitation. It was true that occasionally a subscription was mounted to secure an outstanding painting, but for the most part, as had been the case when the works from the American Academy of Fine Arts had been acquired, the proceeds from the door were used to repay the benefactors. The story of the atheneum from 1850 to 1870 is one of an uphill struggle against poverty to respond to the educational needs of the public.

The directors used novel means to maximize revenue from admissions. Beyond the standard charges of twenty-five cents per person, half-price for children under the age of fourteen, and an annual ticket for $1.00, the directors offered a family annual ticket for $2.50, and a special $4.00 family annual ticket which allowed entry for out-of-town friends.[38]

Apparently, however, the trustees were not blind to the rising cultural imperative for popular education, for by 1856 they offered reduced prices: regular admission was cut from twenty-five to fifteen cents, children's admission from twelve and one-half cents to ten cents, and the special family annual ticket from $4.00 to $3.50.[39] Given their dependence on gate receipts for their very survival, this was the most the trustees could do to accommodate the people. This gesture, however, was not enough to satisfy an idealistic former employee, who soon brought his grievances against the board into the public prints.

Edward Sheffield Bartholomew, a native of Colchester, Connecticut, had been the curator of the atheneum from 1845 to 1848. Two years later, he left for Italy, and settled in Rome with a colony of American sculptors whose most celebrated member was the former Western Museum employee, Hiram Powers. In only a few years, Bartholomew became recognized as a sculptor of great merit, and when he returned to Hartford for a visit in 1856, he was greeted as an American cultural hero.

It undoubtedly came as a tremendous shock to the atheneum's directors when Bartholomew handed them a bluntly critical letter, which detailed and decried their failures as public educators and offered a dramatic solution for the problems. Bartholomew wasted no time in making his point:

> Next in importance to the establishment of Galleries of Art for the culture and improvement of individual and public taste, is the placing of their management upon such a basis as may best subserve the purposes of their creation, and make them productive of the greatest good to the greatest number of people. Convinced that the course adopted by you in the management of the Wadsworth Gallery is the result of erroneous views and calculated to diminish its usefulnesss, I desire to submit to you some remarks on the subject and a proposition, the object of which is to increase the usefulness of the Gallery to the citizens

of Hartford and the State, and to make it more widely instru-
mental in creating and cultivating a taste for art.[40]

Bartholomew proceeded to define how the atheneum's usefulness had been diminished, and the deleterious effects of that dimi-
nution on society as a whole:

> What has been done to increase the intelligence of our people
> by free schools and libraries is well-known; and there is no rea-
> son why they should not be noted for their taste and refinement
> in matters of art as they are for general and sound intellectual
> attainments. . . . There is, it is true, a widespread ignorance
> of Art, but I maintain that the great, if not the only cause of
> the general deficiency on this point, is the want of pure and
> high standards, accessible to all. To hoard up and secrete works
> of art is an offense against humanity, selfish and reprehensible.[41]

Bartholomew left no doubt that he was penning a brief for
popular education by means of the museum. The people, in his
estimation, were perfectly capable of learning, if only they were
given the opportunity to learn. They were being stymied, however, by museums which kept their collections inaccessible to the
masses. An objection might have been raised that the paintings
of the atheneum were not "secreted," since they were available
to anyone who would pay a nominal fee of fifteen cents. But
Bartholomew had a ready answer: "That a person lacks the will
to *pay* for seeing works of art, is the very reason why he should
be induced to look at them, until, elevated by their study, he
becomes a patron,—that a gallery is small and has few attractions
is a valid reason for making it easily accessible, that its attractions
may be increased . . . by increasing the number of those interested
in its objects. By making a gallery free, we tempt the public to
visit it."[42]

Bartholomew evinced a boundless faith in the public's responsiveness to any sort of effort to educate them. If a museum would
welcome them and make an effort to teach them, the people
would respond by becoming patrons of the museum. But none
of this would be possible if access to the museum were not free.

Bartholomew offered an expansive request to the directors to re-move the admission charges:

> I desire to see the Wadsworth Gallery opened to the public, *free.* . . . Free for all classes, it will radiate an artistic and refined feeling among the people. . . . Let it invite the passer-by to while a pleasant instructive hour, in the contemplation of the gems of art, instead of suggesting undisturbed dust and grim solitude; an unappreciated treasure in the midst of an intelligent population. . . . That it may be made free and useful, without involving pecuniary loss, I ask to be allowed to pay into its treasury such an annual sum as shall be equivalent to its present current receipts, until a satisfactory trial has been made of the effect of opening it without restriction, to quiet and orderly visitors, and to students of art, with liberty to study and copy such pictures as they may wish to reproduce.[43]

The treasurer's report of 1857 no longer exists, so it is impossi-ble to determine the gallery's receipts for that year. The closest year for which records are extant, 1862, witnessed a total income of $423.45. If the 1857 gate receipts were of this level, Bartholo-mew's potential expenses were substantial. For this reason alone, Bartholomew's letter would have caused a stir in Hartford's cul-tural circles, but there were deeper reasons for concern, as well. Bartholomew was Hartford's greatest artist; his opinion on such matters carried much weight. As a former curator of the athe-neum, he knew whereof he spoke. The truly significant thing about this outburst was that Bartholomew, a professional artist, did not seek to limit the atheneum to serious students of art. True, he wanted to make the gallery available to budding artists, but he stressed again and again that it must be accessible to people with no artistic ambitions whatsoever. Beyond that, it must be attractive to them. The function of the art museum was not lim-ited, in Bartholomew's estimation, to preserving great art and serving as a drawing school for artists. The art museum must also serve as a great school for the masses, wherein they could absorb the "light and knowledge" that art had to offer. Bartholo-mew was thoroughly in step with the cultural imperative that required the museum to simultaneously function as a school for the populace and as a resource for the professional. Anything that hindered this noble goal, even a nominal admission fee, must go, hence the generous offer to replace lost receipts.

Such a blunt and forceful criticism might have given rise to an angry or impassioned response from the atheneum's trustees. Instead, they maintained an almost complete silence. The newspaper files of the day register no public response, nor do the sketchy surviving records reveal any internal reaction at atheneum meetings. Indeed, the only indirect public comment from an atheneum trustee was highly favorable toward Bartholomew. On November 18, 1857, "a few public-spirited citizens, acting impromptu, provided . . . a dinner in honor of E. S. Bartholomew, the sculptor, and F. E. Church the painter."[44] According to the Hartford *Evening Press*, about sixty people attended, one of whom was atheneum trustee Henry Barnard. Bartholomew's letter had been printed only eleven days before, and one might have expected a sharp rejoinder from Barnard. Instead, he offered warm praise for the sculptor and his ideas:

> Here, and on all occasions, I am the advocate of education of all branches, for all minds and tastes and all men. The germ is found in every soul. . . . I wish that the farmer and mechanic might have the same opportunities to study art as are afforded in the churches, and marketplaces, and highways of the old country. . . . We must have a broader culture in our public schools, a culture so general that artists will no longer be dependent on the contributions of a few rich men, but the whole people loving their work shall join freely in encouraging their creation.[45]

Given Barnard's background as a student of education, it cannot be surprising that he spoke in favor of public education.[46] But he could have done so without echoing Bartholomew's criticisms of the atheneum. By tacitly agreeing that American art was inaccessible, Barnard was in effect admitting that the atheneum had not done enough to attract the common people. Rather than refuting Bartholomew's criticisms, Barnard essentially admitted their truth.

The sparseness of the evidence makes it difficult to determine the reaction of the other atheneum trustees. Surely some must have bristled at Bartholomew's barbs, and some must have been tempted to accept his offer of financial support. The trustees, however, made no public reply, and did not accept his offer. Perhaps they felt that it would be too humiliating to accept Bartholomew's patronage. Some may have worried about the degree of power their former employee would gain by such an arrangement. In any case, Bartholomew's unprecedented offer came to nothing.

The trustees did make attempts to revitalize the institution and render it more educationally useful. At the annual meeting in 1858, it was voted "that Henry Barnard, J.B. Hosmer & Erastus Smith be a committee to inquire into and report the best method of adding to the members & increasing the resources of the Association."[47] This was a far cry from Bartholomew's plea to open the doors to all, but at least it was a step toward responsiveness.

Bartholomew himself indirectly played a role in another effort to make the museum more attractive to the general public. Less than a year after he was feted in Hartford, Bartholomew suddenly died, on May 1, 1858, in Naples. James G. Batterson, one of Hartford's first insurance executives and its earliest collector of European art, raised a subscription, bought the contents of Bartholomew's studio, and presented them to the atheneum. These sculptures were placed in the "Statuary Room," and the proceeds from their exhibition for the first month went to Bartholomew's widow.

Neither committees nor new sculpture brought in the desired patronage, however, and the atheneum's leaders at last experimented with a direct appeal to the public via advertising. The results were indifferent, however, for the total annual receipts of the institution rarely climbed above $500 during the decade of the 1860s.[48]

The trustees never truly transformed the Wadsworth Atheneum into a popular educator; Bartholomew's vision was never fulfilled. Yet, following the dictates of the times, they did succeed in converting the atheneum from a little-visited haven for the art student into a place accessible to a public eager to be educated.

By reducing the admission price, actively seeking more members, judiciously adding to the collection, and advertising for patrons, the trustees succeeded in putting elitism behind them. They were limited by their financial resources and by their own visions, and did not completely achieve the American Compromise as did the Academy of Natural Sciences. There can be little doubt, however, that they were groping toward the vision that Edward Bartholomew had so eloquently articulated, that of fulfilling "a great mission for the diffusion of light and knowledge among men."[49]

The Smithsonian Institution

My idea of a museum . . . is that it should be of special objects and not an *omnium gatherum* of the ods [*sic*] & ends of creation.[50]

By the year 1850, Joseph Henry had grudgingly accepted the notion of a museum at the Smithsonian, but he still wanted it kept small and thoroughly subordinate to the "active operations": original research and publication of its results. In other words, the purpose of the museum was the promotion of professional science, nothing more and nothing less. "The objects of the Smithsonian Institution are not educational," Henry had flatly declared in 1848, and he was still determined in 1850 above all else to promote professional science.[51] But three great convulsions shook the Smithsonian between 1850 and 1865, upheavals that fundamentally altered the institution and led Henry to accept the American Compromise as the basis for the future operation of the Smithsonian. These were the Henry-Jewett feud, the acceptance of the Patent Office collections in 1857, and the Civil War. By 1870, these three experiences had convinced Henry that popular education must take its place beside the promotion of professional science as a legitimate function of the Smithsonian's museum.

The feud between Henry and Jewett had divided the Smithsonian into two camps by the end of the 1840s. Henry firmly believed that James Smithson had intended the Smithsonian to be a small

Charles Coffin Jewett, the first (and only) assistant secretary of
the Smithsonian Institution in charge of the library (Courtesy of
Smithsonian Institution Archives, RU 95, Neg. #841)

organization that would use its funds to discover new scientific
truths and disseminate them. Any other function for the Smithsonian was superfluous and ultimately wasteful of its funds.
Charles Coffin Jewett held to a strict interpretation of the act
establishing the Smithsonian, which provided that one-half of its
income be reserved for a library, gallery of art, lectures, and a
museum. Jewett was determined to build a massive national li-

brary under the aegis of the Smithsonian. A third player in the drama was the new head of the museum, Spencer Baird. Baird looked upon Henry as a mentor, but he was strongly drawn to Jewett's position, for the young naturalist wished to build a comprehensive national museum at the Smithsonian. The two sides finally solidified into the "active operations" camp, led by Henry, and the "big collections" camp, led by Jewett, with Baird informally allied with the librarian.

The story of the struggle between these two camps has been told in detail elsewhere.[52] Due to its importance to Smithsonian history, however, a brief summary is in order. The smoldering feud between Henry and Jewett was fanned into flame late in 1852 when Henry, concerned about the costs of constructing the Smithsonian's "castle," decided to ask the board of regents to repudiate the provision of the Smithsonian Act whereby fifty percent of the income was reserved to the library and museum. Jewett, realizing this would spell an end to his national library dream, reacted angrily, and later openly criticized Henry in his annual report. Henry suppressed the offending passages, and the two communicated only by notes thereafter. Despite Jewett's opposition, Henry asked the regents to abandon the fifty-fifty funding provision, and they appointed a committee of seven to look into the matter.

Baird was just as distressed as Jewett, for Henry's request shattered his dream of a national museum; but while Jewett opposed Henry openly, Baird opposed Henry indirectly. In the September 1853 number of *Putnam's Magazine*, Edward Bissell Hunt, one of Baird's friends, wrote an article critical of the secretary, and closed it with a broad hint that Henry was about to resign. Henry now apparently had two disloyal subordinates, and appeared to be a leader without followers. The secretary immediately counterattacked, calling both Baird and Jewett onto the carpet; Baird apologized, but Jewett blew up at Henry. Jewett then orchestrated, in January 1854, the writing, by a group of his friends, of a series of letters critical of Henry's policies to various Washington newspapers. Until this point, the feud was not widely known outside of Washington, but the board of regents, in February 1854, unwittingly brought the conflict before the entire nation. In an attempt to be impartial, they called upon Baird and Jewett to express their opinions on the proposed alteration of the fifty-fifty funding provision. Baird, perhaps having realized that Henry made a formidable opponent, sent in an innocuous statement. Jewett, however, returned a fifty-page document which blasted Henry and his policies, and even impugned the secretary's honor. The seriousness of the feud was now a matter of public record.

On March 23, 1854, Henry sent a letter to Joseph Leidy at the Academy of Natural Sciences assessing the situation. "I write confidentially to you in relation to the affairs of the Institution which have now reached a crisis," wrote Henry, and he went on to inform Leidy that "without the least shadow of authority Jewett and Baird have usurped the power . . . to undermine the reputation and influence of the Secretary." Henry made clear to Leidy that he detested Jewett, but said of Baird: "He is I think at heart a good fellow," although he suffered from "inordinate ambition." Beleaguered though he was, Henry was confident, telling Leidy, "I do not despair, however, when, I have settled with Jewett, of bringing Baird to a sense of his duty and convincing him that an open and straightforward course is the true one." Despite the duress under which he was operating, Henry pledged to Leidy: "My intention is not to throw overboard the museum, unless we can induce Congress to establish one on a better scale; but to render it subordinate to the active operations. The same with the library. But I am determined that my assistants shall know their places." Even as he was fighting for survival, Henry refused to give up the museum. But he was even more determined to save the active operations, for he closed his letter to Leidy by saying, "Baird must show his hand. He is either my assistant—and supporter or my opponent. I must carry all my measures or leave the Institution. I have made up my mind on that point."[53]

Henry's willingness to fight, and his ability to return to Princeton if he were denied his vision, stopped Jewett in his tracks. On May 20, 1854, the regents committee, by a vote of six to one, repudiated the funding provision, rejected Jewett's library plan, and rebuked him for displaying insubordination in his memorial. Jewett, furious at the decision, launched another letter-writing campaign in an attempt to reverse it. Henry, tiring of his rebellious lieutenant, requested and was granted the power to remove subordinates, and "settled" with Jewett by handing him a summary dismissal in July of 1854.

Jewett's friends, led by regent Rufus Choate, attempted to pressure the regents to overrule Henry and rehire Jewett. At the regents meeting of January 13, 1855, this move was rejected, and Choate resigned in protest. This sparked an uproar that led to investigations by both houses of Congress, both of which cleared Henry of wrongdoing. Thus, by March 3, 1855, Henry had rid himself of Jewett and was firmly in control of the destiny of the Smithsonian.

In theory, Henry was now free to move against Baird and the museum as well. This, however, could not be done without cost. Baird had been less clearly insubordinate than Jewett, and had in fact quietly rejoined the secretary's camp earlier, in August of 1854. In that month's *Putnam's Magazine*, another of Baird's good friends, the ornithologist Thomas Mayo Brewer, authored an article entitled "The Smithsonian Institution: Its Legitimate Mission," which strongly supported Henry's position over that of Jewett, and praised Henry personally. This atoned for Hunt's slurs in the earlier article, and marked Baird's return to Henry's camp. Henry could not eliminate Baird and the museum without another nasty fight, and that was the last thing Henry wanted in 1855. So Baird and the museum would stay, but under what conditions?

Henry's answer to this conundrum fundamentally altered the shape of the Smithsonian Institution. The secretary, in an 1870 letter to his close friend, the Harvard botanist Asa Gray, recalled the solution he decided upon: "After the Jewett [events?] I stated to Professor Baird, if he would render me all of the assistance I might require of him, in carrying out my views of the policy of the Inst*on* I would grant him every facility which the Inst*on* could afford to prosecute any branch of Natural History he might decide to cultivate, but that I could not, without being derelict to the duties devolved upon me and regardless of the experience of the past, give him any share of the management of the Institution. To this he fully and unconditionally agreed."[54]

In short, Henry secured Baird's loyalty once and for all by allowing him to develop the museum as he saw fit. In return, Baird would support Henry's policies for the Smithsonian. The deal worked for both men. Henry gained peace in his own house and Baird's support for the active operations. Baird gained the ability to start building a great museum. The secretary still devoutly hoped that Congress would levy sufficient funds so that the museum could become independent of the Smithsonian, and continued to agitate for such a move in his annual reports. But in the absence of that action by Congress, the deal between Henry and Baird allowed for the sustained growth of the museum.

This first great convulsion, the struggle between Henry and Jewett, changed the Smithsonian from a research institution with a small cabinet to a research-oriented museum. In striking his deal with Baird, Henry realized how profoundly it would change the Smithsonian, but in reality he had little choice but to make the best deal he could manage. The act establishing the Smithsonian had made it the repository for all government collections, including those of the Exploring Expedition and the "National Cabinet of Curiosities" at the Patent Office. Throughout the 1840s and 1850s, the collection at the Patent Office had been growing at an enormous rate, due to the specimens sent back by the army expeditions that were exploring the American West. The federal government had no means to preserve, utilize, or exhibit these objects, and Henry was increasingly pressed to accept the entire aggregation and fulfill the Smithsonian's statutory duty. Henry stoutly refused, citing the expense of properly caring for the collection, and so it languished, unwanted, in the basement of the Patent Office. There was a deeper reason for Henry's refusal to take this gift. He realized that accepting such a massive amount of material would bring with it the obligation to exhibit it to the general public in an educational fashion. He knew this would be a popular move, but because of its expense and its tendency to diffuse rather than create knowledge, he rejected the idea.

Yet, as Marc Rothenberg points out, Henry realized that the Smithsonian was obligated, both to the scientific community and the nation, to make these specimens available for study. If they remained inaccessible, researchers would be deprived of important investigations, and American scientific prestige would suffer. As the flow of specimen barrels from the West increased during the 1850s, it became more imperative to accept the idea of a study museum at the Smithsonian. As early as 1853, therefore, Henry offered to take "temporary" charge of certain of the army collections.[55] Henry's deal with Baird allowed the assistant secretary to build a substantial study collection, not a museum for general exhibition. Even though Henry recognized that his "temporary" acceptance of portions of the collections in the Patent Office was likely to be permanent, he still fought a rearguard action against taking them all.

The second great convulsion, the absorption of the government collections, was nonetheless just a matter of time. By 1857 even Henry had to throw in the towel. The commissioner of patents demanded that the space in his building be cleared to allow him to exhibit patent models. Since the entire aggregation now had to be moved, there was really only one place to move it: the Smithsonian. Henry still held out for the best possible deal, and recorded it in his annual report:

> It was finally concluded that if Congress would make an appropriation for the transfer and new arrangement of the articles then in the Patent Office, and continue the annual appropriation previously made for their care and exhibition while in charge of the Commissioner of Patents, the Institution would under these conditions become the Curator of the national collections. This proposition was agreed to by the government, and the contemplated transfer has accordingly been made.[56]

Henry and Baird both knew that this must radically change the nature of the museum. The collections of the Patent Office had long been opened to the public, and they could hardly be closed now that they were at the Smithsonian. Henry disliked the idea of popular displays, largely because, to his mind, they smacked of sideshows like the Western Museum. He was worried on this score when he wrote Asa Gray, in 1857, about the transfer of the Patent Office collection: "It is necessary to fit up this Museum of the Institution so as to produce a good popular effect or at least that part of the Museum of the Institution which is intended for exhibition. . . . It does not become the dignity of the Institution to do anything for popular effect on its own account but as the custodian of the Government property it will be obligated to do something in the way of display."[57]

The Smithsonian could not possibly put on the gaudy, crowd-pleasing spectaculars so prevalent at catchpenny "museums" like the Western Museum. The dignity of the institution demanded something better. Yet, they must cater to the public in some way. The obvious answer was to set up the exhibits so as to educate the people, which was Baird's particular talent. As Edward Alexander has accurately noted, "Baird thought a United States National Museum would both increase public knowledge of flora and fauna and provide scholars with comparative materials for biological research."[58] Baird set about making the new National Museum a public educator as well as a research institution. Henry allowed Baird to do so, but held back himself, still wedded to the concept of increase rather than diffusion of knowledge, and still searching for another authority to take over the National Museum.

The second convulsion, the absorption of the government collections, in time transformed the National Museum from an exclusively research-oriented institution to one that was primarily research oriented with a component of popular education. The third convulsion was destined to bring the two components into closer balance. The Civil War turned Washington, D.C., into an armed camp from 1861 to 1865. Tens of thousands of civilians and hundreds of thousands of soldiers and sailors passed through the nation's capital during those turbulent years. It was necessary, of course, to provide diversions for these men, and the National Museum was high on everyone's list for a visit, since it was enjoyable, educational, and moral. Baird happily set to work making the museum even more enjoyable and more educational.

Henry, for his part, upon observing the crowds streaming through the museum, seems to have begun to grasp the full educational potential of museums. In his annual report for 1861, he noted an important change in his outlook: "During the past year, Washington has been visited by a greater number of strangers than ever before since the commencement of its history. The Museum has consequently been thronged with visitors, and has been a never-failing source of pleasure and instruction to the soldiers of the Army of the United States quartered in the city or its vicinity. Encouragement has been given them to visit it as often as their duties would permit them to devote the time for this purpose."[59]

This is a far cry from the secretary of 1848, who had proclaimed that the Smithsonian was not an educational institution. Now he not only accepted that function, but even encouraged people to come to the institution for the purpose of diffusing, rather than increasing knowledge. Henry's view of museums had evolved; formerly he had believed that they tended to be either research institutions or sideshows. Now he understood how a museum could include "in its design the encouragement of original study as well as popular instruction and amusement."[60] By the end of the Civil War, Henry wrote that he considered museums "of great importance as a means of intellectual improvement, of rational enjoyment, and as receptacles of interesting materials for the use of the student in any branch of learning."[61] Henry continued his ceaseless quest to transfer the National Museum to another authority, but only because he believed that a truly adequate national museum was beyond the means of the Smithsonian to support, and could be funded only by the national government. In fact, his search was motivated by a desire to see the National Museum established on a grand scale.

The three convulsions had transformed Henry's attitude toward the museum, and transformed the museum itself from a study collection into an institution which both increased and diffused knowledge. This change was reflected in the everyday operations of the institution. For instance, in 1853, when Baird sent the Academy of Natural Sciences duplicate specimens of North

American animals, he did so on condition that the academy would allow "free and unrestricted use to all proper applicants, whether within the hall or elsewhere."[62] In other words, the artifacts had to be made accessible to scholars. Fifteen years later, in 1868, when the Smithsonian transferred its herbarium to the Department of Agriculture, it was done under the following restriction: "that the collection shall, at all times, be accessible to the public, for educational purposes, and to the institution, for scientific investigation."[63] In the space of fifteen years, the emphasis had switched from research exclusively to a balance of research and popular education.

As the decade of the 1860s drew to a close, Joseph Henry reflected on a long career at the Smithsonian, writing one correspondent: "I have now assiduously devoted more than twenty years of my life against much opposition to the development of the plan of the Institution originally proposed in my first report to the Board of Regents and if I can live to see a [?] provision made by Congress for the Museum . . . I shall have fulfilled my mission."[64]

Although he now had a greater appreciation for museums, Henry still fretted that the cost of operating the National Museum would drain the Smithsonian's endowment. The secretary's particular worry in this connection was the annual congressional appropriation for operating the museum. The amount had been set at $4,000 in 1857, and it had remained unchanged ever since, even as the cost of maintaining the collection had continually risen. After much agitation, Henry succeeded in getting the appropriation raised to $10,000 annually in 1870. The secretary noted with relief in his annual report: "This year 1870 may be considered almost an epoch in the history of the Smithsonian Institution, since in this year Congress commenced to recognize the propriety of making something like an adequate appropriation to relieve the Smithson fund from at least a portion of the burden to which it has from the first been subjected in the maintenance and care of the National Museum."[65]

Secure in the knowledge that the museum would not bankrupt the Smithsonian, Henry proceeded to discuss his philosophy of museums more fully than he ever had before or ever would again, taking up five complete pages of his report. He began by showing that he was fully aware of the cultural imperatives of the times: "There is scarcely any subject connected with science and education to which more attention is given at the present day than that of collections of objects of nature and art, known under the general denomination of museums. This arises from their growing importance as aids to scientific investigation and instruction."

Henry obviously recognized the public's demand for popular education in museums, especially in the context of science. The secretary perceived two types of museums, local ones and large central institutions. The local ones must both promote science and educate the people. Large central museums, on the other hand, could afford to specialize. "They may be intended exclusively for scientific research . . . [or] intended almost exclusively for popular instruction and amusement." With regard to the latter type, Henry asserted, "Museums of this kind ought to be established at the public expense in every city or community which can afford the means for their support." There was a third kind of large central museum, those of a "mixed character," which combined scientific investigation with education. Henry made it clear that he now believed that the National Museum should be of the "mixed" variety:

> While the Smithsonian Institution should continue to devote a portion of its own funds to assist in explorations which have for their object the advance of science, the public museum, with the care of which it is instructed by Congress, should, in my opinion, without detracting from its scientific character, largely partake of the popular element. It is to be supported by the Treasury of the United States, and should, therefore, be an object of interest to the large number of visitors who are annually drawn to Washington."[66]

Thus by 1870, the three great convulsions—the feud with Jewett, the absorption of the government collections, and the Civil War—operating in harness with the cultural imperative for popular education, had caused a complete change in the outlook of

Joseph Henry. In 1850 he had grudgingly accepted only a very small study cabinet at the Smithsonian. In 1855, after his deal with Baird, he approved the concept of a museum at the Smithsonian, but only for the purpose of research. By 1858, after accepting the government collections, Henry realized that some provision must be made for popular education in the National Museum. Finally, the Civil War, by bringing vast crowds to the museum, convinced the secretary that popular education was nearly as important as original research at the National Museum. So by 1870, the National Museum was completely in step with the American Compromise, as Henry and Baird sought to balance the claims of scholarly research and popular education. Both the scholar and the student were served, and in accordance with the will of James Smithson, the institution was both "increasing and diffusing knowledge among men."

The "Old Federalists" Fade Away: The New-York Historical Society

The spirit of the age commands us to *march foward.* Advance we *must!* we *cannot* remain *still!* That is stagnation—and stagnation is death. . . . To keep pace with this onward march we must rise *higher* and for *loftier* ends.[67]

During the 1840s, it would have been unthinkable for a sitting president of the New-York Historical Society to make such a ringing call for social change in general, and change within the Historical Society in particular. Yet by 1865, when President Frederic De Peyster, Jr., offered these sentiments in a speech before the society, no one was scandalized; in fact, there was much approbation. The society by the late 1860s had shed much of its elitist aloofness, and had begun to concern itself with the need for popular education. By 1870, the society had, for the most part, embraced the synthesis of popular education and scholarly support that defined the modern American museum.

This transformation from an old Federalist enclave to a more responsive contemporary institution occurred gradually during the late 1840s and early 1850s. A combination of deaths of older members (the Reverend Samuel Miller, the last of the founders, passed away in 1850) and an influx of new members was rapidly changing the face of the society. The death of President Albert Gallatin in August of 1849 opened the way for new leadership, and the members chose Luther Bradish for the post. It would not be proper to say that Bradish represented a younger generation, for he had been born in 1783 and had been a member of the society for more than thirty years; but Bradish was a very different person from most of his contemporaries. Since his retirement in 1842, he had devoted most of his time to educational and philanthropic activities, and he cherished a keen interest in the welfare of the people. Under Bradish, the New-York Historical Society would no longer be a refuge from American society, but a force for change within it.

The transformation in orientation Bradish effected may seem mild unless it is compared to what went before. When the old Federalists held sway, they resisted anything that did not fit their particular world view. A case in point was the meeting of June 20, 1845, called to honor the memory of the recently deceased former president Andrew Jackson. The old Federalists despised "Old Hickory," and they attempted to veto the simple civility of paying respect to his memory. The tribute eventually carried, but not without bitter debate. Member Phillip Hone, a former mayor of New York, recalled, "The resolutions were passed with only two or three dissenting votes, although the meeting was by no means unanimous. But it was one of those things which people did not like to vote against."[68]

The passing of the old Federalists and the elevation of Bradish changed all of this. Bradish served as president from 1849 to 1863, and his incumbency marked a time of explosive growth and fundamental change for the society.

Something of Bradish's personal ideology can be gleaned from an editorial he wrote under the name of "A Friend of the World's Fair" for a pair of New York newspapers. Entitled the "Industrial Exhibition of 1851," the editorial was a warm defense of the London Crystal Palace Exhibition. In it, he showed that he understood the potential of popular education: "The information, which will there be accumulated, will be thence disseminated throughout the world; and knowledge and improvement, now peculiar to one, will thus become general to all. Is there nothing in all this favorable to the Peace, the Progress, and the general amelioration of the condition of the world?"[69]

Bradish sought, within the constraints imposed upon him by an inadequate building, a small staff, and initially, a balky membership, to make popular education a reality at the society. In 1852, when the society moved to its new home at the corner of Second Avenue and Eleventh Street, one impediment was at least partially removed, and the hours of the library and museum were extended from six hours per day to thirteen; henceforth, they would be open from 9:00 A.M. to 10:00 P.M. A visitor still needed to secure a ticket from a society member, but now, for the first time, the institution was open when a working person could visit it.[70] President Bradish was guided in his efforts by the conviction, heretofore so alien to the society, that change was necessary, and he never lost an opportunity to make that point. For instance, he wrote one correspondent in 1851, "We are said to live in an age of *Reform* and I certainly, in my own case, feel both its necessity and its value."[71] Bradish did not mean to exempt the Historical Society from this reform impulse.

The society's move from their cramped quarters at New York University to more commodious ones on Second Avenue made many of Bradish's reforms possible. For the first time in their history, the members had quarters built expressly for them, and enough room to at least partially accommodate a library and a museum. The next fourteen years, from 1853 through 1866, witnessed phenomenal growth in the society's museum, which transformed it from a quaint cabinet of American history to the foremost museum of art and archaeology in America. Some of this growth occurred because of gifts, but significantly, much was the result of purchases, as members grew more responsive to the shifting cultural currents.

The parade of acquisitions began in 1857 when the collection of the late Luman Reed was given to the society by Jonathan

Sturges, Reed's former law partner. It was then the finest collection of American paintings in existence, and it formed the nucleus of the New York Gallery of the Fine Arts, which in effect was merged with the society by this gift. The next year, James Lenox, a member of the society, presented it with thirteen massive marble bas-reliefs from Nineveh. "The Lenox Collection of Nineveh Sculptures," which had cost their donor $3,000, instantly made the society's museum an important archaeological repository. The next acquisition came from the same field. Dr. Henry Abbott, a British subject who had lived in Egypt for twenty years, had gathered a massive collection of Egyptian artifacts and brought them to the United States for exhibition. His attempt to recoup his expenses through exhibition failed, and in 1854 he offered his collection to anyone who could raise $60,000, considerably less than he had spent to acquire it. The Cooper Union made some efforts to procure it, but failed. The society entered the picture in 1859, when the trustees appointed a committee headed by Frederic De Peyster, Jr., to raise money for the purchase. De Peyster, who had earned the undying enmity of the old Federalists when he had sided with David Hosack and John Trumbull in the dispute over the collection in the 1820s, was by now the heir-apparent to Bradish and the society's chief fundraiser. De Peyster set to work with a will and raised the requisite $60,000 within a year. The Abbott Collection, combined with that of Lenox, made the society's archaeology collection by far the best in America.

The acquisitions then returned to art. In December of 1862 Mrs. John James Audubon offered, for $4,000, the original watercolors used by her husband for *The Birds of America*. Once again it was De Peyster who raised the money, and by June of the following year, the paintings were placed in the society's museum. The last of these additions was arguably the most important. Thomas Jefferson Bryan, a wealthy Philadelphian who had been for many years a resident of Paris, made a gift of his collection of art in 1866. Bryan had had the good fortune to live in Paris during the revolutions of 1830 and 1848, and thus had been able to purchase art from many distressed old families. His was the first American cosmopolitan collection of art, one that included old masters as well as good modern paintings. In the early 1850s, Bryan returned to America, took up residence in New York, and established the "Bryan Gallery of Christian Art" on Broadway. When the Cooper Union opened, Bryan deposited his collection there, but withdrew it in disgust in 1863 after he discovered Peter Cooper using the point of his umbrella to convey the merits of one of the paintings to a visitor. Bryan loaned the collection to the society in 1866, but it was not until 1870 that he made the pictures a formal gift. With the Bryan gift added to the Reed bequest, the society had by far the finest art collection of any museum in America.[72]

These acquisitions marked a sharp departure from past practice. The society, which for the first fifty-three years of its existence had purchased very few artifacts, and which since the mid-1820s had not actively solicited gifts to the museum, was suddenly raising money for purchases and aggressively pursuing bequests. The cultural imperatives were emphasizing exhibition and education, and the society's members, with a swiftness that seems to have surprised even them, were responding. The positive attitude of the society of 1857 seemed a different world from the obstructionist society which, a mere dozen years before, could barely agree to pay their respects to a deceased president. In the meantime, as the gifts and purchases accumulated, it rapidly became apparent that even the new building was hopelessly inadequate to exhibit them. If these collections were to be of any use to the people, another building would be necessary, one which could accommodate the crowds they would be sure to attract.

The Historical Society of the 1840s would have packed such collections away and considered public access to them out of the question. In the late 1850s, however, the members of the society's art committee were of a different mind. They were "enthusiastic supporters of the idea of promoting the aesthetic education of the public through free, perpetual exhibitions. They hoped to make the New-York Historical Society and its growing collection of art works an instrument for such a project."[73] The art committee therefore sought a partnership between the society and the state of New York to effect the project. Their idea was simple: the state would make a gift to the society of the disused arsenal building in Central Park, along with an appropriation to renovate it. In return the society would use the arsenal as their museum and render it accessible to the public. The society, however, which was never in good financial condition, did not specifically promise free admission. The art committee sold the commissioners of Central Park on the idea, and in 1862 they received approval for the plan from the state legislature: approval, but no appropriations. There the plan stalled, for in wartime, capital was too tight to think of proceeding without aid from the state.

The society did its best to prod the legislators along. In 1863, they sent another memorial to the legislature, justifying their request in terms of popular education: "The establishment within the Central Park and the City of New York of the Museum of Antiquities and Science and a Gallery of Art would greatly add to its attractions by increasing its means of popular gratification and instruction, and thus contribute to the promotion of its general object."[74]

Not even such arguments of educational value could open the public purse in war time. Meanwhile, another impediment loomed. Several members of the society became concerned that the arsenal sat in a risky location, for it was situated on low ground near a reservoir. The threat of a flood led them to renegotiate the location with the Central Park commissioners. The society's representatives and the commissioners agreed upon a new site, a four-acre tract of the park along Fifth Avenue from Seventy-ninth Street to Eighty-fifth Street. The society's membership, fearful of the cost of erecting a new building, did not accept the arrangement until 1868. The cost did indeed prove insurmountable, and the Historical Society abandoned the site, which was taken by the Metropolitan Museum of Art. Once again, a shortage of money had plagued the society.[75]

The money crisis was a familiar theme at the society, but the attitudes of the members had changed radically from days gone by. No longer was the society swimming against the cultural tides. In 1862, for instance, John R. Peters, Jr., the proprietor of a collection of Chinese artifacts, upon reading that the Historical Society might obtain the arsenal, wrote to Luther Bradish, offering to sell his collection. Bradish's reply reveals that the society was very much in step with the cultural imperative of popular education: "Nothing would be more desirable than the addition of your valuable collection to those already in the Possession of the Society. This would contribute greatly to the general object which the Society has had in view in this Enterprise, that is to contribute as far as possible to increase within the Park the means of popular gratification and instruction, and thus advance the true object of the Park."[76]

Once more, lack of funds prevented this purchase, but impecuniousness obviously did not prevent the society from doing what it could to promote popular education. Bradish was not, however, a person who pursued popular education at the expense of scholarship. Commenting on James Lenox's gift of the sculptures from Nineveh, Bradish said: "In addition to the archaeological testimony from the Nile, this furnished us with valuable material for the Biblical Scholar; and in acknowledging the generous patriotism displayed in the the present instance, illustrated the necessity and propriety of carrying forward all of our interests, intellectual as well as material."[77]

Luther Bradish thus displayed the American Compromise at its best, a balanced appreciation for popular education and for scholarly research. He steered the society firmly in this course, so far as funds allowed, until his death in 1863.

Frederic De Peyster ably picked up Bradish's torch and continued his predecessor's liberal programs. By November of 1865, in an address to the whole society entitled "The Moral and Intellectual Influence of Libraries upon Social Progress," he carried the cultural imperative to synthesize popular education and professional scholarship in museums to its logical conclusion. Speaking to promote the contemplated museum in the arsenal, be began with a clarification: "By libraries, in this address, are to be understood depositories of literature, science and art; in short, all the products of intellect and imagination which can be brought together for the pleasure and instruction of man."[78]

De Peyster wished it clearly to be understood that he was speaking of all repositories of learning, not merely libraries. He went on to consider museums specifically, and voiced strong support for their research function. The museum must conduct itself so that it will be "highly appreciated by students of history," indeed, so that it would be indispensable "to the student in this field of historical research." The museum, however, must be far more than a research institution. As De Peyster put it, "The museum, in its amplitude, will embrace a wider and more extensive field." That wider field was, as the title suggested, social progress.[79]

Social progress could be promoted by the museum's second great function, popular education. The museum could be an efficient educator, and that was crucial, for: "Our country, more than any other in the world, is dependent upon the virtue of the people; and their virtue is largely dependent upon their intelligence and education; and these depend upon the intellectual stimulus which they receive."[80]

In a democracy such as America, only the intelligence and the virtue of the people separated the nation from tyranny on the one hand or anarchy on the other, and only education promoted virtue. The city of New York, as the most populous and wealthiest metropolis in the nation, carried a special burden, for it could exert a vast influence for good or ill over the entire country. It became imperative, then, that the people of New York be educated. De Peyster concluded with an impassioned plea to support a museum that would both promote scholarship and dispense education:

> Taking these two thoughts, the vast influence of the city upon the intellectual and moral character of the nation, and the wonderful destiny which is before it, is there not imposed upon us a most solemn responsibility to make this city a source of intelligence and virtue for the whole land? And what can we do in our sphere towards accomplishing this result better than to lay the foundations of a Library, Museum of Antiquities and Science, and Gallery of Art such as that which I am now advocating—a Library, Museum and Gallery for the whole people such as is commensurate with our greatness and unrivaled

prosperity, one which shall furnish every facility for the student in every department of his investigations, which shall rouse the public mind to noble impulses by the magic influence of genius, which shall stimulate scientific discovery, which shall add strength to all moral and religious institutions and ideas, which shall be a home for the poor for whose elevation our very system of government is designed. Where they who are shut out from so many of the refining effects of social intercourse may silently commune with the great intellects of all ages of the world.[81]

This address perfectly illustrates the remarkable development of the New-York Historical Society in the space of fifteen short years. What had been a haven from the world for the old Federalists was now being proposed as a "home for the poor." The museum was to simultaneously facilitate the investigations of the serious student, and educate the ordinary people to prepare them for the civic duties they faced. In less than two decades, the cultural imperative to synthesize popular education and scholarly research had become the goal of this staid New-York Historical Society. In practical terms, the American Compromise was not achieved at the society until well after 1870, for even the new building did not allow easy access of the people to the collection, but the spirit of the age was motivating the leaders of the society by the end of the 1860s. From that point forward there was no turning back. Eventually, inevitably, both the scholar and everyman must be served. The American democratic culture demanded it.

The Misunderstood Museum: The American Museum of P. T. Barnum

For thirty years I have striven to do good, but (foolishly) stuck my worst side outside until half the Christian Comnity [*sic*] got to believe that I wore horns & hoofs. And now as I have got [old], I begin to feel the desire that present and future generations shall "nothing extenuate or set down aught in malice." Let them show *me as I am*—& God knows, that is bad enough![82]

P.T. Barnum was not quite fifty-five years old in 1865 when he penned these lines, but he obviously was keenly worried about his place in history. The public saw him as "the Prince of Humbugs," an image which he had aggressively fostered in his autobiography and in sundry promotions. But his current status as a successful businessman and the impending judgment of history led Barnum to seek stability and respectability throughout the 1850s and 1860s. Although he continued to offer spectacular entertainments, Barnum eschewed the misleading advertising and outright frauds that he had perpetrated in the 1840s. Instead, he fell in step with the currents in the wider culture, and became more responsive to both professional science and popular education. By the end of the 1860s, he was seriously considering building, beside his American Museum, a high-quality national museum open to the public without charge. Despite his efforts, this part of Barnum's career has been widely misunderstood. Many historians have dismissed Barnum as a huckster and his museums as nothing more than sideshows. They have not appreciated the fact that Barnum's search for respectability caused him to move toward a notion of service to science and promotion of education. Swept along on the cultural currents, Barnum's museums were evolving into educational institutions until two disastrous fires destroyed them in the late 1860s.

The roots of Barnum's quest for respectability in the 1850s and 1860s were many. His success in business had reduced his need for humbug, and his association with the crowned heads of Europe during his tour with General Tom Thumb had induced a longing for respect. Then came the Jenny Lind tour of 1850 which Barnum promoted. The "Swedish Nightingale" became a sensation all across America, and Barnum discovered that he could make high profits from high culture. All of this tended to temper his flair for showmanship.

The signs of Barnum's more serious attitude quickly became manifest in his museums. In 1849, he acquired the Philadelphia Museum from Edmund Peale, and closed the American Museum in New York for renovations. On June 17, 1850, on the occasion of the reopening of the American Museum, he issued a circular letter that contained a revealing passage: "My whole aim and effort is to make my museums totally unobjectionable to the religious and moral community, and at the same time to combine sufficient *amusement* with instruction, to please all proper tastes and to train the mind of youth to reject as repugnant anything inconsistent with moral and refined tastes."[83]

Barnum wished to project an image of moral probity and good taste in his newly refurbished museum, and to make it useful to the community. He obviously felt that the way to accomplish all these objectives was to make the American Museum an educational institution, in name if not completely in practice. In doing so, he was beginning to follow the cultural imperatives.

Barnum unexpectedly received another opportunity to attain respectability in 1854, when the New York Crystal Palace Company begged him to assume the presidency of their faltering enterprise. Barnum hesitated, for the venture seemed doomed. While pondering, he wrote Horace Greeley, "At all events, rest assured that if I work at all it shall be for what I conceive to be the best interests of the exhibition, and of the City of New York & our common country."[84] The temptation to gain respectability as the savior of a great national concern proved enticing, and Barnum took the job. Shortly after assuming the presidency, Barnum proudly proclaimed, "I am now engaged in managing a public enterprise which I hope and believe will be made highly conducive to the interests and reputation of this city and the country at large."[85] Barnum's initial reaction was correct, for the enterprise was too deeply in debt to be rescued. After serving as president for only three months, he resigned, and the whole concern was liquidated shortly thereafter. Barnum's motivation in accepting this thankless task clearly lay in gaining the respect of the community.

In the summer of 1855, with the burden of the Crystal Palace removed, Barnum suddenly sold the American Museum to John Greenwood, Jr. (his assistant manager) and Henry D. Butler for $24,000. The long-term lease on the building, which he assigned to his wife Charity, was sublet to Greenwood and Butler for $19,000 per annum. The profits from his just-published autobiography were starting to roll in. At forty-five, Barnum seemed to be rich and at leisure, truly a gentleman of property, although of uncertain standing.

His prosperity was short-lived. In 1855, Barnum lent money to and signed notes for the Jerome Clock Company, a seemingly successful firm that was considering a move to his hometown, Bridgeport, Connecticut. Their debts proved to be monumental, Barnum's notes were used again and again, and ultimately he owed a succession of creditors approximately $500,000. Both the company and Barnum failed; then he became embroiled in a series of lawsuits.[86] Barnum had no choice but to return to work. He undertook a series of tours of Europe with Tom Thumb, and lectured on "The Art of Money Getting." By 1860, he had recouped his fortune sufficiently to repurchase the American Museum. Nearly twenty years after he had begun, he was starting over again in the museum business.

He was, however, a much different man. The single-minded entertainer of the 1840s had become a sober man of many interests. He was a real-estate developer in Bridgeport, parceling out small lots because he believed that the working classes should become home owners. During the Civil War, Barnum became a leading spokesman for the Union cause. As a member of New York's "Prudential Committee," a home-front vigilante organization dedicated to opposing the pro-Southern "Copperheads," Barnum's life was threatened and, on more than one occasion, he was guarded by Federal troops. In 1863 the American Museum was firebombed by a Confederate agent in revenge for Barnum's activities, but the resulting blaze was quickly extinguished.[87] After the war, Barnum was elected to the Connecticut legislature, where he made a reputation as a strong foe of corporate monopolists. In his one try for national office, he lost a race for Congress in 1867. During the decade of the 1860s, then, Barnum was the soul of respectability outside of his museum career.

He also sought that respect within the museum field. He resumed offering spectacular attractions at the museum, but no longer countenanced outright humbugs. His museum was evolving into something far more valuable. Barnum's correspondence at the time he repurchased the American Museum reveals a certain regret at past actions and a plan for the future: "As a general thing I have not '*duped* the world,' nor attempted to do so; but while I do not attempt to justify all I have done, I know that I have generally given the people the *worth of their money twice told*. The Mermaid, the Wooly Horse, Ploughing Elephants & C. were merely used by me as skyrockets, or advertisements, to attract attention and give notoriety to the *Museum* & such other really valuable attractions as I provide for the public."[88]

Barnum argued that he had not defrauded the people by humbugging them, for they had received more than their money's worth. He went beyond that rationalization, however, to claim that the humbugs had merely served as lures to attract the public. Once inside, they could not fail to learn from his valuable collection. Barnum backed up this sentiment with action. Beginning in the 1860s, he sponsored several expeditions to bring back unknown and unusual animals and fishes. These costly forays made the museum's collection, by the end of the decade, a fascinating trove for the layman and a valuable resource for the professional. The expeditions were not mounted merely to provide popular attractions, for Barnum could easily have found more spectacular offerings at a lower price. They had a more important purpose: the promotion of education and science.

This new emphasis on the educational value of the collection proved to be a theme that Barnum played throughout the 1860s. As the natural history collection grew, he became more and more explicit about its value to the people, especially the young. The museum's handouts and brochures became more exhortatory. One brochure, issued in 1866, echoed Charles Willson Peale in its evocation of the value of natural history: "There is no study that is more important to the youth of a rising generation, or to adult age, than that of Natural History. It teaches man his superiority over brute creation, and creates in his bosom a knowledge of the wisdom and goodness and omnipresence of a supreme and All-Wise Creator. . . . Hence it became necessary that man should study the history of animated nature, make himself master of a science on which his own happiness depended, and which when developed, could not fail to advance the great causes of civilization and learning."[89]

Like Peale, Barnum stressed the educational and the spiritual properties of natural history. By using the American Museum as a school, the people could learn much that would be useful in their lives, while simultaneously having a direct religious experience. The American Museum could function on three levels: as a place of entertainment, as a school, and as a temple. Barnum tried, without notable success, to convince the press of his educational intentions. He wrote plaintively to one editor, "I sadly want & need in your columns a statement of *the facts* concerning the manner in which I am now catering for public *improvement* as well as public amusement."[90] The editors, however, rarely acknowledged any good Barnum was doing, for they could not see past the spectacular attractions Barnum continued to offer. The museum remained misunderstood.

It is fascinating to speculate whether Barnum could have changed his image if given enough time. But time was not something he was destined to have in the museum world. On July 13, 1865, a fire started in the museum's engine room and rapidly engulfed the structure in flames. A few artifacts were saved, but most of the $400,000 collection was destroyed. It was insured for less than $40,000. Barnum, never one to mope, promptly set about forming a new museum.

Barnum the showman had owned four museums in three different cities. All had been devoted, in greater or lesser degrees, to entertainment. Now as he prepared to rebuild the American Museum, he had an audacious idea: why not secure the help of the American and foreign governments to rebuild it? He broached his half-formed plan to his good friend, the author and lecturer Bayard Taylor, in a letter written on July 16, 1865, only three days after the museum fire. After informing Taylor that the museum was destroyed, Barnum talked of replacing it. He was determined that "the next one must be of a much *higher grade* than the other was, although the price must remain thirty cts. for the accommodation of the million." Moreover, it must have a "full collection of specimens of natural history in all its departments."

Once again, Barnum's concern for quality and the educational value of his museum was evident. He lamented, "There is no disputing the fact that the disruption of the Museum is a *national loss* and no living man can command the facilities which I possess to get up a new one." But not even Barnum could do it alone. Therefore, he asked Taylor's help in accomplishing his "great idea," that of persuading every large museum in Europe to contribute artifacts to his new museum. If Taylor were to be his agent, Barnum was confident that he could procure a document signed by President Johnson and his entire cabinet, "stating that the destruction of my museum is a national loss and the American people will duly appreciate the kindness shown by parties abroad in contributing interesting objects to the new museum, & c. & c. & c. & c."[91]

Taylor must have sent an encouraging reply, for Barnum wrote him again just six days later, with an expanded plan. Barnum had just sold his lease on the museum property to James Gordon Bennett of the New York *Herald* for $200,000. Awash in cash and brimming with new confidence, Barnum presented a startling idea to Taylor: he would not only rebuild the American Museum, but would build a national museum beside it. He explained to Taylor, "Astor gave the public a *library*; Cooper gave them an institute." Barnum, too, was ready to take his place among the philanthropists by endowing a useful institution. And given his background, that useful institution had to be a museum: "Why should not Barnum (who in fact was always more of a philanthropist than a humbug) establish a *free museum* for the instruction and edification of the *Youth of America!* In fact, open a fire proof building and open in it a well stocked collection of the works of nature & art, relics & c. open free to the public."[92]

Yet again, Barnum revealed his desire for respectability, both explicitly in his letter and implicitly in his scheme. How better to shed his image as a humbug than to build a great museum that would educate the people? It would only add to this museum's luster if it were established as a national institution, and Barnum made that aim explicit: "I propose to erect a *National Free Museum* which shall contain collections of natural history and shall also contain all specimens of *everything* presented to our govt. in any of its departments." So it was to be a free, national museum, administered by Barnum, but belonging to the people.

The national museum (or institution, for Barnum was still undecided as to what he should name it) was not to stand in solitary splendor. As Barnum put it: "Now alongside of *Barnum's Free National* (something) I propose to erect Barnum's American Museum with its giants, dwarfs, fat women, bearded ladies, baby shows . . . curiosities of all sorts in natural history which I *purchase*, picture gallery & c. & c. To this museum I charge an admission fee of 25 or 30 cts., children half price. Museum open from sunrise to 10:00 P.M. All museum visitors admitted to the *National* (concern) free at all hours from sunrise to 10:00 P.M."[93]

Barnum's plan was simple. He would rebuild the American Museum and confine all of the spectacular and gaudy attractions there. This would raise the capital to allow him to set up a truly valuable National Museum beside it. The American Museum would thus be strictly for entertainment; the National Museum would be for scholarship and education. Barnum won on both counts. The proximity of the National Museum would legitimize Barnum's operation, and the two combined would be a better "draw" than either separately. Barnum wished to make Taylor clearly understand the division, for he wrote, "The National Institution shall be superb, & my pride will be to add to its attractions & conveniences every year & every day and have it perfectly *free* for all well-behaved persons & thus, be an entirely *distinct* thing from the Museum." By promoting such a valuable and respectable enterprise along with his American Museum, Barnum hoped to dispel the air of charlatanism that had lingered about him since his youth, for he closed by telling Taylor that if his plan succeeded, "there shall not be a smell of *humbug* left to my name twelve months hence."[94]

For a time, it appeared as if the dream would come true. Barnum merged with the famous VanAmburgh Menagerie Company, and thus gained a fine collection of African animals. He drew up a memorial calling for the establishment of his National Museum, and sent it off to President Johnson. Despite the signatures of such prominent citizens as Prosper M. Wetmore of the New-York Historical Society, William Cullen Bryant, Henry Ward Beecher, and Horace Greeley, Johnson repeatedly refused to act. Barnum went to Washington, secured an audience with Gideon Welles, and prevailed upon Connecticut Senator Lafayette Forster to intervene on his behalf. Forster persuaded Johnson to issue a directive ordering American ministers, counsels, and commercial agents to give Barnum such assistance as they were able. The National Museum plan was more or less destroyed by this tepid support, and to finish it completely, neither Bayard Taylor nor anyone else was able to go to Europe to solicit museum specimens.

While the National Museum never came to pass, a new American Museum was established on Broadway, opening on November 13, 1865. In combination with VanAmburgh Company, Barnum began energetically rebuilding the collection, and once more the American Museum was the premier place of entertainment in New York. Then once again, disaster struck. On the bitterly cold morning of March 3, 1868, another fire reduced the museum to a charred hulk. The aging showman decided to retire, and never again ran a museum, although he would contemplate doing so on more than one occasion. Instead, when he came out of retirement, it was as a circus manager.

Barnum's retirement was the prelude to a solid century of abuse from historians; as mentioned earlier, his museums were simply dismissed as sideshows. Contemporary views of Barnum's museums, however, effectively refute this negative interpretation. Peter Cooper had used many of Barnum's exhibits as the basis for his museum plans for the Cooper Union. Henry David Thoreau visited the American Museum in 1854, and then several times thereafter. This unlikely confrontation between the "Sage of Walden" and the "Prince of Humbugs" produced admiration for Barnum's natural history collection, especially the aquaria.[95] The notable diarist George Templeton Strong was equally impressed with the aquaria,[96] while Henry James remembered Barnum's lecture room as "the true center of the seat of joy."[97] Great naturalists were also spawned at the museum. John Burroughs traced his first interest in icthyology to competing for $100 in a museum-sponsored trout-catching contest. Dr. Albert S. Bickmore, founder of the American Museum of Natural History, went on his first collecting expedition, to Bermuda in 1862, at Barnum's expense.[98] The list of established scientists who considered Barnum a friend and a source of specimens is impressive: Louis Agassiz, Joseph Henry, Spencer Baird, and Oliver Wendell Holmes, Sr.[99]

Foreign visitors, while generally appalled at the excesses in promotion and exhibition that Barnum occasionally employed, usually found much to praise in the museum. Two 1853 visitors, Francis and Theresa Pulszky, after considering both Barnum's museum and his life outside of it, concluded, "Publicity in America turns 'puffing' sometimes to the public advantage."[100] Captain Oldmixon of the Royal Navy, who was a biting critic of most things American, made no exception for Barnum's Philadelphia Museum, for he was critical of the lecture room, the waxworks, and the musical entertainment. But even he found things to appreciate, noting, "The best things are the Indian dresses, weapons and ornaments, always perfect in their kind, and beautiful."[101] A perceptive Englishwoman named Isabella Lucy Bird may have the last word here. She astutely noticed that the American Museum was really two different things, unfortunately jumbled together. Ms. Bird divided the institution into a "Museum" and a "Palace of Humbug," and lamented, "The museum contains many objects of real interest, particularly to the naturalist and geologist, intermingled with a great deal that is spurious and contemptible."[102] The contemporary judges, both American and foreign, were able to find considerable wheat along with the chaff at the Barnum museums. It was the later historians who invented the museums with no redeeming social value.

Happily, more recent scholars have finally recognized that the American Museum had several positive qualities. John Rickards Betts noted that Barnum had "recognized the appeal of . . . science" and delivered education in natural history "at a time when a knowledge of natural history was considered essential in the schools of a democratic society." Betts also realized that Barnum had provided a "stimulus to the museum movement" by "his popularization of natural history."[103] Neil Harris recognized that Barnum "could promote high art along with vulgar amusements." He also detected "a certain unity to its [the museum's] exotic trappings" that other scholars have ignored. Harris regretted that Barnum's museum career had "ended just as Barnum was returning to the older, scholarly ideals that had animated Charles Willson Peale's museums some 80 years earlier."[104] It was this impulse that caused him, increasingly as the years went by, to employ agents and sponsor expeditions to bring back species unknown to science, the cost of which far outweighed the exhibition value of the specimens returned. It was the same feeling that caused him to employ naturalists to arrange and label his collections, and to write guidebooks for the exhibitions, in order to educate laymen. The scholars, at long last, have begun to be fair to Barnum and his museums.

P.T. Barnum's quest for respectability during the 1850s and 1860s did much to make the American Museum a resource for scientists and students alike. As it happened, Barnum's need for respect dovetailed nicely with the cultural imperative to mix professionalism and popular education. By providing materials for the scientist and enlightenment for the student, Barnum could raise his esteem in the eyes of the community. Neil Harris recognized that Barnum was taking part in the cultural movement to promote education, and pointed out, "In this, as in so many other activities, Barnum followed the taste of his day. . . . Barnum marched in step. With fortune and reputation securely established, he could afford to sound a note of enlightenment."[105] Barnum did more than sound a note; he played a composition of education, chiefly by assembling a magnificent collection of natural history. Barnum and his museums have been misunderstood because it has been too easy to see only the gaudy and fantastic veneer and miss the educational underpinnings. By looking at the collection instead of the freaks, one reaches an understanding of the true value of Barnum's efforts. P.T. Barnum did more than swindle and amuse America at mid-century. He even did more than popularize museums. P.T. Barnum, by the late 1860s, provided an example of the controlling effects of the American democratic culture upon its museums. The American Museum had been evolving toward a good example of the synthesis of popular education and professional science, and had fire not destroyed it, it probably would have achieved the American Compromise.

The American Compromise and the Great Metropolitan Museums

For the people, for education, for science.[106]

The motto of the American Museum of Natural History is nothing more than a concise statement of the American Compromise. This should not be surprising, for the great metropolitan museums, the American Museum of Natural History, the Boston Museum of the Fine Arts, and the Metropolitan Museum of Art, were all founded just as the synthesis between professionalism and popular education was coming to maturity. In short, these great museums are the heirs to more than a century of American museum history, and mark the culmination of that early history. Eighteen-seventy is the watershed year; before that, American museums were struggling to define their purpose and mission, and were relatively modest compared to their European cousins. Very quickly after 1870 the American museum world embraced the American Compromise and launched into an incredible binge of sustained growth. To borrow a term from economics, it is useful to think of 1870 as the "take-off" point. The previous century of American museum history had raised the field to a level of development necessary for exponential growth, and after 1870, museums achieved that level of growth. This development was so sudden that it tended to obscure all that had gone before, to the point that many observers have labeled 1870 as the beginning of museum history in America. To be sure, 1870 is an important date, but all that came after is only a logical extension of all that went before.

The year 1870 marked the take-off point for two reasons. On the one hand, the forces of American democratic culture had impelled the museums in the United States to accept the American Compromise. On the other hand, the great metropolitan institutions were all in the process of being established. The birth of the great museums just as the American Compromise had matured guaranteed that the balance of professionalism and popular education would be a guiding principle of their foundings. These influential institutions, in turn, have served to keep the American Compromise vital and widespread in the American museum community.

The pre-1870 museums had whetted America's appetite for high-quality collections and exhibitions. The early proprietors, like Du Simitière and Peale, had struggled to establish their modest ventures; now newspapers were complaining, "It is lamentable to think that of all the splendid and ambitious cities of this great republic, not one possesses even a creditable gallery of art or a great public museum . . . which the scholar may rank with those of Europe."[107] There was clearly a constituency demanding, by 1870, that first-rate museums be built in America.

The statements of purpose of all three of the great metropolitan museums confirm that they were founded on the basis of the American Compromise. At the opening of the Boston Museum of the Fine Arts, the mayor of the city exclaimed that not only would the museum be a haven for the connoisseur, but also "the crown of our educational system."[108] Similarly, the Act to Incorporate the American Museum of Natural History, which was passed by the New York legislature on April 6, 1869, contained a clear statement of the American Compromise. It proclaimed that the museum was being founded "for the purpose of establishing and maintaining in said city a Museum and Library of Natural History; of encouraging and developing the study of Natural Science; of advancing the general knowledge of kindred subjects, and to that end of furnishing popular instruction and recreation."[109]

The last of these three museums may serve as a case study of the transmittal of the American Compromise from the pre-1870 museum world to the new order that was rising in 1870. The story of the Metropolitan Museum of Art in the years of its founding proves that it, and by extension the modern American museums it has influenced, is a lineal descendant of the pre-1870 museums.

William Cullen Bryant, the venerable poet and editor, set the tone at a meeting called on November 23, 1869, for the expressed purpose of considering the establishment of an art museum in New York. In his address to this meeting, Bryant spelled out, in terms of the American Compromise, the value of such an institution: "The influence of works of art is wholesome, ennobling, instructive. Besides the cultivation of the sense of beauty—in other words, the perception of order, symmetry, proportion of parts . . . the intelligent contemplation of a great gallery of works of art is a lesson in history, a lesson in biography, a lesson in the antiquities of different countries."[110]

According to Bryant, the museum should serve not only those who cultivate beauty, in other words, artists, but also those who sought to learn from art. Ironically, the men who gathered at the Union League Club that evening did not quite realize that they were embracing the American Compromise. Instead they looked across the ocean, to England, for their inspiration. When the Crystal Palace Exposition of 1851 came to a close, the surplus of £186,000 was used to buy eighty-seven acres of land in South Kensington. In 1857, the South Kensington Museum, which would later become the Victoria and Albert, was opened on that site. The South Kensington's vigorous and progressive leader, Sir Henry Cole, was much admired in New York, and the founders of the Metropolitan wished to consciously imitate Cole's methods. Among Cole's innovations were free opening on certain days, access to the museum library for the public, a lecture series, night openings, plentiful labels, traveling exhibitions, and circulating exhibits.[111] Cole devised these ideas without realizing that all but one had already been tried in America. Ironically, even Americans accepted them as completely novel. The Academy of Natural Sciences had allowed free admission to its museum and access to its library as early as 1828. Charles Willson Peale had offered extensive labels and a lecture series by 1800, and had opened in the evenings by 1816. A host of American museum proprietors, including Gardiner Baker in the 1790s and Rembrandt Peale in the 1840s, organized traveling exhibitions. Of all of Cole's "innovations," only circulating exhibits had not already been tried in America.

These facts notwithstanding, the founders sought to consciously imitate Cole's creation. Another speaker at the meeting said forthrightly, "It is our aim to have, at no very future period, a museum similar to the Kensington Museum in London."[112] That the founders explicitly imitated the South Kensington rather than American museums does not in any way diminish the influence of the American Compromise upon them. Bryant and his fellow organizers, for example, had been partially inspired to found an art museum by the example of the New-York Historical Society. After all, it was because the founders were predisposed toward popular education, as a result of their American heritage, that they sought the South Kensington as a model. Ironically, the South Kensington was, in its emphasis on popular education, highly atypical of most British museums of the 1850s and 1860s. Sir Henry Cole himself was a man whose liberal impulses were not widely typical of people of his class. Cole was often "a center of controversy," partially as "a natural result of opposition to his advanced and progressive ideas."[113] The South Kensington was so visible precisely because it was so unusual among British museums at that time. Far from being the product of its natural culture as were American museums, the South Kensington was on the leading edge of a new movement in culture. In fact, it is correct to say that the South Kensington was an American-style museum which happened to reside in England.

There were more than a dozen speakers at the Union League Club that evening, but one after another, they played variations on the theme of the American Compromise. George Fiske Comfort, a young professor from Princeton, pointed out, "The Museum could be visited by classes from the public and other schools, of New York, and adjacent places. . . . And thus the works of art in our Museum will be a means of improving the taste of the rising generation." Nor was this popular education to be limited to the wealthier schools, for Comfort proclaimed, "The Museum will form a place of resort for that large portion of our population which must forever be prevented from providing works of art in their own houses—the poor . . . Freely, and without cost."[114] Comfort's call for a museum accessible to all was echoed by the publisher George P. Putnam, who called for an institution "open to rich and poor and all the world alike."[115] Other art museums were meant for the serious student of art and the connoisseur exclusively; the Metropolitan was to be open to all, to benefit all. There can be no doubt but that the intentions of the founders were in line with the American Compromise, and their actions were consistent with their aims. The American Compromise was even written into the Metropolitan's charter. The legislature, in granting legal status to the museum, charged the trustees as follows: ". . . for the purpose of establishing and maintaining . . . a Museum and library of art, of encouraging and developing the study of the fine arts, and the application of arts to manufactures and practical life, of advancing the general knowledge of kindred subjects, and to that end, of furnishing popular instruction and recreation."[116]

On the one hand, the Metropolitan was to encourage and develop serious scholarship in the domain of the fine arts. On the other, it was to serve the practical function of educating the people in the fine arts and applying the principles of beauty to manufacturing. Thus the American Compromise was defined as the mission of the "Met."

In the 1870s, the Metropolitan made strenuous efforts to live up to its high goals. To support the serious study of art, the students at the Cooper Union, the Art Students League, and the Brooklyn Art Association were given, upon application, free tickets of admission. To accomplish popular education, the trustees encouraged school visits; as the 1865 annual report reveals, they met with much success: "Teachers, accompanied by scholars, frequently visit the Museum to examine illustrations of the immediate subjects of their study, and large numbers of young persons, especially young ladies, are among the most frequent visitors and the most careful students of works of art."[117] The Metropolitan clearly was aiming to balance the professional and the popular.

The American democratic culture had dictated the American Compromise to the Metropolitan, just as it had to the American museums that had come before it. The American Compromise was not invented at the Metropolitan, nor at the American Museum of Natural History, nor at the Boston Museum of the Fine Arts. It had painstakingly evolved from varied sources all over the nation. Charles Willson Peale recognized by 1817 that the museum could be a great tool for popular education and social amelioration. The next year, Daniel Drake began pursuing the vision of a museum as an institution which could educate everyone from the layman to the scholar. William Maclure threw open the doors of the Academy of Natural Sciences in 1828 to all visitors, without charge. Joseph Henry and Spencer Baird melded their respective visions by 1858 to form a National Museum that combined research and popular education. Edward Sheffield Bartholomew, in 1857, made a ringing declaration of the educational value of museums that led to change at the Wadsworth Atheneum. Luther Bradish and Frederic De Peyster, Jr., spent the decades of the 1850s and 1860s breathing new educational vigor into the New-York Historical Society. It was these men, responding to the dictates of the American democratic culture, who hammered out the form of the American Compromise. The great metropolitan museums arrived in 1870 just as this compromise took its final form. They were both the heirs and the culmination of the process. As the heirs, they built on the base of that which had gone before. As the culmination, they came to be credited with originating their inheritance.

The development of the great metropolitan museums fixed the American Compromise as the basis for future museum development in America. This basis has proved elastic; at certain times professionalism has predominated, at others, popular education. At the Metropolitan itself, popular education declined in the later 1880s and 1890s, only to experience a revival in 1905.[118] Vary how it might in externals, however, the underlying basis has remained unchanged since 1870. The evolution of American museums before 1870 truly produced the modern American museum. It is to the pioneers, not to their progeny, that we owe this considerable achievement, for they built great institutions for research and education from nothing but good intentions and the demands of American culture.

Epilogue: The American Compromise and Museum Historiography

The American Compromise came of age just as the great metropolitan museums were being founded. Their headlong rise to prominence in the international community of museums was so unexpected that it tended to make all in America that had gone before, at best, seem merely prologue. It was in the midst of this giddy ascent that the influential pioneers of museum history began to write. One might reasonably expect that their main theme for the early era would be a slow evolution toward the "take-off " point of 1870, but this is not the case. These first historians—George Brown Goode, John Cotton Dana, Theodore Low, and Francis Henry Taylor—were all children of the post-1870 era, museum professionals who looked askance at the times that had antedated the great metropolitan museums. They all agreed that nothing of consequence had occurred in the pre-1870 history of American museums, that for all practical purposes, museum history had begun in 1870. This harsh assessment has proved enormously influential in American museum historiography. It is interesting, however, that these historians have arrived at the same conclusions by means of two contradictory approaches, which may be labeled the professional criticism and the democratic criticism.

The professional criticism charges that the pioneer cabinets sub-

Museums as amateur

ordinated every goal to that of popular exhibition. The legitimate needs of the scholar were ignored, and the level of presentation frequently pandered to the basest instincts of a raucous and unrefined populace. Historians of this ilk were themselves professionals, that is, they made their living working in museums, and they naturally looked askance upon the museum world of 1870, which was pre-professional in two critical ways. First, especially before 1840, the disciplines which comprised the fields of most museums—history, art history, natural history, the physical sciences—were dominated by dilettantes who made their living at other callings. Second, even as late as 1870, a large majority of museum positions were filled by volunteers whose primary occupation lay elsewhere. Moreover, these writers sometimes used their histories as a means to justify and entrench a professional viewpoint that was not yet solidly established. Hence the professional disdain for amateurism permeates the writings of this school of thought.

The democratic criticism charges that museums have long been unresponsive to the needs of the general public, instead serving the desires of elitists drawn from the ranks of such groups as highly educated historians and scientists, or those with unusually acute aesthetic sensibilities, such as artists. At best, say the critics, the museums have failed to take steps to attract the people; at worst they have actually discouraged the public from attending. Realizing just how invidious this antiegalitarianism is in a free country, curators have taken care to disguise their exclusivity as necessary scholarship or efficient professionalism. But they never deceived the public, who understood that they were not welcome in the preserves of the plutocrats.

The professional criticism was the first of the two to develop, and it received its initial full statement from the pioneer in American museum history, George Brown Goode. Goode spent his first two years at the Smithsonian Institution, beginning in 1876, under the administration of Joseph Henry. When Henry died and Spencer F. Baird was elevated to the secretary's position, Goode became assistant secretary in charge of the National Museum. Thus he was exposed to the philosophy of Henry, who favored cabinets for scholars, and that of Baird, who thought that museums should simultaneously serve as research centers and popular educators. These opposing influences tended to make Goode's thought on the subject rather ambivalent. In order to fully understand his position on the professional criticism, it is necessary to first examine the legacy of Joseph Henry.

Joseph Henry was an able scientist who never presumed to be a historian. From the beginning of his tenure, however, he found it necessary to use history as a weapon whenever Congress attempted to establish a national museum under the Smithsonian's aegis. He argued that the institution had been established to increase and diffuse the stock of scientific knowledge, not to establish a museum, which abundant past experience suggested would inevitably become "an indiscriminate collection of objects of curiosity."[1] Henry believed that most popular museums sank to grief by placing sensational objects on exhibit. These tasteless displays attracted the worst elements of the public, and resulted in a "promiscuous collection"[2] of artifacts more suited to the needs of a sideshow than the requirements of science. Later in his career, after he had allowed the National Museum to become part of the Smithsonian, Henry came to appreciate the educational value of popular museums, but this conversion is largely forgotten today. What lingers in museum history is the picture of the critic who aggressively extolled the virtues of collections, "the object of [which] is exclusively the advancement of science. Not being intended for popular exhibition, they need not be mounted, but may be kept in drawers or packed away in labeled boxes or casks, until wanted for a special investigation."[3]

Young George Brown Goode, like the younger Joseph Henry, felt great enthusiasm for the museum as the handmaiden of science. Only eight years after the secretary's death, Goode presented his paper "Museum-History and Museums of History" at the third annual meeting of the American Historical Association. This paper is notable as the first formal work in the history of American museums, and it also marked the real birth of the professional criticism. Like all scholars breaking new ground, Goode inevitably made a few errors. He ignored the beginnings of American museum history by blithely stating, "The first chapter in the history of American museums is short. In colonial days there were none."[4] Goode was apparently unaware that the Charleston Museum had thrown open its doors to the public in 1773, two years before the Revolution. In a similar manner, he identified Charles Willson Peale's Philadelphia establishment, opened in 1785, as the first American public museum, thus ignoring the claims of Charleston and the cabinet of Pierre Eugène Du Simitière, which had been opened to public inspection in 1782. His most serious error, however, lay in an unstated assumption that the early collections were primitive attempts at museum making.

He dismissed Peale's museum by saying, "In 1800 it was full of popular attractions."[5] Considerable scientific work was carried on at Peale's; it can even be said that it was the national museum of its era. Why did Goode not appreciate that fact? The answer is simple: Goode's research in American museum history was limited to secondary sources. He was unaware of the true nature of pre-1870 museums because he had never examined the primary sources indispensable to achieving such an understanding. Only by keeping this fact in mind can the modern reader understand Goode's unintentional but devastating indictment of early cabinets as amateuristic sideshows. He went on to say, "The museum-idea is much broader than it was fifty or even twenty-five years ago. The museum of today is no longer a chance assemblage of curiosities, but rather a series of objects selected with reference to their value to investigators, or their possibilities for public enlightenment. The museum of the future may be made one of the chief agencies of the higher civilization."[6] There, in brief, was Goode's outline of American museum history. From the beginnings until about 1862, they were virtually worthless; from 1862 to 1887 they grew into useful tools for scientists and educators of the public; and in the future they were destined to become one of the locomotives pulling the world toward a better condition. This consideration of a future apotheosis undoubtedly made the realities of the present and the record of the past even less impressive. Perhaps this explains such sweeping denunciations of amateurism as, "The historical museums now in existence contain, as a rule, chance accumulations, like too many natural history museums of the present, like all in the past."[7]

Goode's influence upon museum history has been profound. Virtually every author in the field pays homage to him as the pioneer. Unfortunately most of his successors have also adopted his simplistic lineal view of development and his tendency to rely on the unsupported sweeping assumption in lieu of primary research.

The professional criticism struck a responsive chord in the museum world of the late nineteenth century. In 1891, Newton Horace Winchell, the state geologist of Minnesota, asserted, "The true museum; is that which approaches nearest to the cardinal idea of the Grecian Museum. Its aim is not to amuse, nor to instruct. . . . scientific research, long-continued study, profound contemplation, and conference with the writings of others—these are the purposes of such a museum."[8] In the last two decades of the nineteenth century, as the plutocrats rose to social ascendancy, as the universities began to produce professional scholars, as callings became professions, and as America passed from cultural isolation to cultural competition vis-à-vis Europe, both Goode's and Winchell's views on professionalism seemed quite natural.

Despite the reign of the profesional, the seeds of a new era were well planted in this period. The telegraph and the railroad crisscrossed the nation, giant retail firms began to offer standardized merchandise, and the popular press and penny tabloids catered to everyman. By the dawn of the twentieth century, a profound and sustained popular resurgence was under way, one which has persisted to the present. Such an atmosphere has proved noxious to the professional criticism. To upbraid a museum for catering to the popular taste today seems to smack of virulent elitism. The last scholar to risk this charge, and to apply the professional criticism in a sweeping way, was the witty and often acerbic Francis Henry Taylor, who, at the height of his career, was the director of the Metropolitan Museum of Art.

Taylor was never one to suffer foolishness gladly, and in his slim volume entitled *Babel's Tower* he pulled no punches. Casting a jaundiced professional's eye on the years before 1870, he announced, "The eighteen forties and fifties were rather barren years for museum history."[9] This is an astonishing claim in light of the fact that museums were being founded all over the nation during those two decades, including one of the first public art galleries in 1842 and the National Museum in 1858. Perhaps Taylor confused the state of art museums (which during these decades were relatively less developed than history cabinets) with the state of all museums. In any case, Taylor summarized his view of the cradle age of American museums in a single sentence: "It is prophetic, perhaps, that the foundations of American museums in general, and of the American Museum of Natural History in particular, were laid by Charles Willson Peale . . . and by P. T. Barnum of circus fame. Barnum's dictum 'there's a sucker born every minute' has been one of the mottoes of our profession ever since."[10] Both Taylor's penchant for the flippant remark and his zest for taking a swipe at the competition are only too clear in this statement. Less forgivable is his lapse in historical judgment in misquoting Barnum,[11] and in equating the ethics of the great showman and the great painter. Taylor's contempt for the amateurism and the vulgarity of the pre-1870 museum world could not be clearer.

It is indeed an open question whether Taylor believed that any institution worthy of memory existed in America before the Metropolitan. He declared, "It was not until after the Civil War that America became conscious of her manifest destiny and demanded a share of the artistic treasures of history."[12] Taylor's experience as director of the best art museum in the New World naturally inclined him toward an admiration of professionalism and a contempt for amateurism. But he saw no reason why strong professionalism could not be combined with an attractive appeal to the public. Like Goode, his thinking on the subject was ambivalent, and will be dealt with fully later.

Taylor was the last scholar to embrace truly the professional criticism. Its elitist undertones made it less palatable as the century wore on, and absolutely anathema since the 1960s. Today most scholars reserve it solely for the museums before 1870, "which," as Nathaniel Burt recently put it, "degenerated into more and more rampant, spectacular and vulgar exhibitionism."[13] A residual trace of the professional criticism does sometimes appear in otherwise excellent works of museum history being written today. For example, Kenneth Hudson recently claimed, "It would hardly be an exaggeration to say that until the 1880s the museum world consisted of four countries: France, Germany, England, and Italy. There were, of course, collections elsewhere, including some of great importance, but little innovation was taking place outside these four countries."[14]

Such is the indictment leveled by the professional criticism. Is it an accurate picture? It is undeniable that many early museums sooner or later became sideshows of the most vulgar variety. They exhibited freaks of nature and bizarre creations of man, and generally sought to titillate their visitors rather than enlighten them. Such a stance was almost inevitable for small proprietary concerns in which the gate receipts had to cover expenses. This was, however, hardly the only type of early museum. Even before the turn of the nineteenth century Pierre Eugène Du Simitière and Charles Willson Peale were managing, in Philadelphia, museums focusing, respectively, on history and science. The cabinets of the New-York Historical Society and the museum of the Academy of Natural Sciences of Philadelphia were functioning by 1820. All of these major institutions were serious enterprises of great value to the best scholars of the day. Their proprietors did their best, given their lack of funds, to conduct museums that would be useful in both practical and cultural terms.

Just how well they succeeded is recorded in the accounts left by European visitors to the United States. To be sure, many of these accounts, particularly those which compared American museums to the great establishments of Europe like the Louvre and the British Museum, were critical. But those who took into consideration the youthful age of the American experiment were usually rather impressed. The Englishman William Newnham Blane commented approvingly on his 1822 visit to the Western Museum: "The museum at Cincinnati, though small, is very interesting to a lover of natural history. All the specimens are very neatly arranged."[15] John Melish, another English visitor, praised Peale's museum in Philadelphia as "a very excellent collection, principally of subjects in natural history, and does honour to the ingenuity and taste of the proprietor."[16] Occasionally even as cosmopolitan and sophisticated a traveler as the Spanish diplomat Francisco de Miranda could be moved to enthusiasm over the value of an American museum, in this case Peale's: "It not only offers entertainment and pleasure to the curious and educated traveler, but also sheds light on history and forms patriotic and virtuous ideas in the youth, to whom it presents the worthiest monument which could be erected to the glory of an entire people! Certainly this example should be imitated by all other nations which value virtue and good taste!"[17] Such comments simply do not square with the vision of bumbling amateurs and tasteless peepshows painted for us by Goode and Taylor. They never realized that valuable cabinets existed along with the catchpenny ones, so they tarred all pre-1870 institutions with the same brush. The professional criticism is thus in many ways uncharitable and inaccurate, but it has left a very strong mark upon the historiography of early American museums.

Just as George Brown Goode was the father of the professional criticism, so too was he the first to express the democratic criticism. He probably received the inspiration for the democratic criticism from Spencer Baird, his boss at the Smithsonian. Baird's tenure at the National Museum was marked by devotion to the goal of making the collections more accessible to the general public. He succeeded in his efforts, and it seems likely that young Goode absorbed some of Baird's ideas and opinions on the subject of museums. In "Museum-History and Museums of History," the very article in which he formulated the professional criticism, Goode also spelled out the credo of the democratic criticism.

Goode attacked the sort of museums which Joseph Henry had found so attractive in the 1850s: those cabinets which catered exclusively to the scholar or the connoisseur. Such institutions, while of great value to the specialist, were well-nigh unintelligible to the vast American public.

In place of these museums for the few, Goode envisioned "the people's museum," which should be "designed more thoughtfully to meet the needs of the people, and [be] more intimately intertwined with the policy of national popular education."[18] In short, Goode believed that any museum which catered only to a clientele of scholars was violating the egalitarian ethos of America. Every American should have equal access to the artifacts of a museum, and an equal opportunity to learn from them. One need not be a scholar to need the resources offered by a museum. Goode summed up his credo in a stirring statement which still has a contemporary ring: "The museum of the future in this democratic land should be adapted to the needs of the mechanic, the factory operator, the day-laborer, the salesman, and the clerk, as much as to those of the professional man and the man of leisure."[19]

Thus Goode must be remembered as the first historian to use both the professional and the democratic criticisms. Inevitably, however, he was also the first historian to experience the inherent conflict between them and the first to fail to resolve it. As assistant secretary, and as a highly respected scientist, Goode sought to make the National Museum a center of research for scholars. As a museum professional and a believer in the American Compromise, he wanted to fill his galleries with exhibits that would enlighten the general public. The professionals did not need or want popular education, and the people frequently were attracted by techniques which professionals found vulgar. The two were not easy to mix, and Goode's ambivalence was the honest result of the need to reconcile two very different ideals.

No such misgivings troubled the second great champion of the democratic criticism. John Cotton Dana started his career as a librarian, and he was much acclaimed for his innovative work in that profession. In 1909 he changed careers to become the director of the Newark Museum. Dana was frankly appalled by what he perceived to be the reactionary nature of his new profession, by its exclusivity, by its tendency to value connoisseurship over popular education. He promptly launched several imaginative programs to educate the public and popularize art. He also authored, beginning in 1917, a string of booklets entitled "The New Museum Series," which aimed to demonstrate how museums could be turned into instruments for popular education and recreation.

In the opening sentence in the first booklet he threw down the gauntlet. "There are about eighty live museums in the United States," announced Dana. "Of these, indeed, it is doubtful if the term 'live' can be properly applied to more than fifty."[20] What made a museum "live"? Dana felt that the museum which taught, which advertised, which reached out to its public, was "live." Why did most American museums fail to meet these standards? "It was inevitable," answered Dana, "that the first wish of all our museum enthusiasts should be to produce imitations of the European institutions. Those institutions were, in most cases, long established and greatly admired and they furnished the only illustrations of the museum idea."[21] Dana blamed the aristocratic background of European museums for the tendency to value collection over exhibition and preservation over education. Americans copied this elitist orientation from the very beginning, and by 1909 it was firmly entrenched. Dana lamented, "By no right in reason whatever is the museum a mere collection of things, save by right of precedent. Yet precedent has so ruled in this field that our carefully organized museums have little more power to influence their communities than a painting which hangs on the wall of some sanctuary, a sanctuary which few visit."[22] Precedent decreed that the objects were more important than the people the institution served, and precedents were upheld by dogmatic and inflexibly conservative curators who valued the collection over education.

Dana thus introduced the "corrupted European institution" thesis into museum historiography. American museums were elitist, but the ultimate responsibility for this sad fact lay with their European models. American curators nurtured these examples, and carefully preserved them through the years. Dana could not imagine that such hide-bound organizations could ever have been different in the past, so they must have been absolutely static from the beginning. He thus projected contemporary conditions backward into the past and called it history. He did not, however, attempt to substantiate his claims by research. Unfortunately, despite his unsound methods, the message proved very persuasive to later historians.

Dana's foremost disciple was Theodore L. Low, whose book, *The Museum as a Social Instrument,* first published in 1942, has proved enormously influential, in both a beneficial and a pernicious sense. Low's work was commissioned by the Committee on Education of the American Association of Museums to define the social and educational mission of the museum in America and to measure how well that ideal was being met in practice. Low, at that time a graduate student, produced an indictment of the museum world in the early 1940s, accusing curators of being gluttonous collectors who frankly did not care if the public derived any benefit from their treasures. He went on to outline the proper role of education in museums, and called for the transformation of the museum into a true social instrument, an agency for public improvement through education.

Low's tract did much to galvanize a renaissance for museum education, which was a very important accomplishment. His short section on museum history, however, which forms the classic exposition of the democratic criticism, was a disservice to the discipline. Low's view of history, however, must be understood against the backdrop of social change during the eventful years from the end of World War I to 1942. Three dominant events during this period caught his attention: the ascendancy of mass culture beginning in the 1920s, the depression, and the rise of Fascism and Nazism. From the first, Low concluded that museums must be more accessible to everyone than ever before. From the second, he came to believe that in the new economy of scarcity, museums must justify their existence in terms of their tangible benfits to society. From the third, he became convinced that the rise of institutionalized intolerance was the result of the failure of education, and that museums must play a part in preventing its occurrence in America. Only by understanding these central concerns can the reader fully appreciate *The Museum as a Social Instrument.*

Low's gospel of accessibility, usefulness, and educational value owed much to the influence of John Cotton Dana, for Low quoted

Dana extensively in his work. Unfortunately, Low copied not only Dana's sentiments, but also his fallacious methods of projecting the present upon the past. This is not to say that Low's errors were merely derivative; indeed he committed a novel blunder when he began by announcing that he would "look briefly into the history of museums"[23] in America, and then began his consideration of the subject with the Metropolitan Museum of Art!

To ignore the vital first century of museum history was a serious sin of omission, but Low compounded the transgression by peppering his treatment with such ambiguous terms as "newly-born museums," "the early museum," and "since the beginning." These strongly implied that he was considering museum history in America since its beginning, or 1773, even though his introduction to the historical section suggests that he was actually referring only to the years after 1870. Unfortunately, Low nowhere in the book made his dates explicit, with the result that both the pre-1870 and post-1870 interpretations are possible.

A close reading of *The Museum as a Social Instrument* suggests that Low meant to ignore the first century, and his later ambiguous references were the products of carelessness rather than design. But this confusing exposition, set forth in bold terms in a very influential book, has done violence to pre-1870 museum history. At best, readers of *The Museum as a Social Instrument* form the idea that this period is too insignificant to be mentioned. At worst, they come to believe that the pre-1870 museum world was characterized by the many enormities with which Low really meant to charge the post-1870 milieu.

Since Low's version of the democratic criticism can be so easily misread, it is important to consider it here. No attempt will be made to judge the validity of his criticisms for the post-1870 museum world, but it will quickly become obvious that his argument becomes ludicrous if it is applied to the years before 1870.

When a museum was founded, Low posited, it was natural that its staff should concentrate more on building its collection than on educating the people it served. American museums, however, had continued to stress the former over the latter long after collections had been built up to adequate levels. Low claimed,

"Two factors were largely accountable for this blindness. In the first place, the staff of the early museum was chosen for its scholarship and not for its social consciousness. The second factor was that museum men instinctively turned to Europe for their ideas."[24]

Leaving aside the merit of this argument for the years after 1870, one will quickly see that this position is absurd if taken to apply to the pre-1870 era. Low's first statement is contradicted by the facts. America's earliest museums were run by entrepreneur-virtuosos like Peale, Du Simitière, and Gardiner Baker. Scholars first came onto the scene in small numbers with the founding of the historical societies (Massachusetts in 1791, New-York in 1804), but they did not reach significance in curatorial ranks until the 1840s and did not become dominant until well after the Civil War.

Low's second argument, if applied to the pre-1870 era, contains a grain of truth, but is still much exaggerated. True, the early museum-makers did model some of their techniques and base some of their goals upon European examples. But from the very beginning their cabinets were shaped by the unmistakably American influences of available material and public demand. The standard monographs on the history of art and artists in the United States confirm this assertion. Lillian Miller found that beginning shortly after 1783 a cultural nationalism grew in favor of American efforts. This attitude was reinforced by the War of 1812 and continued to be influential until the late 1850s. Only after the Civil War did a more cosmopolitan outlook emerge.[25] Neil Harris discovered that American artists (many of whom, including Du Simitière, Charles, Raphaelle, Rembrandt and Rubens Peale, John Trumbull, and Hiram Powers, founded or worked in museums) consciously adopted the ideologies and outlooks of their patrons, the "philistine" merchants, bankers, and industrialists. These patrons were highly nationalistic in outlook, and the artists rapidly came to join them in their rejection of European influences.[26]

Low positively identified those responsible for ignoring education in museums: three groups of conservative men who obstinately blocked progressive changes. These were the curators, directors, and trustees. Only the educational staffs had ever stood for progress in the profession, but they had been constantly over-ruled by the archconservatives in the position of power. This is another reason why a pre-1870 interpretation is untenable, for there were no "educational staffs," as such, in American museums before 1870. At any rate, these conservative leaders were "little more than pseudo-Europeans who thought only in terms of European precedents. What they failed to realize was that there could be such a thing as a museum with distinctly American characteristics."[27] Such an attitude was antidemocratic and a betrayal of America's egalitarian ethos; moreover, it flouted Low's doctrines of accessibility, usefulness, and educational value. This statement reflects the strong influence of Dana's "corrupted European institution" thesis upon Low's thought, and the events that had transpired in Europe since Dana had propounded it undoubtedly tended to confirm and justify its xenophobic overtones. To reject European museum history as a totally negative force was not only uncharitable, but also completely incorrect. And to argue that American museums did not display distinctively American characteristics was to ignore reality in order to make a point.

But Low did not shrink from the absurdities of his critique; in fact, he boldly carried it to its logical conclusion:

> The point I wish to make, however, is that museums soon became little more than isolated segments of European culture set in a hostile environment. This fact resulted in an ever-increasing tendency on the part of museums to remain aloof and to look with disdain on the vast majority of Americans whose acquaintance with art was so negligible. Furthermore, this attitude, coupled with the emphasis on scholarship, had the unfortunate faculty of strengthening itself, and the shell which museums somewhat unconsciously had erected around themselves grew thicker and more impenetrable. As a result, museum men have drifted farther and farther away from the public until today it is virtually impossible for many of them to see the problems which confront them in their true light.[28]

This is truly a sweeping indictment. The museum professional is an outsider, alien to and alienated from his native culture. Wrapping himself in a cloak of European custom and higher learning, he looks upon his less fortunate countrymen with scorn. Although he is happy to accept money gathered from the people, he shuts himself off from their needs and concerns. He is an aristocrat in every negative sense of that term, and his museum is a mere playground for the well-off and well-educated, an island of elitist culture set in a hostile democratic sea.

Low's polemic simply unravels when it is critically examined. First, it fails every reasonable test of evidence. Low does not offer a shred of documentation to prove that American museum professionals were unduly influenced by Europeans, nor does he prove that European influence is of necessity a bad thing. In place of solid analysis, Low, like Dana, substituted a presentist and static view of history. Low first assumed (but did not prove) a deplorable state of affairs in the museum world of 1942. By using such words as "tradition," "precedent," and "conservatism," he suggested that the current state of affairs must have prevailed, without variation, from the first moment of museum history. This view is antihistorical, for it projects present conditions onto the past, and it is ahistorical, for it ignores the inevitability of change over time. Devoid of primary evidence and methodologically faulty, Theodore Low's "history" in *The Museum as a Social Instrument* is in reality not history at all, but merely a series of ambiguous, unproven, and mostly inaccurate assertions.

Flimsy as was the argument, however, it struck a responsive chord in a country engaged in a struggle for survival. One man upon whom it had a profound influence was Francis Henry Taylor. The sometime director of the Metropolitan has already been examined as a champion of the professional criticism, but in the same work, *Babel's Tower*, in which he blasted amateurism, Taylor also criticized museums for shunning the public. Taylor was the chairman of the Committee on Education of the American Association of Museums in 1942; he wrote an approving foreword for *The Museum as a Social Instrument* and published the booklet on the Metropolitan's press. The strong influence of Low is very obvious in *Babel's Tower*.

Taylor certainly embraced Low's contempt for the pre-1870 museum world. In his professional criticism, he called the era "barren," compared institutions then in existence to sideshows, and proclaimed that it was only after the Civil War that real museums were founded. On the other hand, he echoed Low in his criticism of elitism in American museums. He asked, "Does it not appear to us that we, of all peoples of history, have had a better, more natural and less prejudiced opportunity to make the museum mean something to the general public? I think we have, and that we have thrown this opportunity away."[29] The chance was squandered in the name of higher learning, but all too often, "scholarship" provided the rationale for snobbery; as Taylor put it, "We have deliberately high-hatted [the public] and called it scholarship."[30]

Despite his feelings about elitism, Taylor had a prescient insight about what the American museum was and always had been: "The American museum is, after all, neither an abandoned European palace nor a solution for storing and classifying the accumulated national wealth of the past. It is an American phenomenon, developed by the people, for the people, and of the people. This is not fascism—it is simple American history."[31] Taylor was quite correct; such a picture did come from simple American history. But he never explained how this reflection and instrument of the people could be at once a catchpenny show pandering to their basest instincts and a stronghold of their social betters, determined to keep them at arm's length. Taylor's ambivalence on this point calls to mind the same difficulty experienced by George Brown Goode, and was yet another manifestation of the difficulty of treading the fine line between democratic sentiments and professional standards in the museum world.

The democratic criticism, invented by Goode and refined by Low and Taylor, remains a vital force in recent museum historiography. Scholars have continued to criticize "elitists" in museums who have failed to be responsive to the needs of the people. No less an authortiy than a former secretary of the Smithsonian decried the day when these scoundrels "first created the public impression [of] something ponderous, dull, musty, dead; a graveyard of old bones of the past."[32] Another scholar bewailed the fact that a museum has become "an alien land," in which "what [the people] saw had little relevance to their lives."[33] The democratic criticism received a boost during the 1960s when many museums were attacked for being tools of the "uptight white establishment." It remains a popular approach in current efforts. But is it a fair critique? Certainly one could cite instances for which it was applicable; the National Museum itself was accessible only to scholars in the early 1850s. But in most cases, constraints on the admission of the general public were dictated by financial considerations. In the rather egalitarian, nationalistic, and democratic culture which arose after the complete breakdown of the deferential mode of society following the War of 1812, the kind of blatant "foreign" behavior described by the democratic critics would never have been tolerated. Moreover, a look at the men who formed the early museums shows that especially after 1820 they tended to come from the middle class—apothecaries, merchants, bankers, physicians—men far more likely to have come from the people than to have despised the people. When one turns to Europe at the same time, one often finds expressions of true elitism which would have been absolutely unthinkable in America. In America museums were opened to the public for nominal admission fees before the Revolution, and as early as 1794 private organizations experimented with opening their cabinets to the gratuitous admission of the public on certain days and at certain times. Compared to present-day standards, that is perhaps somewhat elitist and unresponsive, but we do violence to history when we use present standards in order to judge past events. By the standards of the time, it was very responsive.

In order to dismiss the first century of museum history as having produced nothing more than a playground for the multitude or, alternatively, a sanctuary for the moneyed cognoscenti, the museum historians have made the striking assumption that museums have developed in America independently of American culture. In some mysterious manner, the social, intellectual, political, and economic upheavals of the century from 1770 to 1870 passed museums by. Somehow, the cabinets and galleries remained insulated from war, reaction, reform, and depression, the ferments that profoundly altered all other social institutions. They re-

mained fixed, according to the orientation of the critic, as either
a constant sideshow or a consistent refuge for snobs. Just how
the museums acquired this peculiar cultural immunity, however,
no one has ventured to explain.

Only since the mid-1960s has museum history received more
sympathetic and more sophisticated treatment from scholars. A
mere handful of authors have examined the general history of
museums,[34] while the majority focused on a single institution or
compiled anthologies examining a number of museums individually.[35] These authors have generally been more appreciative of
early museums than a Low or a Taylor, although some employ
the old criticisms occasionally. All, however, share a common
outlook on one point: They believe that there was no museum
movement worth considering in the pre-1870 era. They hold, explicitly or implicitly, that museums grew in a random fashion
and in near-total isolation from one another. They treat the birth
and development of each cabinet separately from all others, as
if each one were a novel idea, culminating in a discrete, indeed
unique institution. Linkages among the network of American museums are neither sought nor explored. They are assumed to have
been as isolated from each other as they supposedly were es-
tranged from American culture in general. Yet these various and
scattered institutions somehow developed in such predictable and
similar ways that many of the same historians have dismissed the
American museum world by means of sweeping general criticisms. This picture of miscellaneous birth and random development producing a monolithic aggregation is found throughout
the literature, and it seems that no one has ever noticed, much
less addressed, the contradiction at its base.

The American museum world prior to 1870 has thus suffered
from a very uncharitable assessment on the part of its historians.
The worst of them have ridiculed its foibles and ignored its accomplishments without even the pretense of a serious investigation. They simply never applied to this subject the ordinary standard of historical proof, which demands extensive work in
primary sources. Even the best of the recent crop of historians,
while more judicious in their evaluation of individual museums,

have continued to treat the history of each in isolation from all of the others. Today, nearly a century after George Brown Goode began writing on the subject of museum history, there is still not a satisfactory general history of museums in America before 1870.

The preceding pages do not comprise that general history, but they can serve as a starting point for that effort. It now seems reasonably clear that the professional criticism is untenable, for there were many museums with high aims and serious purposes before 1870. The democratic criticism is equally inapplicable, for snobbery and elitism were too dangerous to practice during an egalitarian age. Instead, the pre-1870 American museum world sprang from, and developed with, the American democratic culture. In a remarkable fashion, American museums managed to reconcile the incompatible demands of the people for education and scholars for research assistance. This marriage of popular and elite needs, the American Compromise, had fully developed by 1870, and has determined the form of American museums ever since.

The evolution of the American Compromise, the critical formative influence in American museum history, was completed by 1870. Therefore, the first century of that history, far from being the inconsequential era imagined by earlier historians, was the seminal period in American museum history. Much more work needs to be done in this area before we can claim to have a reasonable understanding of it, but the door is at last open. And perhaps at last the lingering negative image fostered by generations of previous historians, an image that early museums did not, in the main, deserve, will at last be dispelled, to be replaced by a more balanced, accurate, and truthful portrait.

Notes

Prologue: Thesis, Definitions, and Structure

1. George Brown Goode, "Museum-History and Museums of History," in *Papers of the American Historical Association* (New York: G. P. Putnam & Sons, 1888), p. 263.
2. Theodore L. Low, *The Museum as a Social Instrument: A Study Undertaken for the Committee on Education of the American Association of Museums* (New York: The Metropolitan Museum of Art, 1942), p. 9.
3. See Ronald P. Formisano, "Deferential-Participant Politics: The Early Republic's Political Culture, 1789–1840," *American Political Science Review* 68 (June 1974): 473–87, for a detailed explanation of the deferential-participant model.
4. The inspiration for the periodization herein employed comes from the thesis of Henry S. May in *The Enlightenment in America* (New York: Oxford University Press, 1976).
5. So argues George Daniels in his perceptive essay, "The Process of Professionalization in American Science: The Emergent Years, 1820–1860," in Nathan Reingold, ed., *Science in America Since 1820* (New York: Science History Publications, 1976), pp. 63–78.
6. The thesis is that of Eric Foner set forth in *Free Soil, Free Labor, Free Men: The Ideology of the Republican Party Before the Civil War* (New York: Oxford University Press, 1970), pp. 34–39, 48–51.

1. The Curio Cabinet Transplanted to the New World, 1740–1780

1. J. Hector St. John Crevecoeur, *Letters from an American Farmer* (London: Thomas Davies & Lockyer Davis, 1782; reprint ed., Garden City, N.Y.: Dolphin Books/Doubleday, undated), p. 49.

2. See Germaine Bazin, *The Museum Age* (New York: Universe Books, 1967).

3. See Henry Steele Commager, *The Empire of Reason: How Europe Imagined and America Realized the Enlightenment* (Garden City, N.Y.: Doubleday, 1977); May, *The Enlightenment in America*; Donald H. Meyer, *The Democratic Enlightenment* (New York: G. P. Putnam's Sons, 1976).

4. Herbert and Marjorie Katz, *Museums, USA: A History and Guide* (Garden City, N.Y.: Doubleday & Company, 1965), p. 1.

5. Elizabeth W. Stone, *American Library Development: 1600–1899* (New York: The H. W. Wilson Company, 1977), pp. 59, 230.

6. Carl and Jessica Bridenbaugh, *Rebels and Gentlemen: Philadelphia in the Age of Franklin* (New York: Reynal and Hitchcock, 1942), p. 330.

7. Brook Hindle, *The Pursuit of Science in Revolutionary America: 1735–1789* (Chapel Hill: University of North Carolina Press, 1956), p. 65.

8. Bridenbaugh and Bridenbaugh, *Rebels and Gentlemen*, p. 273.

9. Two indispensable sources for the history of Harvard's cabinet are David P. Wheatland, *The Apparatus of Science at Harvard: 1765–1800* (Cambridge: Harvard Press, 1968), pp. 3–5, 190–99, and William Hayes Fogg Art Museum, *Early Science at Harvard: Innovators and Their Instruments* (Cambridge: Fogg Art Museum, 1969), pp. 1–40. The best general account of the cabinet's relation to the college is still Samuel Eliot Morison, *Three Centuries of Harvard: 1636–1936* (Cambridge: Harvard University Press, 1936), pp. 92–97, 170–73.

10. Whitfield J. Bell, Jr., "The Cabinet of the American Philosophical Society," in Whitfield J. Bell, Jr., et al., *A Cabinet of Curiosities: Five Episodes in the Evolution of American Museums* (Charlottesville: University Press of Virginia, 1967), pp. 1–34. Quoted material is on pp. 1–2. The best account of the founding of the American Philosophical Society is still Hindle's *Pursuit of Science in Revolutionary America*, pp. 127–45, 263–79.

11. Carl Bridenbaugh, *Cities in Revolt: Urban Life in America, 1743–1776* (New York: Alfred A. Knopf, 1955), p. 416.

12. James. S. Whitehead, ed., "The Autobiography of Peter S. Du Ponceau," *The Pennsylvania Magazine of History and Biography* 63 (November 1939): 432–61.

13. Francois-Jean, Marquis de Chastellux, *Travels in North America in the Years 1780, 1781 and 1782*, 2 vols. (Paris, 1786; reprint ed., Chapel Hill: University of North Carolina Press, 1963), p. 146. Chastellux (1734–1788) was a man of science, a member of both the French Academy and the American Philosophical Society. He was a general in the French army in America, and was at the time of his visit properly the chevalier, not becoming the marquis until the death of his older brother in 1784.

14. Lyman H. Butterfield, ed., *The Adams Papers, Series I: Diaries and Autobiography of John Adams, Vol. 2, Diary 1771–1781* (Cambridge: Belknap Press of Harvard University, 1961), p. 152.

15. Butterfield, *The Adams Papers, Series I: Adams Family Correspondence, Vol. 2: June, 1776–March, 1778* (Cambridge: Belknap Press of Harvard University, 1963), p. 236.

16. Chastellux, *Travels in North America*, p. 146.

17. Evelyn M. Acomb, "The Journal of Baron Von Closen," *William and Mary Quarterly* 10 (April 1953): 206. Baron Ludwig Von Closen (ca. 1752–1830) was a German who served as an aide-de-camp to General Rochambeau, commander of the French army in America.
18. Chastellux, *Travels in North America*, p. 146.
19. Stone, *American Library Development*, pp. 132, 214.
20. Robert Goodwyn Rhett, *Charleston: An Epic of South Carolina* (Richmond: Garrett and Massie, 1940), p. 198.
21. Bridenbaugh, *Cities in Revolt*, p. 384.
22. Katz and Katz, *Museums, USA*, p. 1.
23. Edward P. Alexander, *Museums in Motion: An Introduction to the History and Functions of Museums* (Nashville: American Association for State and Local History, 1979), p. 47.
24. Ibid.
25. George C. Rogers, Jr., *Charleston in the Age of the Pinckneys* (Norman: University of Oklahoma Press, 1969), p. 96.
26. Michael O'Brien and David Moltke-Hansen, *Intellectual Life in Antebellum Charleston* (Knoxville: University of Tennessee Press, 1986), p. 23.
27. See Albert E. Sanders, "The Charleston Museum and the Promotion of Science in Antebellum South Carolina" (Paper presented at the Third Citadel Conference on the South, Charleston, South Carolina, April 25, 1981), and Lester D. Stephens, *Ancient Animals and Other Wondrous Things: The Story of Francis Simmons Holmes, Paleontologist and Curator of the Charleston Museum,* Contributions From The Charleston Museum, no. XVII, February 1988.
28. Bridenbaugh, *Cities in Revolt*, p. 384.
29. Quoted in Hindle, *The Pursuit of Science*, p. 317.

2. The Moderate Enlightenment, 1780–1800: The Museum for the Respectability

1. May, *The Enlightenment in America*, pp. xvi–xvii.
2. Commager, *The Empire of Reason*, pp. xi–xii.
3. May, *The Enlightenment in America*, p. 26.
4. Meyer, *The Democratic Enlightenment*, p. 200.
5. J. R. Pole, "Enlightenment and the Politics of American Nature," in Roy Porter and Mikulas Teich, eds., *The Enlightenment in National Context* (London: Cambridge University Press, 1981), p. 199.
6. Meyer, *The Democratic Enlightenment*, p. xxiv.
7. John Adams to Abigail Adams, August 14, 1776, Butterfield, *Adams Family Correspondence, Vol. 2, June, 1776–March, 1778, p. 96.*
8. Charles Coleman Sellers, *Mr. Peale's Museum: Charles Willson Peale and the First Popular Museum of Natural Science and Art* (New York: W. W. Norton, 1980), p. 12.
9. Pierre Eugène Du Simitière to Colonel Daniel Brodhead, August 29, 1781, Society Miscellaneous Collections, Historical Society of Pennsylvania.
10. Paul Ginsberg Sifton, "Pierre Eugène Du Simitière (1737–1784): Collector

in Revolutionary America" (Ph. D. dissertation, University of Pennsylvania, 1960), p. 13. More recent treatments of Du Simitière include "Pierre Eugène Du Simitière: His American Museum 200 Years After," Catalogue of an exhibition, July to October 1985, Library Company of Philadelphia, and Joel J. Orosz, "Pierre Eugène Du Simitière: Museum Pioneer in America," *Museum Studies Journal* 1 (Spring 1985): 8–18.

11. Memorial of Pierre Eugène Du Simitière to Thomas Wharton, President of the Executive Council of the Commonwealth of Pennsylvania, August 18, 1777, Pierre Eugène Du Simitière Collection, New York Public Library.

12. *The Papers of the Continental Congress*, Foreign Affairs Division, July 22, 1779, National Archives.

13. Edmund A. Burnett, *Letters of Members of the Continental Congress* (Washington, D.C.: The Carnegie Institution of Washington, 1921), 1: 209.

14. Pierre Eugène Du Simitière to Nathaniel Scudder, August 20, 1780, Du Simitière Letter Book, Peter Force Papers, Series 8d, Library of Congress.

15. Acomb, "Journal of Von Closen," p. 207.

16. Ibid.

17. Chastellux, *Travels in North America*, p. 145.

18. Ibid.

19. Pierre Eugène Du Simitière to Monsieur Gerard, September 12, 1782, Du Simitière Letter Book, Peter Force Papers, Series 8d, Library of Congress.

20. Pierre Eugène Du Simitière, Broadside dated June 1, 1782, Library Company of Philadelphia.

21. Ibid.

22. Ibid.

23. Ibid.

24. Ibid.

25. See Lillian Miller, *Patrons and Patriotism: Encouragement of the Fine Arts in America, 1790–1860* (Chicago: University of Chicago Press, 1966), pp. 8–23, and Neil Harris, *The Artist in American Society: The Formative Years, 1790–1860* (New York: George Braziller, 1966), pp. vii–xi, 295–98.

26. Acomb, "Journal of Von Closen," p. 207.

27. Chastellux, *Travels in North America*, p. 145.

28. Johann David Schoepf, *Travels in the Confederation [1783–1784]* (Philadelphia, 1911; reprint ed., trans. and ed. Alfred J. Morrison, New York: Bergman Publishers, 1968), pp. 85–86. Schoepf (1752–1800) was a physician with a keen interest in natural history. He was in America from 1777 to 1784 as a surgeon with troops from Ansbach.

29. Du Simitière to Monsieur Gerard, September 12, 1782.

30. Schoepf, *Travels in the Confederation*, p. 86.

31. Sifton, "Pierre Eugène Du Simitière," p. 450 n.

32. Thomas Jefferson to Martha Jefferson, February 18, 1784, in Julian P. Boyd, ed., *The Papers of Thomas Jefferson* (Princeton: Princeton University Press, 1950), 6: 543.

33. Hans Huth, "Pierre Eugène Du Simitière and the Beginnings of the American Historical Museum," *The Pennsylvania Magazine of History and Biography* 69 (October 1945): 321.

34. Charles Willson Peale to Rembrandt Peale, October 28, 1812, in Lillian B. Miller, ed., *The Collected Papers of Charles Willson Peale and his Family on Microfiche* (Millwood, N.Y.: Kraus Microforms, 1981), Series II-A, Card 15. Citations to this source will be given hereafter as *PPF*, for "Peale Papers on Fiche."

35. Charles Willson Peale, "1826 Autobiography," *PPF*, Series II-C, Card 14.

36. Pierre Eugène Du Simitière, *Scraps*, no. 92, p. 14, Historical Society of Pennsylvania.

37. Charles Willson Peale to the American Philosophical Society, March 7, 1797, *PPF*, Series II-A, Card 21.

38. Sellers, *Mr. Peale's Museum*, p. 23.

39. See *Charles Willson Peale* (New York: Charles Scribner's Sons, 1969) and *Mr. Peale's Museum*, previously cited. Seller's research is impeccable and his conclusions, though colored by filial loyalty, are basically sound.

40. C. W. Peale to David Ramsay, October 18, 1786, *PPF*, Series II-A, Card 14.

41. Lillian B. Miller, "Charles Willson Peale: A Life of Harmony and Purpose," in Edgar P. Richardson, ed., *Charles Willson Peale and His World* (New York: Harry N. Abrams, 1983), p. 171.

42. C. W. Peale, "1826 Autobiography," *PPF*, Series II-C.

43. C. W. Peale, Introductory Lecture on Natural History, 1799, *PPF*, Series II-D, Card 2.

44. Sellers, *Mr. Peale's Museum*, p. 15.

45. Miller, "A Life of Harmony," p. 196.

46. C. W. Peale to Mr. Seagrave, March 23, 1796, *PPF*, Series II-A, Card 20.

47. C. W. Peale to the American Philosophical Society, March 7, 1797, *PPF*, Series II-A, Card 21.

48. C. W. Peale to Timothy Matlack, March 9, 1800, *PPF*, Series II-A, Card 23.

49. Richardson, "Charles Willson Peale and His World," p. 87.

50. C. W. Peale to [?], June 29, 1796, *PPF*, Series II-A, Card 22.

51. C. W. Peale, Second Lecture, 1799, *PPF*, Series II-D, Card 2.

52. C. W. Peale to Moses Finley, February 18, 1800, *PPF*, Series II-A, Card 23.

53. C. W. Peale to Representatives of the State of Massachusetts in Congress, December 14, 1799, *PPF*, Series II-A, Card 22.

54. Miller, *Patrons and Patriotism*, p. 8.

55. Richardson, "Charles Willson Peale and His World," p. 87.

56. C. W. Peale to Beale Bordley, December 5, 1786, *PPF*, Series II-A, Card 14.

57. C. W. Peale to Rembrandt Peale, February 12, 1826, *PPF*, Series II-A, Card 71.

58. C. W. Peale, "Address to the Directors of the Library Company of Philadelphia," October 5 and November 5, 1795, *PPF*, Series II-B, Card 1.

59. C. W. Peale to Mordecai Lewis, April 12, 1796, *PPF*, Series II-A, Card 20.

60. C. W. Peale to Thomas Jefferson, February 6, 1797, *PPF*, Series II-A, Card 21.
61. C. W. Peale to Edmond Jennings, December 28, 1800, *PPF*, Series II-A, Card 23.
62. C. W. Peale, Diary June 17–December 19, 1798, *PPF*, Series II-B, Card 15.
63. Joseph J. Ellis, *After the Revolution: Profiles of Early American Culture* (New York: W. W. Norton, 1979), p. 34.
64. C. W. Peale to the American Philosophical Society, March 7, 1797, *PPF*, Series II-A, Card 21.
65. C. W. Peale to Ambroise Palisot de Beauvois, June 16, 1799, *PPF*, Series II-A, Card 22.
66. C. W. Peale, "Introductory Lecture on Natural History, 1799," *PPF*, Series II-D, Card 2.
67. C. W. Peale to Moses Finley, February 18, 1800, *PPF*, Series II-A, Card 22.
68. Ibid.
69. Pierre Eugène Du Simitière, *Scraps*, no. 102, Historical Society of Pennsylvania.
70. Isaac Newton Phelps Stokes, *The Iconography of Manhattan Island, 1498–1909* (New York: Robert H. Dodd, 1915; reprint ed., New York: Arno Press, 1967), 6: 47.
71. Ibid., 5: 1275.
72. Society of Tammany or Columbian Order, Committee of Amusement, Minutes, October 24, 1791–February 23, 1795, New York Public Library.
73. Broadside dated June 1, 1791, issued by the Tammany Society. Reproduced in Winifred E. Howe, *A History of the Metropolitan Museum of Art: With a Chapter on the Early Institutions of Art in New York* (New York: Metropolitan Museum of Art, 1913), 1: 2.
74. Ibid.
75. Stokes, *Iconography*, 5: 1280.
76. Broadside reproduced in Howe, *A History of the Metropolitan*, 1: 2.
77. Robert M. and Gale S. McClung, "Tammany's Remarkable Gardiner Baker: New York's First Museum Proprietor, Menagerie Keeper and Promoter Extraordinary," *New-York Historical Society Quarterly* 62 (April 1958): 143.
78. C. W. Peale, "1826 Autobiography," *PPF*, Series II-C, Card 16. Recent scholars have noted that there is no independent confirmation of Peale's explanation. See Robert I. Goler, "'Here the Book of Nature is Unfolded'": The American Museum and the Diffusion of Scientific Knowledge in the Early Republic," *Museum Studies Journal* 2 (Spring 1986): 21.
79. Stokes, *Iconography*, 5: 1323.
80. Charles Willson Peale, Diary no. 11, June 6, 1791, *PPF*, Series II-B, Card 12.
81. Stokes, *Iconography*, 5: 1297.
82. Ibid.

83. See Sellers, *Mr. Peale's Museum*, pp. 26–28.
84. Stokes, *Iconography*, 5: 1321.
85. Gardiner Baker to John Pintard, February 11, 1797, John Pintard Papers, New-York Historical Society.
86. Ibid.
87. C. W. Peale, Diary no. 16, ca. June 28, 1798, *PPF*, Series II-B, Card 14.
88. Gardiner Baker to John Pintard, March 4, 1798, John Pintard Papers, New-York Historical Society.
89. Ibid.
90. Ibid.
91. McClung and McClung, "Tammany's Gardiner Baker," p. 167.

3. The Didactic Enlightenment, 1800–1820: The Decline of the Respectability

1. Douglas T. Miller, *The Birth of Modern America, 1820–1850* (New York: Western Publishing Company, 1970), p. 21.
2. Gilman Ostrander, *The Rights of Man in America, 1606–1861* (Columbia: University of Missouri Press, 1960), p. 156.
3. Robert H. Wiebe, *The Opening of American Society: From the Adoption of the Constitution to the Eve of Disunion* (New York: Alfred A. Knopf, 1984), p. 255.
4. Ibid., p. 143.
5. John W. Francis, M.D., *Old New York: Or Reminiscences of the Past 60 Years. Anniversary discourse delivered before the New-York Historical Society, November 17, 1857* (1865; reprint, New York: Benjamin Blom, 1971), pp. 124–25.
6. Rita Susswein Gottesman, *The Arts and Crafts in New York, 1800–1804, Collections of the New-York Historical Society for the Year 1949, Vol. 82* (New York: New-York Historical Society, 1950), p. 22.
7. Ibid., pp. 22–23.
8. Ibid., p. 26.
9. Ibid.
10. Stokes, *Iconography*, 5: 1518.
11. Quoted in Loyd Haberly, "The American Museum from Baker to Barnum," *New-York Historical Society Quarterly* 63 (July 1959): 279.
12. Quoted in Howe, *A History of the Metropolitan*, 1: 76.
13. Ibid., p. 20. Dr. John Griscom was a Quaker physician who delivered lectures in chemistry frequently at the New York Institution.
14. John Pintard to Eliza Noel Pintard Davidson, April 15, 1817, *Letters from John Pintard to His Daughter, Eliza Noel Pintard Davidson, 1816–1837* (New York: New-York Historical Society, 1940), 1: 60–61.
15. Haberly, "The American Museum," p. 280.
16. Howe, *A History of the Metropolitan*, 1: 76.
17. John Pintard to Eliza Noel Pintard Davidson, July 4, 1819, *Letters from John Pintard*, 1: 203.
18. Charles Willson Peale, Diary no. 22, ca. June 1, 1817, *PPF*, Series II-B, Card 22.

19. Ibid., June 4, 1817.
20. Ibid., ca. June 10, 1817.
21. John Pintard to Eliza Noel Pintard Davidson, May 18, 1818, *Letters from John Pintard*, 1: 123.
22. Ibid., August 9, 1821, 2: 73.
23. Charles Willson Peale to Raphaelle Peale, June 6 and 7, 1807, *PPF*, Series II-A, Card 41.
24. C. W. Peale to Andrew Ellicot, February 28, 1802, *PPF*, Series II-A, Card 25.
25. C. W. Peale to John Hawkins, October 7, 1804, *PPF*, Series II-A, Card 32.
26. C. W. Peale to Rembrandt Peale, October 28, 1809, *PPF*, Series II-A, Card 48.
27. Thomas Jefferson to C. W. Peale, May 5, 1802, *PPF*, Series II-A, Card 25.
28. C. W. Peale to Thomas Jefferson, June 6, 1802, *PPF*, Series II-A, Card 26.
29. Ibid.
30. C. W. Peale to Thomas Jefferson, February 26, 1804, *PPF*, Series II-A, Card 29.
31. "Address delivered by Charles W. Peale to the Corporation and Citizens of Philadelphia on the 18th day of July, 1816," *PPF*, Series XI-A, Card 5.
32. C. W. Peale to Raphaelle Peale, ca. May 1806, *PPF*, Series II-A, Card 38.
33. C. W. Peale to Thomas Jefferson, September 2, 1808, *PPF*, Series II-A, Card 43.
34. C. W. Peale to James Madison, April 30, 1809, *PPF*, Series II-A, Card 46.
35. "Address delivered by Charles W. Peale," *PPF*, Series XI-A, Card 5.
36. Ibid.
37. Ibid.
38. Ibid.
39. Rembrandt Peale to Thomas Jefferson, July 13, 1813, *PPF*, Series VI-A, Card 2.
40. Wilbur Harvey Hunter, *The Story of America's Oldest Museum Building* (Baltimore: The Peale Museum, 1964), p. 11.
41. John Pintard to De Witt Clinton, August 28, 1812, American Academy of Fine Arts Papers, New-York Historical Society.
42. Remark of Rufus King, unofficial Federalist candidate for president of the United States, 1812, quoted in Paul F. Boller, *Presidential Campaigns* (New York: Oxford University Press, 1984), p. 30.
43. David Hackett Fischer, *The Revolution of American Conservatism: The Federalist Party in the Era of Jeffersonian Democracy* (New York: Harper & Row, 1965), pp. 192–96.
44. See Ostrander, *The Rights of Man in America*, pp. 112–13.
45. Fischer, *The Revolution of American Conservatism*, p. 197.
46. "To the Public: The Address of the New-York Historical Society, Issued February 12, 1805," quoted in R. W. G. Vail, *Knickerbocker Birthday: A*

Sesqui-Centennial History of the New-York Historical Society, 1804–1954 (New York: New-York Historical Society, 1954), p. 452.

47. Pintard to Clinton, August 28, 1812, American Academy of Fine Arts Papers.

48. Vail, *Knickerbocker Birthday*, p. 48.

49. Pintard to Clinton, August 28, 1812, American Academy of Fine Arts Papers.

50. Ibid.

51. De Witt Clinton to [?], February 24, 1807, De Witt Clinton Collection, New York Public Library.

52. New-York Historical Society Meeting, March 11, 1817, Minutes of the New-York Historical Society on Microfilm, New-York Historical Society.

53. Circular dated March 6, 1817, from George Gibbs to Charles Willson Peale, *PPF*, Series II-A, Card 59; Circular dated March 11, 1817, from Samuel Latham Mitchill to Jeremy Robinson, Peter Force Papers, Series 8d, Items 148.1-.3, Reel 60, Library of Congess; Circular dated June 16, 1817, ibid. The "& C. & C." was the nineteenth-century equivalent of our usage of "etc., etc."

54. Circular dated March 6, 1817, from George Gibbs to Charles Willson Peale, *PPF*, Series II-A, Card 59.

55. Quoted in Vail, *Knickerbocker Birthday*, p. 210.

56. Charles Willson Peale, Diary no. 22, May 23–June 14, 1817, *PPF*, Series II-B, Card 21.

57. Ibid.

58. Ibid.

59. John Pintard to Eliza Noel Pintard Davidson, August 13, 1816, *Letters from John Pintard to His Daughter*, 1: 25–26.

60. Daniel Drake, *Anniversary Discourse on the State and Prospects of the Western Museum Society: Delivered . . . June 10, 1820, on the Opening of the Museum* (Cincinnati: Western Museum Society, 1820), pp. 31–32, Pamphlet in collection of the Cincinnati Historical Society.

61. Christine Chapman Robbins, *David Hosack: Citizen of New York* (Philadelphia: American Philosophical Society, 1964), p. 27.

62. Quoted in letter from Cornelia Tyler to Christine Chapman Robbins, September 11, 1962, Christine Chapman Robbins Collection (Collection 346), American Philosophical Society.

63. John C. Greene, *American Science in the Age of Jefferson* (Ames: Iowa State University Press, 1984), p. 100.

64. Memorial of David Hosack to the Senate and Assembly of the State of New York [April 5, 1808], Christine Chapman Robbins Papers (Collection 346), American Philosophical Society.

65. Ibid.

66. [T.?] Coleman to Mr. Croswell, January 28, 1810, Misc. Mss., David Hosack, New-York Historical Society.

67. David Hosack to Amos Eaton, August 30, 1810, Christine Chapman Robbins Papers (Collection 346), American Philosophical Society.

68. Ibid.

69. See Edward Pessen, *Riches, Class and Power Before the Civil War* (Lexington, Mass.: D.C. Heath, 1973), pp. 120–29.

70. Patsy A. Gerstner, "The Academy of Natural Sciences of Philadelphia, 1812–1850," in Alexandra Oleson and Sanborn C. Brown, ed., *The Pursuit of Knowledge in the Early American Republic: American Scientific and Learned Societies from Colonial Times to the Civil War* (Baltimore: John Hopkins University Press, 1976), pp. 174–75.

71. George Ord, "Memoir of Thomas Say," quoted in Edward J. Nolan, "History of the Academy, 1812–1912," Unpublished Manuscript (Collection 463), Academy of Natural Sciences of Philadelphia, p. 10. One must be cautious when assessing Ord's statements, for he was excessively opinionated and prone to writing uncharitable assessments of his contemporaries.

72. Venia T. and Maurice E. Phillips, eds., *Minutes and Correspondence of the Academy of Natural Sciences of Philadelphia, 1812–1924* (Philadelphia: Academy of Natural Sciences of Philadelphia, 1963), Microfilm, Reel 1, Frame 015.

73. Ibid., March 17, 1812, Frame 034.

74. Ibid., Frame 032.

75. Ibid., Frame 034.

76. Ibid., Frame 046.

77. Ibid., Frame 006.

78. Ibid., Frame 021.

79. Ibid., February 26, 1817, Frame 340.

80. Elijah Slack, James Findlay, William Steele, Jesse Embree, Daniel Drake, "An Address to the People of the Western Country," *The American Journal of Science* 1 (1819): 203–206. See also Samuel Latham Mitchill to Daniel Drake, August 2, 1819, Daniel Drake Papers, Cincinnati Historical Society.

81. See Rubens Peale to Daniel Drake, August 2, 1819, and Rubens Peale to Titian Peale, August 4, 1819, *PPF*, Series VII-A, Card 3.

82. Greene, *American Science*, p. 118.

83. Ibid., p. 219.

4. The Age of Egalitarianism, 1820–1840: The Ideal of Popular Education

1. See Alice Felt Tyler, *Freedom's Ferment: Phases of American Social History to 1860* (Minneapolis: University of Minnesota, 1944), and Ronald G. Walters, *American Reformers: 1815–1860* (New York: Hill and Wang, 1978).

2. Ralph Waldo Emerson, "New England Reformers," in *The Prose Works of Ralph Waldo Emerson*, 2 vols. (Cambridge: Harvard University, 1870), 1: 551; Edwin C. Rozwenc, ed., *Ideology and Power in the Age of Jackson* (Garden City, N.Y.: Anchor Books, 1964), p. 171.

3. James Fenimore Cooper, *The American Democrat* (Cooperstown: H. & E. Phinney, 1838), p. 79; Rozwenc, *Ideology and Power*, p. 130.

4. See Pessen, *Riches, Class and Power Before the Civil War*, pp. 1–6, 151–67.

5. Dr. Thomas L. Nichols, *Forty Years of American Life* (London: John Maxwell & Co., 1864; reprint ed., New York: Negro Universities Press, 1968), p. 58.

6. Horace Mann, "The Necessity of Education in a Republican Government" (1838); Rozwenc, *Ideology and Power*, p. 145.

7. Carl Bode, *The American Lyceum: Town Meeting of the Mind* (New York: Oxford University Press, 1956), pp. 12–13.

8. Charles Willson Peale, "Lectures on Natural History, the Museum, Health, Domestic Happiness," and "A Voice in Behalf of the Oppresed," *PPF*, Series II-D, Card 28.

9. William Maclure to Benjamin Silliman, July 18, 1824, reproduced in "Letters from William Maclure," *The American Journal of Science and Arts* 9 (1825): 162–63.

10. "Trustees of the Philadelphia Museum Company to the Select Council of Philadelphia," April 11, 1821, *PPF*, Series VII-A, Card 3.

11. C. W. Peale to Rembrandt Peale, April 18, 1821, *PPF*, Series II-A, Card 65. Charles Willson Peale was an early supporter of women's rights, and thus was always gratified to see women in the audience.

12. C. W. Peale to Rubens Peale, March 23, 1823, *PPF*, Series II-A, Card 67.

13. C. W. Peale to Angelica Peale Robinson, March 10, 1823, *PPF*, Series II-A, Card 67.

14. C. W. Peale to Philadelphia Museum Trustees, May 5, 1821, *PPF*, Series II-A, Card 65.

15. "To Our Readers," *The Philadelphia Museum or Register of Natural History and the Arts* 1 (January 1824): 14, *PPF*, Series XI-A, Card 17.

16. Ibid., p. 16.

17. "History of the Museum," *The Philadelphia Museum* p. 3.

18. "To Our Readers," *The Philadelphia Museum*, p. 15.

19. C. W. Peale to Thomas Jefferson, September 10, 1825, *PPF*, Series II-A, Card 69.

20. Rubens Peale to James Thomas Carey, July 14, 1835, *PPF*, Series XI-C, Card 1. Hosack was at this time the president of the New-York Historical Society, and a leader in both the medical and museum fields.

21. *Patron Book*, Peale's New York Museum, 1825, *PPF*, Series VII-A, Card 5. All of the above-named gentlemen were members of the New-York Historical Society.

22. Rubens Peale to Franklin Peale, April 25 and 28, 1826, *PPF*, Series VII-A, Card 5.

23. Rubens Peale to Franklin Peale, March 5, 1829, *PPF*, Series VII-A, Card 6.

24. Rembrandt Peale, "Prospectus of a Museum of Arts and Sciences, to be Established in Baltimore" (1824), *PPF*, Series VI-A, Card 4.

25. Ibid.

26. Titian R. Peale to the Board of Trustees of the Philadelphia Museum Company, March 20, 1834, *PPF*, Series VIII-A, Card 3.

27. Ibid., April 17, 1834.

28. Rembrandt Peale to the President and Directors of the Philadelphia Museum Company, May 5, 1836, *PPF*, Series VI-A, Card 8.
29. Sellers, *Mr. Peale's Museum*, p. 288.
30. Ibid., p. 250.
31. Patsy A. Gerstner, "The 'Philadelphia School' of Paleontology: 1820–1845" (Ph.D. diss., Case Western Reserve University, 1967), pp. 222–27.
32. William Maclure, "An Epitome of the Improved Pestalozzian System of Education . . . ," *The American Journal of Science and Arts* 10 (1826): 145.
33. Ibid. p. 149.
34. Isaac Lea, "On the Pleasure and Advantage of Studying Natural History," *The American Journal of Science and Arts* 11 (1826): 218.
35. Ibid., p. 221.
36. "Report of the Committee to Devise Rules for the Preservation of the Library & C.," October 28, 1823, Collection 940, no. 23, Academy of Natural Sciences of Philadelphia.
37. Isaac Hays, Titian Peale, John Vaughn (Annual Report of the Curators of the Academy of Natural Sciences), December 26, 1826, *PPF*, Series VIII-A, Card 2.
38. Samuel George Morton, John P. Wetherill, George Ord, Samuel Merrick, and Walter Johnson, "Report of the Committee on Erecting a Building for the Doorkeeper," August 5, 1828, Collection 940, no. 5, Academy of Natural Sciences.
39. Ibid.
40. William Maclure to Samuel George Morton, April 3, 1830, Samuel George Morton Papers, Collection 475, American Philosophical Society. Most of these letters were written to Morton from Mexico. There is no record of Morton's replies.
41. Ibid., March 26, 1835.
42. Ibid., December 27, 1836.
43. Ibid., June [?], 1837.
44. Ibid., December 27, 1836.
45. George Ord to Titian Peale, January 18, 1829, Ord-Peale Correspondence, Historical Society of Pennsylvania.
46. Richard Harlan to John James Audubon, November 19, 1828, Misc. Mss.—Harlan, New-York Historical Society.
47. Samuel George Morton to Gideon Mantell, August 14, 1831, Mantell Collection, Alexander Turnbull Library, Wellington, New Zealand.
48. William Maclure to Samuel George Morton, June 15, 1839, Samuel George Morton Papers, Collection 475, American Philosophical Society.
49. Samuel George Morton, Chairman, Committee on Maclure's Letter, *Minutes of the Academy of Natural Sciences*, November 21, 1839, Academy of Natural Sciences Microfilm, Reel 3.
50. Ibid.
51. Draft of Letter from Joseph Henry to J. B. Varnum, June 22, 1847, Record Unit 7001, Box 8, Smithsonian Institution Archives.

52. Daniel Drake, "Anniversary Discourse," pp. 30–31.

53. Ibid., pp. 24–25.

54. Ibid., pp. 33–34.

55. Ibid., p. 34.

56. Alice Ford, ed., *Audubon, By Himself: A Profile of John James Audubon* (Garden City, N.Y.: The Natural History Press, 1969), p. 87.

57. Elizabeth R. Kellogg, "Joseph Dorfeuille and The Western Museum," *The Journal of the Cincinnati Society of Natural History* 22 (April 1945): 4.

58. William Newnham Blane, *An Excursion Through the United States and Canada During the Years 1820–23 by an English Gentleman* (London: Baldwin, Graddock & Co., 1824; reprint ed., New York: Negro Universities Press, 1969), p. 126.

59. Poem by "P." (probably Joseph Dorfeuille), Cincinnati *Literary Gazette,* March 13, 1824, p. 88. The original is in the collection of the Cincinnati Historical Society.

60. Frances Trollope, *Domestic Manners of Americans* (London: Whitaker, Treacher & Co., 1832; reprint ed., ed. Donald Smalley, New York: Alfred Knopf, 1949), p. 62. For the full story of the "Regions," see Donald Smalley's Introduction, pp. xxiv–xxxiv.

61. Linden Ryder to Hiram Powers, November 21, 1835, Hiram Powers Papers, Cincinnati Historical Society.

62. Linden Ryder to Hiram Powers, March 3, 1837, Hiram Powers Papers, Cincinnati Historical Society.

63. Lewis Leonard Tucker, "'Ohio Show-Shop': The Western Museum of Cincinnati, 1820–1867," in Whitfield J. Bell et al., *A Cabinet of Curiosities: Five Episodes in the Evolution of American Museums* (Charlottesville: University Press of Virginia, 1967), pp. 96–97.

64. Charles Augustus Murray, *Travels in North America* (London: Richard Bentley, 1839), 1: 203–204; Roland Bartel and Edwin R. Bingham, eds., *America Through Foreign Eyes, 1827–1842* (Boston: D. C. Heath and Company, 1956), p. 98.

65. Haberly, "The American Museum from Baker to Barnum," p. 282.

66. Gideon Welles, "Diary of a Trip to Philadelphia and New York, May 2, 1823 to the Autumn of 1823," p. 69, Gideon Welles Collection, Connecticut Historical Society.

67. Nichols, *Forty Years of American Life,* p. 64.

68. George Wilson Pierson, *Tocqueville and Beaumont in America* (New York: Oxford University Press, 1938), p. 150.

69. John Pintard to Dr. John W. Francis, January 14, 1819, quoted in Vail, *Knickerbocker Birthday,* p. 57.

70. Vail, *Knickerbocker Birthday,* pp. 55–57.

71. New-York Historical Society *Minutes,* March 9, 1824, Microfilm at New-York Historical Society.

72. Ibid., April 13, 1824, and May 13, 1824, and Vail, *Knickerbocker Birthday,* pp. 63–67.

73. New-York Historical Society *Minutes,* May 18, 1825.

74. Frederic De Peyster, Jr., to Frederic De Peyster, Sr., June 17, 1817,

Frederic De Peyster, Jr., Papers, New-York Historical Society.

75. See "Agreement with Three Dinghams to Let, 1828," Frederic De Peyster, Jr., Papers, New-York Historical Society.
76. New-York Historical Society *Minutes*, June 14, 1825.
77. John Trumbull to John B. Beck, June 15, 1825, John Trumbull Papers, New-York Historical Society.
78. De Witt Clinton to John Pintard, April 12, 1821, De Witt Clinton Collection, New York Public Library.
79. Robert Hendre Kelby, *The New York Historical Society, 1804–1904* (New York: New-York Historical Society, 1905), p. 32.
80. De Witt Clinton, "Diary Attributed to De Witt Clinton," Misc. Mss., New-York Historical Society, p. 1.
81. "Petition of the New-York Athenaeum and the New-York Historical Society Library to the Mayor and Aldermen of New York," New-York Historical Society *Minutes*, May 27, 1828.
82. Vail, *Knickerbocker Birthday*, pp. 76–80.

5. The Age of Professionalism, 1840–1850: The Scientists Lead the Way

1. The discussion that follows relies heavily upon the thesis of George H. Daniels, first explicated in his 1967 article in *ISIS*, "The Process of Professionalization in American Science: The Emergent Period, 1820–1960." The article was reprinted in Nathan Reingold, ed., *Science in America Since 1820* (New York: Science History Publications, 1976), pp. 63–78.
2. Greene, *American Science in the Age of Jefferson*, pp. 409–412.
3. See William Stanton, *The Great United States Exploring Expedition of 1838* (Berkeley: University of California Press, 1975), pp. 1–72.
4. Sally Gregory Kohlstedt, *The Formation of the American Scientific Community: The American Association for the Advancement of Science, 1848–1860* (Urbana: University of Illinois Press, 1976), p. 57.
5. Vladimir Clain-Stefanelli, *History of the National Numismatic Collections*, Contributions from the Museum of History and Technology, Paper 31, Bulletin 229 (Washington, D.C.: U. S. Government Printing Office, 1968), p. 4.
6. Kohlstedt, *The Formation of the American Scientific Community*, pp. 56–58.
7. Robert V. Bruce, *The Launching of Modern American Science, 1846–1876* (New York: Alfred A. Knopf, 1987), pp. 252–53.
8. Daniels, "The Process of Professionalization," pp. 67–68.
9. Bode, *The American Lyceum*, p. 134.
10. Patsy A. Gerstner, "The Academy of Natural Sciences of Philadelphia, 1812-1850," in Oleson and Brown, eds., *The Pursuit of Knowledge in the Early American Republic*, p. 188.
11. Phillips and Phillips, eds., *Minutes and Correspondence of the Academy of Natural Sciences*, Reel 4, October 27, 1840 (Frame 85); December 29, 1840 (Frame 99); February 16, 1841 (Frame 109).

12. Nolan, *A History of the Academy of Natural Sciences*, p. 237, Collection 463, Academy of Natural Sciences.
13. John Speakman to John Price Wetherill, February 8, 1845, Collection 530, Academy of Natural Sciences.
14. John Speakman, "To the Academy of Natural Sciences," November 4, 1845, Collection 530, Academy of Natural Sciences.
15. Joseph Leidy to S. S. Haldeman, February ?, 1847, Leidy Collection, Collection 1, p. 1, Academy of Natural Sciences. "Mr. Gambel" was William Gambel, a physician and ornithologist. Leidy triumphed with the aid of John Cassin, an influential member of the academy.
16. Phillips and Phillips, eds., *Minutes and Correspondence of the Academy of Natural Sciences*, May 4, 1847, Reel 4, Frames 61–62.
17. Nolan, *History of the Academy of Natural Sciences*, p. 321, Collection 463, Academy of Natural Sciences.
18. Phillips and Phillips, eds., *Minutes and Correspondence of the Academy of Natural Sciences*, March 28, 1848, Reel 4, Frame 181.
19. Gerstner, "The Academy of Natural Sciences," p. 188.
20. Mary Bartlett Cowdrey, *American Academy of Fine Arts and American Art Union: 1816–1852, with the History of the American Academy by Theodore Sizer* (New York: The New-York Historical Society, 1953), pp. 3–7.
21. John F. Fulton and Elizabeth H. Thompson, *Benjamin Silliman, 1779–1864: Pathfinder in American Science* (New York: Henry Schuman, 1947), pp. 164–72.
22. Regarding the visit to Scudder's, see Daniel Wadsworth to Mehitabel Wadsworth, May 17, 1815, Wadsworth Family Papers, Connecticut Historical Society. The visit to Peale's is evidenced by the presence in the collection of the Connecticut Historical Society of a silhouette of Daniel Wadsworth embossed with the stamp of Peale's Philadelphia Museum (Uncatalogued item, Connecticut Historical Society).
23. Richard Saunders with Helen Raye, *Daniel Wadsworth: Patron of the Arts* (Hartford: Wadsworth Atheneum, 1981), pp. 30–31.
24. Ibid., pp. 31–32.
25. Ibid., *Daniel Wadsworth*, pp. 13–14.
26. Frances H. Grund, *The Americans and their Moral, Social and Political Relations* (Boston: Marsh, Capon and Lyon, 1837; reprint ed., New York: Johnson Reprint Corporation, 1968), pp. 85–86.
27. C. C. Beecker to Daniel Wadsworth, n.d. (ca. 1826), Letters to Daniel Wadsworth, 1826–1831, Wadsworth Atheneum Loan Collection, Connecticut Historical Society.
28. Marian G. M. Clarke, *David Watkinson's Library: 100 Years in Hartford, Connecticut, 1866–1966* (Hartford: Trinity College Press, 1966), pp. 29–30.
29. "Minutes of the Meetings of the Board of Trustees of Wadsworth Atheneum, 1844–1922, along with Minutes of the Annual Meeting of the Stockholders of the Atheneum, 1862–1922," undated, p. 1, Wadsworth Atheneum Archives.
30. Saunders and Raye, *Daniel Wadsworth*, p. 33.

31. Ibid., pp. 35–36.
32. Gideon Welles, "Diary of a Trip to Philadelphia and New York, May 2, 1823, to the Autumn of 1823," Gideon Welles Collection, Connecticut Historical Society.
33. "Wadsworth Gallery," *Hartford Courant*, August 10, 1844, p. 2.
34. *Catalogue of Paintings now Exhibiting in Wadsworth Gallery, Hartford* (Hartford: Elihu Geer, 1844), Wadsworth Atheneum Archives.
35. Wilcomb E. Washburn, "A National Museum," in *The Smithsonian Experience* (Washington, D.C.: The Smithsonian Institution, 1977), pp. 20–27. See also Wilcomb E. Washburn, ed., *The Great Design: Two Lectures on the Smithson Bequest by John Quincy Adams* (Washington, D.C.: The Smithsonian Institution, 1965).
36. Washburn, "A National Museum," p. 22.
37. Quoted in S. Dillon Ripley, *The Sacred Grove: Essays on Museums* (New York: Simon and Schuster, 1969), pp. 52–53.
38. Joseph Henry, "Journal of a Trip to West Point in New York," June 22, 1826, *PPF*, Series XI-C, Card 1.
39. Joseph Henry, "Record of Experiments," May 9, 1835, *The Papers of Joseph Henry, vol. 2: The Princeton Years Nov. 1832–Dec. 1835,*, ed. Nathan Reingold (Washington, D.C.: Smithsonian Institution Press, 1975), p. 391.
40. Joseph Henry, Address on Charles Willson Peale, n.d. but delivered in Philadelphia in 1876 according to Nathan Reingold, *PPF*, Series II-A, Card 76, pp. 41–42.
41. Ibid., pp. 11–12.
42. Joseph Henry to Alexander Dallas Bache, September 6, 1846, Record Unit 7001, Box 8, quoted in Wilcomb Washburn, "Joseph Henry's Conception of the Purpose of the Smithsonian Institution," in *A Cabinet of Curiosities*, pp. 108–09.
43. Joseph Henry to J. B. Varnum, June 22, 1847, in ibid., pp. 111–12.
44. Washburn, "Joseph Henry's Conception," pp. 129–52.
45. Peter Force et al., "Memorial of the National Institution," November 14, 1848, Peter Force Papers, Series 8d, no. 109.2, Library of Congress.
46. Joseph Henry, "Third Annual Report of the Secretary, 1849," in *The Fourth Annual Report of the Board of Regents of the Smithsonian Institution . . . During the Year 1853* (Washington, D.C.: A.O.P. Nicholson, 1854), p. 173.
47. Joseph Henry, "Fourth Annual Report of the Secretary, 1850," in *The Fifth Annual Report of the Board of Regents of the Smithsonian Institution . . . During the Year 1850* (Washington, D.C.: A. Boyd Hamilton, 1851), p. 8.
48. See Washburn, "Joseph Henry's Conception," pp. 134–36.
49. George P. Marsh to Spencer F. Baird, June 7, 1849, Spencer F. Baird Papers, Record Unit 7002, Box 24, Smithsonian Institution Archives.
50. George P. Marsh to Spencer F. Baird, August 23, 1850, Spencer F. Baird Papers, Record Unit 7002, Box 24, Smithsonian Institution Archives.
51. Sellers, *Mr. Peale's Museum*, pp. 298–99.
52. Walter Muir Whitehill, Introduction to Whitfield Bell, Jr., *A Cabinet of Curiosities*, pp. vi–vii.

53. "Minutes of the Philadelphia Museum Company, 1827–1840," January 10, 1840, p. 191, *PPF*, Series XI-A, Card 24.
54. "Minutes of the Philadelphia Museum Company, January 8, 1841–June 10, 1845," December 19, 1842, p. 260, *PPF*, Series XI-A, Card 24.
55. Ibid., p. 261.
56. Toby A. Appel, "Science, Popular Culture and Profit: Peale's Philadelphia Museum," *Journal of the Society for the Bibliography of Natural History* 9 (Winter 1980): 628.
57. Ibid., p. 619.
58. Jennette Dorfeuille to Samuel George Morton, September 19, 1840, Samuel George Morton Papers, American Philosophical Society.
59. Tucker, "'Ohio Show-Shop,'", p. 97.
60. Vail, *Knickerbocker Birthday*, p. 90.
61. Kelby, *The New York Historical Society*, p. 45.
62. Albert Gallatin to Pierre Eugène Du Simitière, November 12, 1783, Albert Gallatin Papers, Box 522, Library of Congress. Sellers described Gallatin as a "friend" of the Philadelphia Museum. See Sellers, *Mr. Peale's Museum*, p. 168.
63. Draft of New-York Historical Society Memorial, April 1846, Albert Gallatin Papers, New York University Microfilm Collection, Reel 44, Frame 103, Library of Congress.
64. Final Draft of New-York Historical Society Memorial, May 7, 1846, ibid., Frame 109.
65. A. H. Saxon, ed., *Selected Letters of P. T. Barnum* (New York: Columbia University Press, 1983), p. xiv.
66. Neil Harris, *Humbug: The Art of P. T. Barnum* (Boston: Little, Brown and Company, 1973), p. 33.
67. Sellers, *Mr. Peale's Museum*, p. 304.
68. John Rickards Betts, "P. T. Barnum and the Popularization of Natural History," *Journal of the History of Ideas* 20 (1959): 359.
69. Harris, *Humbug*, p. 181.
70. Alexander, *Museums in Motion*, p. 50.
71. Saxon, *Selected Letters*, p. xv.
72. Ibid., p. xvii.
73. P. T. Barnum to Moses Kimball, February 2, 1848, quoted in Saxon, *Selected Letters*, p. 39.
74. Harris, *Humbug*, p. 36.
75. Ibid., p. 105.
76. Ibid.
77. P. T. Barnum, *Barnum's Own Story*, ed. Waldo R. Browne (New York: Dover Publications, 1961), pp. 104–108.
78. P. T. Barnum to Moses Kimball, January 30, 1843, in Saxon, *Selected Letters*, p. 13.
79. P. T. Barnum to Moses Kimball, February 2, 1848, in Saxon, *Selected Letters*, p. 39.
80. Barnum, *Barnum's Own Story*, p. 101.
81. Harris, *Humbug*, p. 4.

82. P. T. Barnum to Moses Kimball, August 18, 1846, P. T. Barnum Papers, New York Public Library.

83. P. T. Barnum, undated handbill (ca. 1850), Misc. Mss.—Barnum, New-York Historical Society. The bill mentions "my museum in Philadelphia," which Barnum operated from 1849 to 1851, hence the approximate date.

84. P. T. Barnum to Moses Kimball, October 18, 1846, P. T. Barnum Papers, New York Public Library.

85. P. T. Barnum to Moses Kimball, April 3, 1846, P. T. Barnum Papers, New York Public Library.

86. Dr. Albert C. Koch, *Journey Through a Part of the United States of America in the Years 1844–1846* (Dresden, 1847; reprint ed., trans. and ed. Ernst A. Stadler, Carbondale, Ill.: Southern Illinois University Press, 1972), p. 9.

6. The American Compromise, 1850–1870: The Synthesis of Popular Education and Professionalism

1. John Higham, *From Boundlessness to Consolidation: The Transformation of American Culture, 1848–1860* (Ann Arbor: William L. Clements Library, 1969), p. 15.

2. Ibid., p. 8.

3. Daniel H. Calhoun, *Professional Lives in America: Structure and Aspiration, 1750–1850* (Cambridge: Harvard University Press, 1965), p. 180.

4. Daniels, "The Process of Professionalization," p. 75.

5. Ibid., p. 77.

6. Foner, *Free Soil, Free Labor, Free Men*, pp. 11–39.

7. Higham, *From Boundlessness to Consolidation*, p. 18.

8. Charles B. Hosmer, *Presence of the Past: A History of the Preservation Movement in the United States Before Williamsburg* (New York: G. P. Putnams Sons, 1965), pp. 46–62. See also Edward P. Alexander, *Museum Masters: Their Museums and Their Influence* (Nashville: The American Association for State and Local History, 1983), pp. 177–204.

9. For the Great Exposition of the Industry of all Nations see Kenneth W. Luckhurst, *The Story of Exhibitions* (London: Studio Publications, 1951), and Alexander, *Museum Masters*, pp. 146–51. For the New York Crystal Palace, see Luckhurst, *The Story of Exhibitions*, and J. E. Canter, "The Museum in the Park," *The Metropolitan Museum of Art Bulletin* 26 (April 1968): 332–40. A good contemporary description is William Chambers, *Things as They Are in America* (London: W. R. Chambers, 1854; reprint ed., New York: Negro University Press, 1968), pp. 200–203.

10. Edward C. Mack: *Peter Cooper: Citizen of New York* (New York: Duell, Sloan, & Pearce, 1949), pp. 40, 89, 259.

11. Ibid., p. 266.

12. Edward Lurie, *Louis Agassiz: A Life in Science* (Chicago: The University of Chicago Press, 1960), p. 115.

13. Ibid., p. 231.

14. Ibid., p. 239.
15. Ibid., p. 236.
16. George M. Frederickson, *The Inner Civil War: Northern Intellectuals and the Crisis of the Union* (Evanston: Harper & Row, 1965), pp. 201–202.
17. Sir Charles Lyell to [?] Horner, July 15, 1853, quoted in Joseph Leidy II, "Manuscript Biography of Joseph Leidy," Joseph Leidy II Papers, Collection 166, Academy of Natural Sciences.
18. George Ord to Titian Peale, January 27, 1852, Ord-Peale Papers, Historical Society of Pennsylvania.
19. Gerstner, "The Academy of Natural Sciences," p. 189.
20. Ibid., p. 193, note 63.
21. Phillips and Phillips, eds., *Minutes and Correspondence of the Academy of Natural Sciences*, July 29, 1851; October 14, 1851; October 21, 1851; Reel 5, Frames 20, 60, and 64.
22. Ibid., "A Museum in Philadelphia," Philadelphia *Inquirer*, Saturday, January 28, 1854, Reel 33, Frame 0488.
23. Ibid., Frame 0489.
24. "Regulations, Hall of the Academy of Natural Sciences of Philadelphia," June 1, 1855, in Nolan, "A History of the Academy of Natural Sciences," Collection 463, Academy of Natural Sciences.
25. Phillips and Phillips, eds., *Minutes and Correspondence*, April 26, 1859, and June 28, 1859, Reel 5, Frames 614 and 629.
26. J. H. Slack, M.D., ed., *Handbook of the Museum of the Academy of Natural Sciences of Philadelphia* (Philadelphia: Collins, 1862), pp. 7–8, Library Company of Philadelphia.
27. Phillips and Phillips, eds., *Minutes and Correspondence*, March 8, 1864, Reel 6, Frame 312.
28. Ibid., October 31, 1865, Reel 6, Frame 128.
29. Ibid., March 27, 1866, Reel 6, Frame 413.
30. Ibid., June 19, 1866, Reel 6, Frame 424.
31. Philadelphia *American and Gazette*, January 17, 1867, William Ruschenberger Papers, Collection 97, Academy of Natural Sciences.
32. William S. W. Ruschenberger (Chairman of the Board of Trustees of the Academy of Natural Sciences) to J. Vaughan Merrick, Esq., May 10, 1867, Phillips and Phillips, eds., *Minutes and Correspondence*, Reel 29, Frame 739.
33. Ibid., Frame 740.
34. Philadelphia *American and Gazette*, October 24, 1867, William Ruschenberger Papers, Collection 97, Academy of Natural Sciences.
35. Philadelphia *Sunday Dispatch*, July 28, 1867, William Ruschenberger Papers, Collection 97, Academy of Natural Sciences.
36. Clipping, unidentified and undated, William Ruschenberger Papers, Collection 97, Academy of Natural Sciences.
37. Edward Sheffield Bartholomew, "Copy of a Letter to the Directors of the Wadsworth Gallery, Hartford, Conn.," in Hartford *Evening Press*, Saturday, November 7, 1857, p. 1, Connecticut Historical Society.

38. *Catalogue of Paintings in Wadsworth Gallery, Hartford* (Hartford: E. Gleason, 1850), unnumbered title page, and ibid., 1851.
39. *Catalogue of Paintings in Wadsworth Gallery, Hartford* (Hartford: Case, Tiffany & Company, 1856), unnumbered title page.
40. Bartholomew, "Copy of a Letter," p. 1.
41. Ibid.
42. Ibid.
43. Ibid., pp. 1–2.
44. Hartford *Evening Press*, Thursday, November 19, 1857, p. 2, Connecticut Historical Society.
45. Ibid.
46. See Clarke, *David Watkinson's Library*, p. 148.
47. Minutes of Annual Meeting of the Stockholders of the Wadsworth Atheneum, June 5, 1858, *Minutes of Meetings . . . of the Wadsworth Atheneum*, p. 35, Wadsworth Atheneum.
48. *Treasurer's Reports, 1862–63, 1867–75*, Wadsworth Atheneum.
49. Bartholomew, "Copy of a Letter," p. 1.
50. Joseph Henry to Ephriam George Squier, December 5, 1850, Library of Congress.
51. Joseph Henry, "Report of the Secretary," in *Third Annual Report of the Board of Regents of the Smithsonian Institution . . . During the Year 1848* (Washington, D.C.: 1849), p. 33.
52. See Joel J. Orosz, "Disloyalty, Dismissal and a Deal: The Development of the National Museum at the Smithsonian Institution," *Museum Studies Journal* 2 (Spring 1986): 22–23.
53. Joseph Henry to Joseph Leidy, March 23, 1854, Joseph Leidy Papers, Academy of Natural Sciences.
54. Joseph Henry to Asa Gray, May 29, 1870, Historic Letter File, Folder: Joseph Henry, Gray Herbarium Library, Harvard University.
55. Marc Rothenberg, Associate Editor, Joseph Henry Papers, letter to the author, July 29, 1986.
56. Joseph Henry, "Report of the Secretary," in *Annual Report of the Board of Regents of the Smithsonian Institution for the Year 1858* (Washington, D.C.: Smithsonian Institution, 1859), p. 14.
57. Joseph Henry to Asa Gray, April 6, 1857, Historic Letter File, Folder: Joseph Henry, Gray Herbarium Library, Harvard University.
58. Alexander, *Museums in Motion*, p. 55.
59. Joseph Henry, *1861 Annual Report*, p. 44.
60. Ibid., 1862, p. 34.
61. Ibid., 1865, p. 60.
62. Spencer Baird to John L. Le Conte, November 26, 1853, Record Unit 53, vol. 7, no. 240, Smithsonian Institution Archives.
63. Agreement between Horace Capron and Joseph Henry, January 1, 1868, William J. Rhees Collection, Record Unit 7081, Box 31, Folder: National Herbarium, Smithsonian Institution Archives.
64. Joseph Henry to Felix Flugel, March 18, 1869, Record Unit 33, vol. 13, p. 652, Smithsonian Institution Archives.

65. Joseph Henry, *1870 Annual Report*, p. 13.
66. Ibid., pp. 31–34.
67. Frederic De Peyster, Jr., *The Moral and Intellectual Influence of Libraries Upon Social Progress* (New York: New-York Historical Society, 1866), p. 48.
68. Philip Hone, *The Diary of Philip Hone, 1828–1851* (New York: Dodd Mead & Company, 1927; reprint ed., ed. Allan Nevins, New York: Kraus Reprint Co., 1969), p. 734.
69. Luther Bradish, "Industrial Exhibition of 1851," to the editor of the New York *Courier* and New York *Enquirer*, Luther Bradish Collection, Box 16, New-York Historical Society.
70. Printed sheets, "New-York Historical Society Library: New-York, October 28, 1856," and "New-York Historical Society Circular to Members: New-York, September 28, 1860," New York Public Library Microfilm Collection, New-York Historical Society.
71. Luther Bradish to Dr. John D. Russ, undated but ca. June 1851, Luther Bradish Collection, Box 16, New-York Historical Society. Dr. Russ was the secretary of the New York Juvenile Asylum.
72. See Vail, *Knickerbocker Birthday*, pp. 108–12 and 126–28.
73. Ibid., pp. 118–19.
74. New-York Historical Society *Minutes*, May 12, 1863.
75. Ibid., March 6, 1866, and April 3, 1866. See also Vail, *Knickerbocker Birthday*, p. 119.
76. Luther Bradish to John R. Peters, Jr., April 15, 1862, Luther Bradish Papers, New-York Historical Society.
77. New-York Historical Society *Minutes*, December 7, 1858.
78. Frederic De Peyster, Jr., *The Influence of Libraries*, p. 46.
79. Ibid., pp. 47–48.
80. Ibid., p. 85.
81. Ibid., p. 90.
82. P. T. Barnum to Theodore Tilton, May 29, 1865, Misc. Mss.—Barnum, New-York Historical Society.
83. P. T. Barnum, printed circular letter, ca. June 1850, in Saxon, *Selected Letters*, p. 43.
84. P. T. Barnum to Horace Greeley, March 8, 1854, P. T. Barnum Papers, New York Public Library.
85. P. T. Barnum to James Gordon Bennett, April 28, 1854, in Saxon, *Selected Letters*, p. 75.
86. Harris, *Humbug*, pp. 150–152.
87. Irving Wallace, *The Fabulous Showman: The Life and Times of P. T. Barnum* (New York: Alfred Knopf, 1959), pp. 187–91.
88. P. T. Barnum to Messrs. R. Griffin & Co., January 27, 1860, in Saxon, *Selected Letters*, p. 103.
89. Betts, "Barnum and the Popularization of Natural History," p. 358.
90. P. T. Barnum to Robert Bonner, February 5, 1862, Barnum Collection, New York Public Library.
91. P. T. Barnum to Bayard Taylor, July 16, 1865, in Saxon, *Selected Letters*, pp. 137–38.

92. P. T. Barnum to Bayard Taylor, July 22, 1865, in Saxon, *Selected Letters*, pp. 140–41.

93. Ibid.

94. Ibid., pp. 141–43.

95. Betts, "Barnum and the Popularization of Natural History," p. 355.

96. Harris, *Humbug*, p. 167.

97. Wallace, *The Great Showman*, p. 115.

98. Betts, "Barnum and the Popularization of Natural History," p. 362.

99. Ibid., p. 362.

100. Francis and Theresa Pulszky, *White, Red, Black: Sketches of Society in the United States During the Visit of Their Guests* (New York: Trubner & Co., 1853; reprint ed., New York: Negro Universities Press, 1968), 3: 167.

101. Captain Oldmixon, R.N., *Transatlantic Wanderings, or, A Last Look at the United States* (London: George Routledge & Co., 1855; reprint ed., New York: Johnson Reprint Co., 1970), p. 54.

102. Isabella Lucy Bird, *The Englishwoman in America* (London: John Murray, 1856; reprint ed., Madison: University of Wisconsin Press, 1966), p. 354.

103. Betts, "Barnum and the Popularization of Natural History," p. 368.

104. Harris, *Humbug*, pp. 4, 57, 172.

105. Ibid., p. 173.

106. Motto of the American Museum of Natural History, quoted in Grace Fisher Ramsey, "The Development, Methods and Trends of Educational Work in Museums of the United States" (Ph.D. diss., New York University, 1938), pp. 10–11.

107. "Causes of Absenteeism," article in an unidentified Philadelphia newspaper, ca. 1868, William Ruschenberger Papers, Collection 97, Academy of Natural Sciences.

108. Quoted in Calvin Tomkins, *Merchants and Masterpieces: The Story of the Metropolitan Museum of Art* (New York: E. P. Dutton & Co., 1970), p. 59.

109. Quoted in Ramsey, "Educational Work in Museums," p. 11.

110. Quoted in Howe, *A History of the Metropolitan Museum of Art*, 1: iii.

111. See Alexander, *Museum Masters*, pp. 158–160.

112. George Fiske Comfort, speech printed in *A Metropolitan Art Museum in the City of New York: Proceedings of a Meeting Held at the Theater of the Union League Club. Tuesday Evening, November 23, 1869* (New York: Printed for the Committee, 1869), p. 17, Metropolitan Museum of Art Archives.

113. Alexander, *Museum Masters*, p. 157.

114. George Fiske Comfort, speech printed in *A Metropolitan Art Museum*, p. 15.

115. George P. Putnam, ibid., p. 4.

116. Quoted in Howe, *A History of the Metropolitan*, 2: xi.

117. Ibid., 1:174.

118. "Educational Work in the Museum: A Review," *Bulletin of the Metropolitan Museum of Art* 7 (September 1912): 158–60.

Epilogue: The American Compromise and Museum Historiography

1. *Annual Report of the Board of Regents of the Smithsonian Institution for the Year 1850* (Washington, D.C.: Smithsonian Institution, 1851), p. 8.
2. Ibid., 1851, p. 24.
3. Ibid., 1870, p. 33.
4. Goode, "Museum-History and Museums of History," p. 258.
5. Ibid., p. 260.
6. Ibid., p. 263.
7. Ibid., p. 274.
8. Newton Horace Winchell, "Museums and Their Purposes," *Science* 18 (1891): 44.
9. Francis Henry Taylor, *Babel's Tower: The Dilemma of the Modern Museum* (New York: Columbia University Press, 1945), p. 20.
10. Ibid.
11. There is simply no evidence that Barnum ever made such a statement.
12. Taylor, *Babel's Tower*, pp. 20–21.
13. Nathaniel Burt, *Palaces for the People: A Social History of the American Art Museum* (Boston: Little, Brown & Co., 1977), p. 33.
14. Kenneth Hudson, *Museums of Influence* (Cambridge: Cambridge University Press, 1987), p. 7.
15. Blane, *An Excursion Through the United States and Canada*, p. 126.
16. John Melish, *Travels Through the United States of America in the Years 1806, 1807 and 1809, 1810 & 1811* (Philadelphia, 1815; reprint ed., New York: Johnson Reprint Corporation, 1970), p. 127.
17. Francisco de Miranda, *The New Democracy in America: Travels of Francisco Miranda in the United States, 1783–84* (1785; reprint ed., Norman: University of Oklahoma Press, 1963), p. 43.
18. Goode, "Museum History," p. 262.
19. Ibid., p. 263.
20. John Cotton Dana, *The New Museum, no. 1 of The New Museum Series* (Woodstock, Vt.: The Elm Tree Press, 1917), p. 12.
21. John Cotton Dana, *The New Museum, no. 2 of The New Museum Series* (Woodstock, Vt.: The Elm Tree Press, 1917), p. 12.
22. Ibid., p. 25.
23. Low, *The Museum as a Social Instrument*, p. 7.
24. Ibid., p. 9.
25. Miller, *Patrons and Patriotism*, pp. 8–23, 142–43.
26. Harris, *The Artist in American Society*, pp. vii–xi, 295–98.
27. Low, *The Museum as a Social Instrument*, p. 9.
28. Ibid.
29. Taylor, *Babel's Tower*, p. 22.
30. Ibid.
31. Ibid., p. 21.
32. Ripley, *The Sacred Grove*, p. 38.
33. Alma Wittlin, *Museums: In Search of a Useable Future* (Cambridge: M.I.T. Press, 1970), pp. 118–19.

34. For example, Herbert and Marjorie Katz, *Museums, U.S.A.*, is a book compiled almost entirely from secondary sources provided by the museums themselves. It presents short and uncritical institutional histories of numerous museums. Nathaniel Burt's *Palaces for the People* is an immensely readable volume, but suffers from errors of fact and of interpretation. Edward Alexander's *Museums in Motion* is by far the finest book on general museum history yet published. Unfortunately, the entire world history of museums is covered in only 100 pages, so the treatment is necessarily very abbreviated.

35. The best work on a single museum is Charles Coleman Sellers, *Mr. Peale's Museum*, a first-rate history of this important institution. The best collection is Whitfield Bell, Jr., et al. *A Cabinet of Curiosities: Five Episodes in the Evolution of American Museums*. Another good collection is Sanborn Brown and Alexandra Oleson, eds., *The Pursuit of Knowledge in the Early American Republic: American Scientific and Learned Societies from Colonial Times to the Civil War*, which contains valuable information on several early cabinets, especially that of the Academy of Natural Sciences of Philadelphia. Edward Alexander's *Museum Masters: Their Museums and Their Influence* offers solid chapters on Charles Willson Peale, Ann Pamela Cunningham, the Smithsonian Institution, and John Cotton Dana's Newark Museum.

Selected Bibliography

The following bibliography is not an exhaustive list of every manuscript collection consulted or every book examined, but rather a listing of those most relevant and most important to the topic. It is divided into two sections, Manuscript Sources and Secondary Sources. The Manuscript Sources section is subdivided by manuscript repository. The Secondary Sources section is subdivided according to subject. Manuscript collections that have been published (such as *The Peale Family Papers on Microfiche* or *The Joseph Henry Papers*) are listed as secondary sources under the appropriate subject heading.

Manuscript Sources

Academy of Natural Sciences of Philadelphia

Committees, Reports of. Collection 940.
Lea, Isaac. Correspondence. Collection 452.
Leidy, Joseph. Collection. Collection 1.
Leidy, Joseph, II. Papers. Collection 166.
Morton, Samuel George. Papers. Collection 30.
Nolan, Edward James. Reminiscences of the Academy. Collection 970.
Nolan, Edward James. Manuscript History of the Academy. Collection 463.
Ord, George. Papers. Collection 280.
Ruschenberger, William S. W. Correspondence. Collection 207.
Ruschenberger, William S. W. Papers. Collection 97.
Speakman, John. Collection. Collection 530.

American Philosophical Society, Philadelphia

Hosack, David. Papers. Collection 347.
Maclure, William. Papers. Collection 428.
Morton, Samuel George. Papers. Collection 475.
Ord, George. Letters on Audubon. Collection 503.
Ord, George—Waterton, Charles. Correspondence. Collection 502.
Robbins, Christine Chapman. Christine Chapman Robbins Collection. Collection 346.
Say, Thomas. Papers. Collection 656.

Cincinnati Historical Society, Cincinnati

Drake, Daniel. Collection.
Powers, Hiram. Papers.

Connecticut Historical Society, Hartford

Evening Press, Hartford. Back issues.
Loan Collection, Wadsworth Atheneum.
Wadsworth Family. Papers.
Wadsworth, Daniel. Papers.
Welles, Gideon. Collection,.

Gray Herbarium Library, Harvard University, Cambridge

Henry, Joseph. Historic Letter File.

Historical Society of Pennsylvania, Philadelphia

Du Simitière, Pierre Eugène. Papers.
Ord, George—Peale, Titian. Papers.
Poinsett, Joel Roberts. Papers.
Society Miscellaneous Collections.

Library Company of Philadelphia

Du Simitière, Pierre Eugène. Papers.

Library of Congress, Washington, D.C.

Barnum, P. T. Papers.
Force, Peter. Papers.
Gallatin, Albert. Papers.
New York University Microfilm Collection.
Welles, Gideon. Collection.

Maryland Historical Society, Baltimore

Gilmor, Robert, Jr. Papers.

Metropolitan Museum of Art, New York City

Metropolitan Museum of Art Archives.

New-York Historical Society, New York City

American Academy of Fine Arts. Papers. Ms. 1619.
Barnum, P. T. Miscellaneous Manuscripts.
———. Papers. Ms. 2578.
Bradish, Luther. Papers. Ms. 1589.
Clinton, De Witt. Correspondence. Ms. 1188.
———. Miscellaneous Manuscripts.
Francis, Dr. John W. Papers. Ms. 1902.
Gallatin, Albert. Papers. Ms. 1314.
Hosack, David. Correspondence. Ms. 1661.
———. Miscellaneous Manuscripts.
Mitchill, Samuel Latham. Papers. Ms. 1314.
Moore, George Henry. Correspondence. Ms. 2670.
New York Crystal Palace Papers. Ms. 2832.
New-York Historical Society Minutes.
New York Public Library Microfilm Collection.
Pintard, John. Correspondence. Ms. 978.
Tammany Society or Columbian Order Records. Ms. 1736.
Trumbull, John. Correspondence. Ms. 717.

New York Public Library, New York City

Barnum, P. T. Papers.
Clinton, De Witt. Letters.
Clinton, De Witt—Remsen, Henry. Correspondence.
Du Simitière, Pierre Eugène. Collection.
Francis, Dr. John W. Collection.
Moore, George Henry. Papers.
Pintard, John—Clinton, De Witt. Correspondence.
Strong, George Templeton. Diary.
Tammany Society or Columbian Order, Minutes of Proceedings, 1791–1795.
Trumbull, John. Papers.

The Peale Museum, Baltimore

Peale Museum Archives.

Smithsonian Institution Archives, Washington, D.C.

Baird, Spencer F., Assistant Secretary. Outgoing Correspondence, 1850–1877. RU 53.
Baird, Spencer F. Papers. RU 7002.
Columbian Institute Records. RU 7051.
Goode, George Brown. Collection. RU 7050.
Henry, Joseph. Collection. RU 7001.
National Institute Records. RU 7058.
Office of the Secretary, Outgoing Correspondence. RU 33.
Office of the Secretary, Register of Correspondence. RU 42.
Rhees, William J. Collection. RU 7081.
Secretary and Assistant Secretary, Register of Correspondence. RU 57.
United States Exploring Expedition Collection. RU 7186.
Varden, John. Papers. RU 7063.

Wadsworth Atheneum, Hartford

Minutes of the Annual Meeting of the Stockholders of the Atheneum, 1862–1922.
Minutes of the Board of Trustees, 1844–1922.
Treasurer's Reports, 1862, 1863, 1867, 1868, 1869, 1870, 1871, 1872, 1873, 1874, 1875.

Secondary Sources

The Moderate and the Didactic Enlightenments

Bridenbaugh, Carl. *Cities in Revolt: Urban Life in America, 1743–1776.* New York: Alfred A. Knopf, 1955.
Bridenbaugh, Carl, and Jessica. *Rebels and Gentlemen: Philadelphia in the Age of Franklin.* New York: Reynal and Hitchcock, 1942.
Commager, Henry Steele. *The Empire of Reason: How Europe Imagined and America Realized the Enlightenment.* Garden City, N.Y.: Doubleday, 1977.
Crevecoeur, J. Hector St. John. *Letters from an American Farmer.* London: Thomas Davies & Lockyer Davis, 1782. Reprint. Garden City, N.Y.: Dolphin Books/Doubleday.
Ellis, Joseph J. *After the Revolution: Profiles of Early American Culture.* New York: W. W. Norton & Company, 1979.
Fischer, David Hackett. *The Revolution of American Conservatism: The Federalist Party in the Era of Jeffersonian Democracy.* New York: Harper & Row, 1965.
Formisano, Ronald T. "Deferential-Participant Politics: The Early Republic's Political Culture, 1789–1840." *Political Science Review* 68 (June 1974): 473–87.
May, Henry S. *The Enlightenment in America.* New York: Oxford University Press, 1976.

Meyer, Donald H. *The Democratic Enlightenment*. New York: G. P. Putnam's Sons, 1976.

Ostrander, Gilman. *The Rights of Man in America, 1606–1861*. Columbia: University of Missouri Press, 1960.

Pole, J. R. "Enlightenment and the Politics of American Nature." In *The Enlightenment in National Context*, edited by Roy Porter and Mikulas Teich, pp. 192–214. London: Cambridge University Press, 1981.

Wiebe, Robert H. *The Opening of American Society: From the Adoption of the Constitution to the Eve of Disunion*. New York: Alfred A. Knopf, 1984.

The Age of Egalitarianism

Miller, Douglas T. *The Birth of Modern America, 1820–1850*. New York: Western Publishing Company, 1970.

Nichols, Dr. Thomas L. *Forty Years of American Life*. 2 vols. London: John Maxwell and Company, 1864. Reprint. New York: Negro Universities Press, 1968.

Pessen, Edward. *Riches, Class and Power Before the Civil War*. Lexington, Mass.: D.C. Heath, 1973.

Rozwenc, Edwin C., ed. *Ideology and Power in the Age of Jackson*. Garden City, N.Y.: Anchor Books/Doubleday, 1964.

The Age of Professionalism

Bruce, Robert V. *The Launching of Modern American Science, 1846–1876*. New York: Alfred A. Knopf, 1987.

Calhoun, Daniel H. *Professional Lives in America: Structure and Aspiration, 1750–1850*. Cambridge: Harvard University Press, 1965.

Daniels, George. "The Process of Professionalization in American Science: The Emergent Period, 1820–1860." In *Science in America Since 1820*, edited by Nathan Reingold, pp. 63–78. New York: Science History Publications, 1976.

———. "The Pure-Science Ideal and Democratic Culture." *Science* 156 (June 30, 1967): 1699–1705.

Dupree, A. Hunter. *Science in the Federal Government: A History of Policies and Activities to 1940*. New York: Harper & Row, 1964.

Gerstner, Patsy A. "The 'Philadelphia School' of Paleontology: 1820–1845." Ph.D. dissertation, Case Western Reserve University, 1967.

Greene, John C. *American Science in the Age of Jefferson*. Ames, Iowa: State University Press, 1984.

Hindle, Brooke. *The Pursuit of Science in Revolutionary America: 1735–1789*. Chapel Hill: University of North Carolina Press, 1956.

Jacob, Margaret C. *The Cultural Meaning of the Scientific Revolution*. New York: Alfred A. Knopf, 1988.

Kohlstedt, Sally Gregory. *The Formation of the American Scientific Community: The American Association for the Advancement of Science, 1848–1860.* Urbana: University of Illinois Press, 1976.

Lurie, Edward. *Louis Agassiz: A Life in Science.* Chicago: University of Chicago Press, 1960.

Miller, Lillian B. *The Lazzaroni: Science and Scientists in Mid-Nineteenth Century America.* Washington, D.C.: Smithsonian Institution Press, 1972.

Poesch, Jessie. *Titian Ramsay Peale, 1799–1885: And His Journals of Wilkes Expedition.* Memoirs of the American Philosophical Society for Promoting Useful Knowledge, vol. 52. Philadelphia: American Philosophical Society, 1961.

Porter, Charlotte M. *The Eagle's Nest: Natural History and American Ideas, 1812–1842.* University, Ala.: University of Alabama Press, 1986.

Stanton, William. *The Great United States Exploring Expedition of 1838.* Berkeley: University of California Press, 1975.

The American Compromise

Foner, Eric. *Free Soil, Free Labor, Free Men: The Ideology of the Republican Party Before the Civil War.* New York: Oxford University Press, 1970.

Frederickson, George M. *The Inner Civil War: Northern Intellectuals and the Crisis of the Union.* Evanston: Harper & Row, 1965.

Higham, John. *From Boundlessness to Consolidation: The Transformation of American Culture, 1848–1860.* Ann Arbor: William L. Clements Library, 1969.

Pre-1783 American Cabinets

Bell, Whitfield J., Jr. "The Cabinet of the American Philosophical Society." In *A Cabinet of Curiosities: Five Episodes in the Evolution of American Museums,* no editor, pp. 1–34. Charlottesville: University Press of Virginia, 1967.

William Hayes Fogg Art Museum. *Early Science at Harvard: Innovators and their Instruments.* Cambridge: Fogg Art Museum, 1969.

Morison, Samuel Eliot. *Three Centuries of Harvard: 1636–1936.* Cambridge: Harvard University Press, 1936.

O'Brien, Michael, and David Moltke-Hansen. *Intellectual Life in Antebellum Charleston.* Knoxville: University of Tennessee Press, 1986.

Rhett, Robert Goodwyn. *Charleston: An Epic of South Carolina.* Richmond: Garrett and Massie, 1940.

Rogers, George C., Jr. *Charleston in the Age of the Pinckneys.* Norman: University of Oklahoma Press, 1969.

Sanders, Albert E. "The Charleston Museum and the Promotion of Science in Antebellum South Carolina." Paper presented at the Third Citadel Conference on the South, Charleston, South Carolina, April 25, 1981.

Stephens, Lester D. *Ancient Animals and Other Wondrous Things: The Story of Francis Simmons Holmes, Paleontologist and Curator of the Charleston Museum.* Contributions From The Charleston Museum, no. XVII, February 1988.

Stone, Elizabeth L. *American Library Development: 1600–1899.* New York: H. W. Wilson Company, 1977.

Wheatland, David P. *The Apparatus of Science at Harvard: 1765–1800.* Cambridge: Harvard University Press, 1968.

Whitehead, James S., ed. "The Autobiography of Peter S. Du Ponceau." *The Pennsylvania Magazine of History and Biography* 63 (November 1939): 432–61.

Du Simitière's Museum

Boyd, Julian P., ed. *The Papers of Thomas Jefferson*, vol. 6. Princeton: Princeton University Press, 1950.
Burnett, Edmund A. *Letters of Members of the Continental Congress*. Washington, D.C.: The Carnegie Institution of Washington, 1921.
Butterfield, Lyman H., ed. *The Adams Papers, Series I: Correspondence, Vol. 2: June, 1776–March, 1778*. Cambridge: Belknap Press of Harvard University, 1963.
———. *The Adams Papers, Series I: Diaries and Autobiography of John Adams, Vol. 2, Diary, 1771–1781*. Cambridge: Belknap Press of Harvard University, 1961.
Huth, Hans. "Pierre Eugène Du Simitière and the Beginnings of the American Historical Museum." *The Pennsylvania Magazine of History and Biography* 69 (October 1945): 315–25.
Library Company of Philadelphia. "Pierre Eugène Du Simitière: His American Museum 200 Years After." Catalogue of an Exhibition, July to October 1985. Philadelphia: Library Company of Philadelphia, 1985.
Orosz, Joel J. "Pierre Eugène Du Simitière: Museum Pioneer in America." *Museum Studies Journal* 1 (Spring 1985):8–18.
Patterson, Richard S., and Richardson Dougall. *The Eagle and the Shield: A History of the Great Seal of the United States*. Washington, D.C.: U.S., Government Printing Office, 1978.
Potts, William John. "Du Simitière, Artist, Antiquary and Naturalist, Projector of the First American Museum, with Some Extracts from his Notebook." *Pennsylvania Magazine of History and Biography* 13 (October 1889): 341–75.
Sifton, Paul Ginsberg. "A Disordered Life: The American Career of Pierre Eugène Du Simitière." *Manuscripts* 25 (1973): 235–53.
———. "Pierre Eugène Du Simitière (1737–1784): Collector in Revolutionary America." Ph.D. dissertation, University of Pennsylvania, 1960.

The Peale Museums

Appel, Toby A. "Science, Popular Culture and Profit: Peale's Philadelphia Museum." *Journal of the Society for the Bibliography of Natural History* 9 (Winter 1980): 619–34.
Hindle, Brooke. "Charles Willson Peale's Science and Technology." In *Charles Willson Peale and his World*, edited by Edgar P. Richardson, pp. 106–69. New York: Harry N. Abrams, 1983.
Hunter, Wilbur Harvey. *The Peale Family and Peale's Baltimore Museum, 1814–1830*. Baltimore: Peale Museum, 1965.
———. *The Story of America's Oldest Museum Building*. Baltimore: Peale Museum, 1964.

Miller, Lillian B. "Charles Willson Peale: A Life of Harmony and Purpose."
 In *Charles Willson Peale and His World*, edited by Edgar P. Richardson, pp.
 170–233. New York: Harry N. Abrams, 1983.
————, ed. *The Collected Papers of Charles Willson Peale and His Family on Mi-
crofiche*. Millwood, N.Y.: Kraus Microforms, 1981.
Richardson, Edgar P. "Charles Willson Peale and His World." In *Charles Will-
son Peale and His World*, edited by Edgar P. Richardson, pp. 22–105. New
 York: Harry N. Abrams, 1983.
Sellers, Charles Coleman. *Charles Willson Peale*. New York: Charles Scribners
 Sons, 1969.
————. *Mr. Peale's Museum: Charles Willson Peale and the First Popular Museum
of Natural Science and Art*. New York: W. W. Norton, 1980.
————. "Peale's Museum and 'The New Museum Idea.'" *Proceedings of the
American Philosophical Society Held at Philadelphia for Promoting Useful
Knowledge* 124 (February 29, 1980): 25–34.

The American Museum (under Baker and Scudder)

Goler, Robert I. "'Here the Book of Nature is Unfolded': The American Mu-
seum and the Diffusion of Scientific Knowledge in the Early Republic."
 Museum Studies Journal 2 (Spring 1986): 10–21.
————. "Natural History in the Early American Republic: A Study of the
 American Museum in New York City, 1790–1798." Graduate Research
 Project, Case Western Reserve University, 1984.
Gottesman, Rita Susswein. *The Arts and Crafts in New York, 1800–1804*. Col-
lections of the New-York Historical Society for the Year 1949, vol. 82.
 New York: New-York Historical Society, 1950.
Haberly, Loyd. "The American Museum from Baker to Barnum." *New-York
Historical Society Quarterly* 63 (July 1959): 273–87.
McClung, Robert M., and Gale S. "Tammany's Remarkable Gardiner Baker:
 New York's First Museum Proprietor, Menagerie Keeper and Promotor
 Extraordinary." *New-York Historical Society Quarterly* 62 (April 1958):
 142–69.
Stokes, Isaac Newton Phelps. *The Iconography of Manhattan Island, 1498–1909*.
 New York: Robert H. Dodd, 1915. Reprint. New York: Arno Press, 1967.

The American Museum (under Barnum)

Betts, John Rickards. "P. T. Barnum and the Popularization of Natural His-
tory." *Journal of the History of Ideas* 20 (1959): 353–68.
Browne, Walter R., ed. *Barnum's Own Story*. New York: Dover Publications,
 1961.
Harris, Neil. *Humbug: The Art of P. T. Barnum*. Boston: Little, Brown &
 Company, 1973.
Saxon, A. H., ed. *Selected Letters of P. T. Barnum*. New York: Columbia Uni-
versity Press, 1983.

Wallace, Irving. *The Fabulous Showman: The Life and Times of P. T. Barnum.* New York: Alfred A. Knopf, 1959.

The New-York Historical Society

De Peyster, Frederic, Jr. *The Moral and Intellectual Influence of Libraries Upon Social Progress.* New York: New-York Historical Society, 1866.

Francis, John W., M.D. *Old New York: Or Reminiscences of the Past 60 Years.* Anniversary discourse delivered before the New-York Historical Society, November 17, 1857. New York: New-York Historical Society, 1865. Reprint. New York: Benjamin Blom, 1971.

Hone, Phillip. *The Diary of Phillip Hone, 1828–1851.* New York: Dodd, Mead & Company, 1927. Reprint, Allan Nevins, ed. New York: Kraus Reprint Company, 1969.

Kelby, Robert Hendre. *The New York Historical Society, 1804–1904.* New York: New-York Historical Society, 1905.

Letters from John Pintard to his Daughter, Eliza Noel Pintard Davidson, 1816–1837. 4 vols. New York: New-York Historical Society, 1940.

Smit, Pamela Richards. "The New-York Historical Society Library: A History, 1804–1978." Ph.D. dissertation, Columbia University, 1979.

Vail, R. W. G. *Knickerbocker Birthday: A Sesqui-Centennial History of the New-York Historical Society, 1804–1954.* New York: New-York Historical Society, 1954.

The Elgin Botanical Garden

Robbins, Christine Chapman. *David Hosack: Citizen of New York.* Philadelphia: American Philosophical Society, 1964.

The Academy of Natural Sciences of Philadelphia

Gerstner, Patsy A. "The Academy of Natural Sciences of Philadelphia, 1812–1850." In *The Pursuit of Knowledge in the Early American Republic: American Scientific and Learned Societies from Colonial Times to the Civil War,* edited by Alexandra Oleson and Sanborn C. Brown, 174–93. Baltimore: Johns Hopkins University Press, 1976.

Lea, Isaac. "On the Pleasure and Advantage of Studying Natural History." *American Journal of Science and Arts* 11 (1826): 218–21.

Leidy, Joseph II. "Manuscript Biography of Joseph Leidy." Joseph Leidy II Papers, Academy of Natural Sciences.

Maclure, William. "An Epitome of the Improved Pestalozzian System of Education . . . " *American Journal of Science and Arts* 10 (1826): 139–51.

———. "Letters from William Maclure." *American Journal of Science and Arts* 9 (1825): 160–67.

Phillips, Venia T., and Maurice E. Phillips, eds. *Minutes and Correspondence of the Academy of Natural Sciences of Philadelphia, 1812–1924.* Microfilm, 38 reels. Philadelphia: Academy of Natural Sciences, 1963.

Ruschenberger, W. S. W. *Notice of the Origin, Progress and Present Condition of the Academy of Natural Sciences of Philadelphia*. Philadelphia: T. K. and P. G. Collins, Printers, 1852.

Slack, J. H., M.D. *Handbook of the Museum of the Academy of Natural Sciences of Philadelphia*. Philadelphia: Collins, 1862.

The Western Museum of Cincinnati

Adams, Alexander B. *John James Audubon: A Biography*. New York: G. P. Putnam's Sons, 1966.

Drake, Daniel. "Anniversary Discourse on the State and Prospects of the Western Museum Society: Delivered . . . June 10, 1820, on the Opening of the Museum." Cincinnati: Western Museum Society, 1820.

Ford, Alice, ed. *Audubon, By Himself: a Profile of John James Audubon*. Garden City, N.Y. Natural History Press, 1969.

Hendrickson, Walter B. "The Western Museum Society." *Historical and Philosophical Society of Ohio Bulletin* 7 (1949): 99–110.

Horine, Emmet Field, M.D. *Daniel Drake (1785–1852) Pioneer Physician of the Midwest*. Philadelphia: University of Pennsylvania Press, 1961.

Kellogg, Elizabeth R. "Joseph Dorfeuille and the Western Museum." *Journal of the Cincinnati Society of Natural History* 22 (April 1945): 3–29.

Shapiro, Henry and Zane L. Miller, eds. *Physician to the West: Selected Writings of Daniel Drake on Science and Society*. Lexington: University Press of Kentucky, 1970.

Slack, Elijah, James Findlay, William Steele, Jesse Embree, and Daniel Drake. "An Address to the People of the Western Country." *American Journal of Science* 1 (1819): 203–06.

Trollope, Frances. *Domestic Manners of the Americans*. London: Whittaker, Treacher & Co., 1832. Reprint, edited by Donald Smalley. New York: Alfred Knopf, 1949.

Tucker, Lewis Leonard. "'Ohio Show-Shop': The Western Museum of Cincinnati, 1820–1867."In Whitfield J. Bell et al., *A Cabinet of Curiosities: Five Episodes in the Evolution of American Museums*. Charlottesville: University Press of Virginia, 1967.

The Wadsworth Atheneum

Catalogue of Paintings in Wadsworth Gallery, Hartford. Hartford: E. Gleason, 1850.

———. 1851.

Clarke, Marian G. M. *David Watkinson's Library: 100 Years in Hartford, Connecticut, 1866–1966*. Hartford: Trinity College Press, 1966.

Fulton, John F., and Elizabeth H. Thompson. *Benjamin Silliman, 1779–1864: Pathfinder in American Science*. New York: Henry Schuman, 1947.

Saunders, Richard, and Helen Raye. *Daniel Wadsworth: Patron of the Arts*. Hartford: Wadsworth Atheneum, 1981.

The National Museum of the Smithsonian Institution

Annual Report of the Board of Regents of the Smithsonian Institution. Washington, D.C.: Smithsonian Institution, 1849–1871.

Borome, Joseph A. *Charles Coffin Jewett.* Chicago: American Library Association, 1951.

Cohen, Marilyn S. "American Civilizations in Three Dimensions: The Evolution of the Museum of History and Technology of the Smithsonian Institution." Ph.D. dissertation, George Washington University, 1980.

Goode, George Brown. *An Account of the Smithsonian Institution: Its Origin, History, Objects and Achievements.* Washington, D.C. Smithsonian Institution, 1895.

————. "A Memorial of George Brown Goode with a Selection of His Papers." In *Annual Report of the Board of Regents of the Smithsonian Institution for 1897, Part 2.* Washington, D.C.: Smithsonian Institution, 1901.

————, ed. *The Smithsonian Institution, 1846–1896: The History of the First Half Century.* Washington, D.C.: Smithsonian Institution, 1897.

Hinsley, Curtis M., Jr. *Savages and Scientists: The Smithsonian Institution and the Development of American Anthropology, 1846–1910.* Washington, D.C.: Smithsonian Institution Press, 1981.

Oehser, Paul. *Sons of Science: The Story of the Smithsonian Institution and its Leaders.* New York: Henry Schuman, 1949.

Orosz, Joel J. "Disloyalty, Dismissal and a Deal: The Development of the National Museum at the Smithsonian Institution." *Museum Studies Journal* 2 (Spring 1986): 22–33.

Reingold, Nathan. "The New York State Roots of Joseph Henry's National Career." *New York History* 54 (April 1973): 132–44.

————, ed. *The Papers of Joseph Henry.* 3 vols. Washington, D.C.: Smithsonian Institution Press, 1972–.

Rhees, William Jones. *The Smithsonian Institution: Documents Relative to its Origin and History.* 2 vols. Washington, D.C.: Smithsonian Institution, 1879.

Washburn, Wilcomb E. "A National Museum." In *The Smithsonian Experience.* Washington, D.C.: Smithsonian Institution, 1977.

————. "Joseph Henry's Conception of the Purpose of the Smithsonian Institution." In Whitfield J. Bell et al., *A Cabinet of Curiosities: Five Episodes in the Evolution of American Museums.* Charlottesville: University Press of Virginia, 1967.

The Metropolitan Museum of Art

Howe, Winifred E. *A History of the Metropolitan Museum of Art: With a Chapter on the Early Institutions of Art in New York.* 2 vols. New York: Metropolitan Museum of Art, 1913.

A Metropolitan Museum of Art in the City of New York: Proceedings of a Meeting Held at the Theater of the Union League Club, Tuesday Evening, November 23, 1869. New York: Printed for the Committee, 1869.

Tomkins, Calvin. *Merchants and Masterpieces: The Story of the Metropolitan Museum of Art.* New York: E. P. Dutton, 1970.

General Museum History

Alexander, Edward P. *Museum Masters: Their Museums and Their Influence.* Nashville: American Association for State and Local History, 1983.
————. *Museums in Motion: An Introduction to the History and Functions of Museums.* Nashville: American Association for State and Local History, 1979.
Bazin, Germain. *The Museum Age.* New York: Universe Books, 1967.
Clain-Stefanelli, Vladimir. *History of the National Numismatic Collections.* Contributions from the Museum of History and Technology, Paper 31, Bulletin 229. Washington, D.C.: U.S. Government Printing Office, 1968.
Dana, John Cotton. *The New Museum, Numbers 1 and 2.* Woodstock, Vt.: Elm Tree Press, 1917.
Goode, George Brown. "Museum-History and Museums of History." In *Papers of the American Historical Association*, edited by Herbert Baxter Adams, 3: 497–520. New York: G. P. Putnam's Sons, 1888.
Hudson, Kenneth. *Museums of Influence: The Pioneers of the Last 200 Years.* Cambridge: Cambridge University Press, 1987.
Katz, Herbert, and Marjorie. *Museums, U.S.A.: A History and Guide.* Garden City, N.Y.: Doubleday & Company, 1965.
Lord, Clifford L., ed. *Keepers of the Past.* Chapel Hill: University of North Carolina Press, 1965.
Low, Theodore L. *The Museum as a Social Instrument: A Study Undertaken for the Committee on Education of the American Association of Museums.* New York: Metropolitan Museum of Art, 1942.
Miller, Edward. *That Noble Cabinet: A History of the British Museum.* Athens, Ohio: Ohio University Press, 1975.
Ramsey, Grace Fisher. "The Development, Methods and Trends of Educational Work in Museums of the United States." Ph.D. dissertation, New York University, 1938.
Ripley, S. Dillon. *The Sacred Grove: Essays on Museums.* New York: Simon and Schuster, 1969.
Taylor, Francis Henry. *Babel's Tower: The Dilemma of the Modern Museum.* New York: Columbia University Press, 1945.
Van Tassel, David D. *Recording America's Past.* Chicago: University of Chicago Press, 1960.
Wittlin, Alma. *Museums: In Search of a Usable Future.* Cambridge: M.I.T. Press, 1970.

Art in America

Burt, Nathaniel. *Palaces for the People: A Social History of the American Art Museum.* New York: Little, Brown & Company, 1977.
Cowdrey, Mary Bartlett. *American Academy of Fine Arts and American Art*

Union: 1816–1852, with the History of the American Academy by Theodore Sizer. New York: New-York Historical Society, 1953.

Grindhammer, Lucille Wrubel. "Art and the Public: The Democratization of the Fine Arts in the United States, 1830–1860." Ph.D. dissertation, Case Western Reserve University, 1973.

Harris, Neil. *The Artist in American Society: The Formative Years, 1790–1860.* New York: George Braziller, 1966.

Miller, Lillian. *Patrons and Patriotism: Encouragement of the Fine Arts in America, 1790–1860.* Chicago: University of Chicago Press, 1966.

Related Organizations and Movements

Bode, Carl. *The American Lyceum: Town Meeting of the Mind.* New York: Oxford University Press, 1956.

Hosmer, Charles B. *Presence of the Past: A History of the Preservation Movement in the United States Before Williamsburg.* New York: G. P. Putnam's Sons, 1965.

Mack, Edward C. *Peter Cooper: Citizen of New York.* New York: Duell, Sloan & Pearce, 1949.

Accounts of Foreign Visitors

Acomb, Evelyn M. "The Journal of Baron Von Closen." *William and Mary Quarterly, 3rd Series* 10 (April 1953): 196–236.

Bird, Isabella Lucy. *The Englishwoman in America.* London: John Murray, 1856. Reprint. Madison: University of Wisconsin Press, 1966.

Blane, William Newnham. *An Excursion Through the United States and Canada During the Years 1820–23 by an English Gentleman.* London: Baldwin, Graddock & Company, 1824. Reprint. New York: Negro Universities Press, 1969.

Chambers, William. *Things as They Are in America.* London: W. R. Chambers, 1854. Reprint. New York: Negro Universities Press, 1968.

Chastellux, Francois-Jean, Marquis de. *Travels in North America in the Years 1780, 1781 and 1782.* 2 vols. Paris, 1786. Reprint. Chapel Hill: University of North Carolina Press, 1963.

Grund, Francis J. *The Americans and their Moral, Social and Political Relations.* Boston: Marsh, Capon & Lyon, 1837. Reprint. New York: Johnson Reprint Corporation, 1968.

Koch, Dr. Albert C. *Journey Through a Part of the United States of America in the Years 1844–1846.* Dresden, 1847. Reprint, translated and edited by Ernst A. Stadler. Carbondale, Ill.: Southern Illinois University Press, 1972.

Melish, John. *Travels Through the United States of America in the Years 1806, 1807, 1809, 1810 & 1811.* Philadelphia, 1815. Reprint. New York: Johnson Reprint Corporation, 1970.

Miranda, Francisco de. *The New Democracy in America: Travels of Francisco Miranda in the United States, 1783–84.* William Spence Robertson, ed. *The Diary of Francisco de Miranda.* New York: Hispanic Society of America,

1928. Reprint. Norman: University of Oklahoma Press, 1963.

Murray, Charles Augustus. *Travels in North America*. 2 vols. London: Richard Bentley, 1839. Reprint, edited by Roland Bartel and Edwin R. Bingham, *America Through Foreign Eyes, 1827–1842*. Boston: D. C. Heath and Company, 1956.

Oldmixon, Captain R. N. *Transatlantic Wanderings, or, a Last Look at the United States*. London: George Routledge & Company, 1855. Reprint. New York: Johnson Reprint Corporation, 1970.

Pierson, George Wilson. *Tocqueville and Beaumont in America*. New York: Oxford University Press, 1938.

Pulszky, Francis and Theresa. *White, Red, Black: Sketches of Society in the United States During the Visit of Their Guests*. 3 vols. New York: Trubner & Company, 1853. Reprint. New York: Negro Universities Press, 1968.

Schoepf, Johann David. *Travels in the Confederation, 1783–1784*. Philadelphia, 1911. Reprint, translated and edited by Alfred J. Morrison. New York: Bergman Publishers, 1968.

Index

ular education, 55–56, 57, 110, 167,
168; losing audience, 115, 118–19, 165;
caters to popular interests, 165, 166;
Committee of Investigation, 166–68;
and professionalism in the sciences, 167;
collection sold, 168, 178, 221
Peale's Utica Museum, 85, 117, 118
Penn, William, 58
Penn Squares, 192–94
Pennsylvania, University of, 22, 45, 51, 105
Pennsylvania Hospital in Philadelphia, 16,
18, 20, 21, 22, 25, 31
Perry, Oliver Hazard, 76
Pestalozzi, Johann Heinrich, 104, 120
Pestalozzian System of Education, 120–21
Peters, John R., Jr., 217–18
Philosophes, 12, 13, 27
Philosophy Chamber (Harvard), 17, 18
Philosophy School (Harvard), 17
Phoenix, Daniel, 72
Pinckney, Charles Coatsworth, 23
Pintard, John, 65, 66, 76–77, 80, 92, 102,
134, 135, 137, 138, 170; establishes
Tammany museum, 58–59; leaves Tam-
many Society, 61; and New-York His-
torical Society, 88; and New York In-
stitution, 89; elitist views, 90, 91; meets
with Charles Willson Peale, 93; concep-
tion of museum's social function,
94–95; and American Museum, 132–33
"Pleasurable instruction," 7, 28, 86
Poinsett, Joel Roberts, 141, 142, 143
Pole, J. R., 28
Powers, Hiram, 129–31, 168, 196, 250
Preservation movement, 8, 182
Princeton University, 158, 204
Professional criticism, 1, 238–45, 246,
252, 256. *See also* Goode, George
Brown; Taylor, Francis Henry
Professionalism, 3, 8, 125, 140, 169, 180,
181, 186, 187, 231–32, 235–36
Professionalism, Age of, 8, 44, 179
Professionalism in the Sciences, viii,
141–42; and Academy of Natural Sci-
ences, 145, 188, 192–93; and Smithson-
ian Institution, 160, 161–62, 164–65,
201, 207, 210; and Peale's Philadelphia
Museum, 166–67, 168; and Western

Museum, 168–69; and New-York Historical Society, 169, 170–71; and American Museum, 172, 176, 177–78, 179,
221, 224–31; and American Compromise, 180, 193; avoids conflict with religion, 181; and Cooper Union, 184; and
Museum of Comparative Zoology,
185–86; and American Museum of Natural History, 231, 232
"Prudential Committee," 223
Public library, 7
Public school, 7, 143, 183
Putnam, George P., 235

Quakers, 16

"Rational amusement," 7, 28, 51, 58,
81–82, 87, 96, 103
Reed, Luman, 214, 216
Reform impulse, 7, 109
Republicanism, 46, 50, 55. *See also* Peale,
Charles Willson
Republicans, Jeffersonian, 61, 80
Respectability, 7, 28, 50, 58, 62, 66, 67,
69, 71, 73, 82, 91, 95, 96, 101, 105,
129; decline of, ix, 5, 57, 68, 70, 80,
107, 108; as museum owners, 26, 49;
denied access to European cabinets, 29;
role in deferential model, 48; attempts
to control "lower orders," 99
Revolution, American, 9, 15, 19, 23, 25,
29, 32, 44; Du Simitière collection dur-
ing, 30
Revolution, French, 7, 55, 68, 69, 71, 83
Rittenhouse, David, 31, 45, 53
Rodgers, John R. B., 58
Rousseau, Jean Jacques, 46
Royal Society, 18
Ruschenberger, William S. W., 189
Rush, Benjamin, 31, 141
Russ, Dr. John D., 277 (n. 71)
Ryder, Linden, 131

St. Cecilia Society, 22
Sanitary Fair, 8, 186; at Philadelphia, 190
Savage, Edward, 73–74, 75, 79, 183
Say, Thomas, 101, 102, 113, 121, 124, 162
Schoepf, Johann David, 39, 40, 260 (n. 28)